# COMMUNICATING EFFECTIVELY DURING A HEALTH CRISIS

Exploring how and why communication breakdowns occur during pandemics and world disasters, this book offers solutions for improving communication and managing future public health crises.

A compilation of evidence-based lessons learned, this book shows how to effectively convey critical lifesaving information during a pandemic. It assesses how trust in leaders and governments during a public health crisis is formed and the impact this has on how information is perceived by the public. Using the COVID-19 pandemic as a case study, the book demonstrates how informative policy decisions and health risk messages can be better communicated for the handling of future pandemics. At a macro-level, the book looks at issues concerning situational awareness, how different countries managed or mismanaged the pandemic, and the lessons readers can learn from those occurrences. At a micro-level, it examines individual differences in public health message perceptions and corresponding actions taken or not taken.

An interdisciplinary critique of the delivery and reception of messages during global disasters, this text is suitable for undergraduate and graduate courses in Communication Studies, Health Communication, Risk Communication and Public Health, Psychology, Sociology, and Disaster Management.

**Devjani Sen** is an Instructor in the Department of Social Sciences at Algonquin College, Canada.

**Rukhsana Ahmed** is an Associate Professor in the Department of Communication in the College of Arts and Sciences at the University at Albany, State University of New York, USA.

# COMMUNICATING EFFECTIVELY DURING A HEALTH CRISIS

## A Critical Examination of Communication Breakdowns During the COVID-19 Pandemic

*Devjani Sen and Rukhsana Ahmed*

Routledge
Taylor & Francis Group
NEW YORK AND LONDON

Designed cover image: sv_sunny / © Getty Images

First published 2025
by Routledge
605 Third Avenue, New York, NY 10158

and by Routledge
4 Park Square, Milton Park, Abingdon, Oxon, OX14 4RN

*Routledge is an imprint of the Taylor & Francis Group, an informa business*



ISBN: 978-1-032-49684-9 (hbk)
ISBN: 978-1-032-49682-5 (pbk)
ISBN: 978-1-003-39498-3 (ebk)

DOI: 10.4324/9781003394983

Typeset in Times New Roman
by codeMantra

# CONTENTS

# PREFACE

Let us consider the ominous prediction of Bill Gates during his TED Talks in Vancouver, Canada in 2015:

If anything kills over 10 million people in the next few decades, it's more likely to be a highly infectious virus rather than a war. Not missiles, but microbes. Now, part of the reason for this is that we have invested a huge amount in nuclear deterrence, but we've actually invested very little in a system to stop an epidemic.

> ...And as you look at what went on, the problem wasn't that there was a system that didn't work well enough. The problem was that we didn't have a system at all.
>
> ...In fact, there are some pretty obvious key missing pieces. We didn't have a group of epidemiologists ready to go who would have gone, seen what the disease was, see how far it had spread. The case reports came in on paper. It was very delayed before they were put online, and they were extremely inaccurate. We didn't have a medical team ready to go. We didn't have a way of preparing people.
>
> There was no one there to look at treatment approaches. No one to look at the diagnostics, no one to figure out what tools should be used. As an example, we could have taken the blood of survivors, processed it, and put that plasma back in people to protect them, but that was never tried. So there was a lot that was missing, and these things are really a global failure.
>
> ...The failure to prepare could allow the next epidemic to be dramatically more devastating than Ebola.

~ Excerpt from Bill Gates: "The Next Outbreak? We're Not Ready" TED talks, Vancouver, Canada 2014.

How was the world to know how his ominous prediction would come true and the disastrous impacts on global history?

## What Is Unique about the COVID-19 Pandemic?

In their analysis of the COVID-19 pandemic, Jankelová et al. (2021) point out that current tools of crisis and prevention planning did not work in the context of the COVID-19 pandemic because of its highly unpredictable nature. In essence managers had little choice but to act efficiently quickly and deliberately which was challenging given the feelings of anger, fear, and anxiety caused by the constant changes and unpredictability of how things changed so quickly during COVID-19 (Liu and Lang, 2018; Myer et al., 2007; as cited in Jankelova et al., 2021).

## Assumptions about the COVID-19 Pandemic

Arguably, traditional management of disaster events emphasize control, yet a pandemic comprises a lot of unexpected situations that are complex and ambiguous, demanding new forms of communicative approaches (Heide & Simonnson, 2020). Heide and Simonnson argue that a change in focus is needed where there is a greater focus on internal communication versus external communication with stakeholders, where individuals are the recipients of information:

> The pandemic is an example of a wicked problem that involves a lot of ambiguity. Often organizations try to handle wicked problems by trying to control it through traditional management skills and practices. A pandemic demands a strong leadership and a communicative approach that highlights the importance of coworkers. In the studied organization the authors found knowledge and rhetoric about the value of coworkers and communicative coworkership
>
> *(p. 256)*

## The Change in the Public's Role during Crisis Events

Collins et al. (2020) argue that given the plethora of information that exists in our current world, crisis communication needs to convey accurate and otherwise credible information to gain quick control of the situation and, in turn, the trust of the public. They further argue about how the community is an integral aspect of the communication that takes place about a given crisis in that information is now received and transmitted vertically and horizontally among all parties as opposed to coming only from the top-down approach as in the past. With the public now playing a key role in emergency management, this information can be disseminated and evaluated in real time – a key transformation that has recently taken place with the advent of information about a crisis coming from social media.

Historically, speaking, COVID-19 is not our first pandemic, there have been other global public health disasters such as the plague, Spanish influenza, HIV, and Ebola. So, what makes COVID-19 different?

With the plethoric rise in social media use, arguably the COVID-19 pandemic is one where the public has played a more active part in the creation of knowledge and in the determination of active truth. To effectively learn from past mistakes, perhaps what is needed is to ask ourselves different questions, for example: what is helpful information about the pandemic, and how do we as a society distinguish between authentic and false information? What do we do with the information we receive? Do all groups in society have equal access to pertinent health communications during a global crisis such as the COVID-19 pandemic? How do we process this information? What are some of the barriers we face?

## Limitations of Current Literature on Crisis Management

In his evaluation of the literature on crisis management, Jong (2020) has stated that despite the need for a comprehensive framework to assess crisis communication during a pandemic, there are no such guidelines within existing assessment studies on crisis management. Indeed, it has been argued that "the pandemic is not a purely biological catastrophe that can only be treated from a medical point of view. The pandemic is a critical event that acquires its meaning within different political, economic and social contexts."

## How This Book Will Enhance Our Understanding of the COVID-19 Pandemic

Returning to our discussion of Bill Gates' prediction of the COVID-19 pandemic during his 2014 speech, what went wrong in the management of our current pandemic, more specifically, what could we have improved in terms of crisis communication? Since December 2023, over 600 million have been infected by COVID-19 with an estimated death toll of nearly 7 million people world-wide. Scholars have argued that given many countries have adopted different communication strategies during the COVID-19 crisis, effective crisis and risk communication is especially important for developing countries as they cope with disease management with fewer resources than developed countries.

Arguably effective crisis management which may entail dealing well with regional, cultural, linguistic, and ethnic diversity considerations will lead to building trust, credibility, honesty, transparency, and accountability (Ataguba & Ataguba, 2020). This book will provide readers with relevant theoretical frameworks and the current empirical research findings on how and why communication breakdowns occur during world disasters and crises, and their ramifications on the population at large. It is evident that there are a number of challenges encountered in research in this area, leading to the questions, what are some of the challenges in most effectively framing risk? Is critical information being transmitted effectively, efficiently and is it leading to a reasonable information/action ratio? Material used from this book may be used to train those working in media, as well as students of media studies, health communication, public health, and disaster management to better understand how to most effectively frame risk messages during pandemics such as the COVID-19 pandemic.

An interdisciplinary approach is taken to our exploration of how communication breakdowns occur during a pandemic. This book explores the area of risk communication from a psychological perspective (e.g., how do we most effectively frame health risk messages, are they being framed to maximize comprehensive factors by the common populace? Are messages conveying vital lifesaving information about safety being accessed and understood by the majority of people in our society?). At a macro-level, we look at issues relating to situational awareness as it relates to the pandemic but also how different countries managed or mismanaged the pandemic and what lessons we can learn from those occurrences. At a micro-level we explore individual differences in public health message perceptions and corresponding actions taken or not taken.

## A Better Understanding of Communication Breakdowns during the COVID-19 Pandemic

We begin this book with an exploration of how communication breakdowns may take place. Drawing heavily on literature from the management of disaster events Chapter 1 *Towards a Better Understanding of Communication Breakdowns during the COVID-19 Pandemic,* we explore what can go wrong during a pandemic. From this we explore risk communication and how we can interact as effectively as possible during disaster events.

During the early stages of a pandemic especially, it is critical that authentic fact-based information about self-care is disseminated as quickly and efficiently as possible; the lives of millions of people world-wide are contingent upon doing so. The danger of widespread misinformation, especially during a public health crisis, is that it undermines collective sense making and collective action (West & Bergstrom, 2020). Indeed, given that misinformation has been growing fast and has reached crisis proportions, it has been a serious risk in undercutting public support for policies to control the spread of severe acute respiratory syndrome coronavirus 2 (SARS-CoV-2) (West & Bergstrom, 2020). While there is a plethora of credible information about vaccination and other life-saving measures for disease prevention, there is also a lot of untruthful, or misinformation. In Chapter 2 *The Dangers of the Infodemic: The Spreading of False Information About the COVID-19 Pandemic*, we will investigate questions such as how do we effectively locate the sources of this misinformation, and slow or stop its spread? Who are more susceptible to be persuaded by misinformation? How can we make the public more aware of this misinformation and encourage information seeking behaviors that lead to more credible information dissemination?

It is imperative that health information is trusted to promote disease prevention. In the case of a global public health crisis like the Covid-19 pandemic, vaccination information may come from a variety of sources such as family, friends, work colleagues, neighbors and other associates, government agencies, healthcare givers, the media, and government sources. In Chapter 3 *Trust in the Government During the COVID-19 Pandemic: How to Be a Good Leader*, we review existing studies to examine if available information is trusted and factors that may be impeding public trust. Some questions of interest include, is it the source of the information and can information sources be made more credible? And how can more effective information sharing take place if certain information sources are less trusted than others?

In an ideal world, authentic health information on measures about how to contain the COVID-19 virus is dispersed quickly and efficiently and is subsequently processed by people world-wide who implement these guidelines for their own and others' safety. But how is this information processed? With the plethora of information at our disposal, how do we discriminate between fake and authentic information about the COVID 19 virus? Conspiracy beliefs regarding dangers specific to public health has been rampant and widespread (Oliver & Wood, 2014). The danger of conspiracy beliefs is that they can lead people to ignore or otherwise disregard appropriate health-related behaviors (Jolley & Douglas, 2014), endangering the lives of people world-wide. By better understanding questions such as *who* believes in conspiracy theories and misinformation about pandemics such as the COVID-19 and *why* they have such beliefs, we can better create strategies to alleviate the harmful effects of the beliefs to be better prepared for the next pandemic (Uscinkski et al., 2020).

Indeed, during a global disaster like the COVID-19, information is only empowering if it is understood properly and ultimately used to prevent further infections and deaths. There is a growing need for public health communication research to be employed in the identification of the information needs of the populace at large, which can then use this information to take better control of their health and self-care (Kreps & Maibach, 2008). An important question that needs to be considered is what causes certain people to not comply with (or even incite rebellion against) measures to mitigate the spread of the virus? Some studies suggest that defiance of COVID-19 mitigation guidelines may be a combination of emotions and rational choice considerations (Burruss et al., 2021).

It is evident that there are a number of challenges encountered in research in compliance behavior leading to the question, what are some of the challenges in most effectively framing risk? A related question entails, is critical information being transmitted effectively, efficiently and is it leading to reasonable actions to safeguard one's health?? In their systematic review of literature on vaccine hesitancy, Larson et al. (2014) conclude that some of the limitations of the current research include: (1) the complex nature of vaccine hesitancy is not easily understood as it is driven by a variety of context-specific factors, (2) the majority of studies on vaccine hesitancy were conducted in Europe and the Americas, and (3) the frameworks used as determinants of vaccine hesitancy are in large part taken from traditional models such as the Health Belief Model which do not adequately account for contextual influences.

In Chapter 4 *Pandemic Compliance ‚Non-Compliance: A Review of Theory and Empirical Studies,* we will overview theoretical and empirical literature to help us better understand the information-action ratio as it pertains to the COVID-19 pandemic. We consider how information we have processed about the pandemic and/or otherwise have been exposed to, leads to actions we take regarding self-protective measures during the pandemic? In order to address these questions, the chapter will overview various theories of misinformation such as Conspiracy and Religion-Based theories regarding the spread of the COVID-19 virus. While a number of studies will be reviewed, we will draw heavily from the thematic analysis of Berg et al.'s (2022) study which provides a wealth of insights into understanding how COVID-19 health risk messages have been misconstrued by the public. After reviewing relevant literature on factors that motivate people to comply with COVID-19 non-pharmaceutical intervention (NPIs), we proceed to a discussion of motivators of non-compliance with self-protective measures by reviewing the literature on key drivers of compliant behavior during the pandemic. This discussion will lead to an in-depth discussion on how risk perception has been a key driver of compliance with health-preventative behaviors across the world. We will explore how the public perceives health messages to take proactive measures to safe-guard one's health during the pandemic.

Clearly certain countries performed better than others in managing the Covid-19 pandemic. For example, in the case of Japan, which was once proclaimed to be a leader in its pandemic management prowess, the country was later criticized for its weak strategic communications during the pandemic, specifically for failing to adequately depict the true reality of the status of the coronavirus within the country with widespread documentation of infection numbers and sufficient testing for the presence of the virus (Snow, 2022) In this case, what may have been more effective means of managing public health crisis at a global level? How do we optimize the communication of guidelines more effectively across different countries? In Chapter 5 *Cross Cultural and*

*Gender Differences in Crisis Management Styles: Lessons from the COVID-19 Pandemic,* we will explore these questions by looking at the management styles of how various countries managed during the COVID-19 pandemic. Continuing with this exploration, we will analyze gender differences in leadership styles across major global speeches during the COVID-19 pandemic.

Pictorial information captures and conveys important messages that can supplement textual information. When a strange and new experience occurs, it is human nature to attempt to make the foreign familiar and in so doing, 'make sense' of our new reality. In this way, cultural narratives have been created during the COVID-19 pandemic. These narratives have broken our old reality, creating a new 'normal.' In Chapter 6 *'Framing Risk': An In-Depth Exploration of the Role of Semiotic Analysis in Message Persuasion,* we will explore how a number of COVID-19 messages convey important narratives through semiotic analysis.

Employing data gathered during the peak phase of the COVID-19 pandemic and compared with data taken when the lockdown was lifted, Kimhi et al. (2020) found that certain psychological attributes may help lower the negative impacts of the COVID-19 pandemic. The study conducted in Israel found that the higher an individual's resilience and well-being, the lower their sense of danger, and distress during the pandemic. Positive Psychology, first introduced in 1998 by psychologist Martin Seligman, is the scientific study of what makes people happy in life, with a focus on individual as well as societal well-being. One of the tenets of Positive Psychology is that times of uncertainty and transition may provide opportunities for personal growth and potentially even enhance well-being. There are some studies that suggest this may be the true during the aftermaths of COVID-19 (Cohen-Louck & Levy, 2021; Fiengold et al., 2022). In Chapter 7 *Positive Psychology: Enhancing Well-Being During COVID-19,* using Positive Psychology as a theoretical framework, we will review literature and theory aiming to identify potential factors that may help to protect and create feelings of well-being during the COVID-19 pandemic.

Many social groups have become more vulnerable during the COVID-19 pandemic. For example, due to the nature of their work, front-line workers have been placed at higher risk of acquiring the virus, while other groups such as older adults, ethnic minority groups, and disabled individuals may find access to healthcare information more challenging. Isolated populations such as the incarcerated may find further isolation during the pandemic further detrimental to their mental health. In Chapter 8 *Moving Forward: Re-Thinking Communication during and Post COVID-19 with Special Consideration to Marginalized Populations,* we explore how many vulnerable individuals are further disadvantaged by the pandemic and proactive steps that can be taken to empower these groups with improved access to facilities to support their unique healthcare needs.

In our final Chapter *Lessons Learned from Past Pandemics*, we explore the issue of what we can learn from past global level disaster events? Through synthesis of many studies reviewed for this book we will explore some of the important lessons for planning and managing future pandemics.

## *Bibliography*

Akram, U., Fülöp, M. T., Tiron-Tudor, A., Topor, D. I., & Căpuşneanu, S. (2021). Impact of digitalization on customers' well-being in the pandemic period: Challenges and opportunities for the retail industry. *International Journal of Environmental Research and Public Health, 18*(14), 7533.

Ardolino, M., Bacchetti, A., & Ivanov, D. (2022). Analysis of the COVID-19 pandemic's impacts on manufacturing: A systematic literature review and future research agenda. *Operations Management Research, 15*, 551–566. doi: 10.1007/s12063-021-00225-9

Ataguba, O. A., &Ataguba, J. E. (2020). Social determinants of health: The role of effective communication in the COVID-19 pandemic in developing countries. *Global Health Action, 13*(1), 1788263.

Berg, S. H., Shortt, M. T., Thune, H., Røislien, J., O'Hara, J. K., Lungu, D. A., & Wiig, S. (2022). Differences in comprehending and acting on pandemic health risk information: A qualitative study using mental models. *BMC Public Health, 22*(1), 1–15.

Bhandari, D., Kotera, Y., Ozaki, A., Abeysinghe, S., Kosaka, M., & Tanimoto, T. (2021). COVID-19: Challenges faced by Nepalese migrants living in Japan. *BMC Public Health, 21*(1), 1–14.

Burruss, G. W., Jaynes, C. M., Moule, J., & Fairchild, R. (2021). Modeling individual defiance of COVID-19 pandemic mitigation strategies: Insights from the expanded model of deterrence and protection motivation theory. *Criminal Justice and Behavior, 48*(9), 1317–1338. doi: 10.1177/00938548211010315

Coccia, M., & Benati, I. (2018). Comparative evaluation systems. In A. Farazmand (Ed.), *Global encyclopedia of public administration, public policy, and governance*. Cham: Springer International Publishing AG. doi: 10.1007/978-3-319-31816-5_1210-1

Cohen-Louck, K., & Levy, I. (2021). Viruism: The need for a new term describing COVID-19 impact in context of viral victimization. *Psychological Trauma: Theory, Research, Practice, and Policy, 13*(1), 1–8.

Collins, A. B., Ndoye, C. D., Arene-Morley, D., & Marshall, B. D. (2020). Addressing co-occurring public health emergencies: The importance of naloxone distribution in the era of COVID-19. *International Journal of Drug Policy, 83*, 102872.

Dai, R., & Hu, L. (2022). Inclusive communications in COVID-19: A virtual ethnographic study of disability support network in China. *Disability & Society, 37*(1), 3–21.

Delardas, O., Kechagias, K. S., Pontikos, P. N., & Giannos, P. (2022). Socio-economic impacts and challenges of the coronavirus pandemic (COVID-19): An updated review. *Sustainability, 14*(15), 9699.

De Luca Picione, R., Martini, E., Cicchella, S., Forte, S., Carranante, M., Tateo, L., & Rhodes, P. (2021). The impact of Covid-19 pandemic: Psycho-social perception of the crisis and sense-making processes. *Community Psychology in Global Perspective, 7*(2), 103–128.

Dryhurst, S., Schneider, C. R., Kerr, J., Alexandra L., Freeman, J., Recchia, G., van der Bles, A. M., Spiegelhalter, D., & van der Linden, S. (2020). Riskperceptions of

COVID-19 around the world. *Journal of Risk Research, 23*(7–8), 994–1006. doi: 10.1080/13669877.2020.1758193

Feingold, J. H., Hurtado, A., Feder, A., Peccoralo, L., Southwick, S. M., Ripp, J., & Pietrzak, R. H. (2022). Posttraumatic growth among health care workers on the frontlines of the COVID-19 pandemic. *Journal of Affective Disorders, 296*, 35–40.

Gates, B. (2014). "The next outbreak? we're not ready" TED talks, Vancouver, Canada. Retrieved from: https://www.youtube.com/watch?v=6Af6b_wyiwI

Germain, S., & Yong, A. (2020). COVID-19 highlighting inequalities in access to healthcare in England: A case study of ethnic minority and migrant women. *Feminist Legal Studies*, 28(3), 301–310.

Hale, T., Angrist, N., Goldszmidt, R. et al. (2021). A global panel database of pandemic policies (Oxford COVID-19 Government Response Tracker). *Nature Human Behaviour, 5*, 529–538. doi: 10.1038/s41562-021-01079-8

Haley, E., Caxaj, S., George, G., Hennebry, J., Martell, E., & McLaughlin, J. (2020). Migrant farmworkers face heightened vulnerabilities during COVID-19. *Journal of Agriculture, Food Systems, and Community Development, 9*(3), 35–39.

Heide, M., & Simonsson, C. (2021). What was that all about? On internal crisis communication and communicative coworkership during a pandemic. *Journal of Communication Management, 25*(3), 256–275.

Jankelová, N., Joniaková, Z., Blštáková, J., Skorková, Z., & Procházková, K. (2021). Leading employees through the crises: Key competences of crises management in healthcare facilities in coronavirus pandemic. *Risk Management and Healthcare Policy, 14*, 561–573. doi: 10.2147/RMHP.S288171

Jolley, D., & Douglas, K. M. (2014). The effects of anti-vaccine conspiracy theories on vaccination intentions. *PloS One*, 9(2), e89177.

Jong, W. (2020). Evaluating crisis communication. A 30-item checklist for assessing performance during COVID-19 and other pandemics. *Journal of Health Communication, 25*(12), 962–970.

Kimhi, S., Eshel, Y., Marciano, H., & Adini, B. (2020). A renewed outbreak of the COVID-19 pandemic: A longitudinal study of distress, resilience, and subjective wellbeing. *International Journal of Environmental Research and Public Health*, 17(21), 7743.

Kreps, G. L., & Maibach, E. W. (2008). Transdisciplinary science: The nexus between communication and public health. *Journal of Communication, 58*(4), 732–748. doi: 1111/j.1460-2466.2008.00411.x

Liu, X., & Yang, J. (2018). The research on influence of public security insignificant emergency and management-QCA analysis based on Web crawler data of 32 events. *Journal of Risk Analysis Disaster Crisis Research*, 1, 137–158.

Magomedov, I. A., Khaliev, M. S., & Khubolov, S. M. (2020, November). The negative and positive impact of the pandemic on education. *Journal of Physics: Conference Series, 1691*(1), 012134 (IOP Publishing).

Moreland, C. J., Ruffin, C. V., Morris, M. A., & McKee, M. (2021). Unmasked: How the COVID-19 pandemic exacerbates disparities for people with communication-based disabilities. *Journal of Hospital Medicine, 16*(3), 185–188.

Myer, R. A., Conte, C., & Peterson, S. E. (2007). Human impact issues for crisis management in organizations. *Disaster Prevention Management, 16*, 761–770. doi:10.1108/09653560710837055

Okorie, O., Subramoniam, R., Charnley, F., Patsavellas, J., Widdifield, D., & Salonitis, K. (2020). Manufacturing in the time of COVID-19: An assessment of barriers and enablers. *IEEE Engineering Management Review, 48*(3), 167–175.

Oliver, E., & Wood, T. (2014). Medical Conspiracy Theories and Health Behaviors in the United States. *JAMA Internal Medicine, 174*(5), 817–818. doi:10.1001/jamainternmed.2014.190

Onyema, E. M., Eucheria, N. C., Obafemi, F. A., Sen, S., Atonye, F. G., Sharma, A., & Alsayed, A. O. (2020). Impact of Coronavirus pandemic on education. *Journal of Education and Practice, 11*(13), 108–121.

Özvarış, Ş. B., Kayı, İ., Mardin, D., Sakarya, S., Ekzayez, A., Meagher, K., & Patel, P. (2020). COVID-19 barriers and response strategies for refugees and undocumented migrants in Turkey. *Journal of Migration and Health, 1*, 100012.

Schimmenti, A., Billieux, J., & Starcevic, V. (2020). The four horsemen of fear: An integrated model of understanding fear experiences during the COVID-19 pandemic. *Clinical Neuropsychiatry, 17*(2), 41–45. doi: 10.36131/CN20200202.

Shakespeare, T., Watson, N., Brunner, R., Cullingworth, J., Hameed, S., Scherer, N., & Reichenberger, V. (2022). Disabled people in Britain and the impact of the COVID-19 pandemic. *Social Policy & Administration, 56*(1), 103–117.

Snow, N. (2022). Japan's strategic miscommunications: In the shadow of the pandemic Olympics. *Place Branding and Public Diplomacy, 18*, 30–32.

Uscinski, J.E., Enders, A. M. Klofstad, C., Seelig, M., Funchion, J. Everett, C., & Wuchty, S. (2020). Why do people believe COVID-19 conspiracy theories? HKS Misinformation Review. https://misinforeview.hks.harvard.edu/article/why-do-people-believe-covid-19-conspiracy-theories/

Uscinski, J.E., Enders, A. M. Klofstad, C., Seelig, M., Funchion, J. Everett, C., & Wuchty, S. (2020). Why do people believe COVID-19 conspiracy theories? *HKS Misinformation Review*. https://misinforeview.hks.harvard.edu/article/why-do-people-believe-covid-19-conspiracy-theories/

West, J. D., & Bergstrom, C. T. (2021). Misinformation in and about science. *Proceedings of the National Academy of Sciences, 118*(15), e1912444117.

# 1

# TOWARD A BETTER UNDERSTANDING OF COMMUNICATION BREAKDOWNS DURING THE COVID-19 PANDEMIC

## Chapter Learning Objectives

- Describe what is meant by risk communication
- Explain how the Mental Models Approach can help us understand communication gaps
- Discuss its importance to understand situational awareness in the context of a pandemic such as the COVID-19
- Discuss some of the elements of an effective leader when working virtually, in terms of building trust among team members and in the leader

## Introduction

As of December, 2023, over 7 million people have died from the COVID-19 outbreak and there are nearly 700K confirmed cases in 229 countries and territories around the world; as of February 12, 2023, there has been a +600% surge in new cases (Worldometer, 2023). In this chapter we conceptualize the COVID-19 as a natural disaster which is in line with other current scholarship (Madhav et al., 2018; Clark, 2020; Seddighi, 2020). In order to prevent or slow the spread of future pandemics, we need to better understand the miss steps that took place during the COVID-19 pandemic.

We begin this chapter by examining how communication takes place during disaster events. We explore the role of power structures during a pandemic and how they can create challenges in effective communication during these events.

We then explore what we can learn about communicating better during disaster events from past studies where natural disasters have taken place and the public responses to these events. This review is followed by exploring some

DOI: 10.4324/9781003394983-1

critical questions of how communication may take place during these events. Some questions to ponder: how do we seek information, process it, and equip ourselves for good decision-making during a public health crisis? It may depend on situational awareness which will enable a more holistic understanding of what is going on during the complexities of a disaster event. Here we discuss the critical issue of sense-making.

This leads to a discussion of what is meant by risk communications. After this we explore communication gaps during disaster events through the lens of a Mental Models Approach. After discussing if we are asking the correct questions we explore a case study of how the pandemic was handled in the United Arab Emirates, particular how communication was intentionally made as transparent as possible to the public.

Given the complexities of a disaster event, the formation of trust is an important aspect of communication. A pandemic is fraught with many types of change, including changes to social structures. In the case of the COVID-19 pandemic, much of our work now takes place virtually, and this is true for many countries all around the world. When interaction take place virtually a host of social cues are no longer present, and certainly this will impact how the creation of trust among co-workers within a virtual workplace team. To explore this in more detail, we will discuss virtual workplaces, and how communication takes place in these spaces, and if the role of the leader changed in post-pandemic workplaces?

We conclude the chapter with reflections about whether or not we need new ways of communicating. Some recommendations are discussed.

## Challenges in Communication and Power Structures during a Pandemic

Risk mitigation during the COVID-19 pandemic comprises many challenges as a number of different actions needed to be considered including knowing how to evaluate, plan, implement, and maintain risk mitigation measures, along with appropriately deciding various coordination measures including decisions about the chain of command, and channeling communication (DeBruin et al., 2020). Communication and information sharing take place across a number of different agencies, including governments and sectors, (e.g., stakeholders such as decision-makers, scientists, practitioners, and citizens), and between different levels of society (such as international, national, regional, and local) (Tompkins et al., 2008, as cited in DeBruin). Support for this assertion can be found in a small-scale study comprising the administration of 2,883 surveys at an Australian university conducted by Seale et al. (2011). In this study university officials were required to warn staff and students about the spreading of the flu virus on campus. Seale et al. (2011) identified a major challenge for navigating a middle ground between inciting unnecessary fear and promoting complacency. Thus, information needs to be communicated clearly too various audiences and stakeholders, in a manner which is quick and easy to understand to various people around the world. To better understand how we process a plethora of information during such events, we look at the concept of sense-making.

### *Sense-Making*

It has been said that the resiliency of a society facing disaster events is contingent upon how its individual members cope with their anxiety and fears (Schimmenti et al., 2020).

Schimmenti and colleagues (2020) identified four kinds of fear in the COVID-19 pandemic context, including fear: (1) of the body and fear for the body, (2) of and for significant, (3) of knowing and not knowing what is ahead, and (4) of taking action and not taking action.

Arguably fear can be lessened through clarification of the unknown. Let us now return to our question of what information we need/is pertinent during a pandemic.

### *Building a Communication Gap Model – Are We Asking the Correct Questions?*

A study by Henrich and Holmes (2011) using focus groups, for which a pandemic situation was simulated, identified the following three areas regarding what people want to know about the pandemic, specifically about information relating to the available drugs and vaccines:

1. What are the socio-demographic characteristics of people who have been infected and where has the infection spread? How has the virus spread? How can infections be avoided?
2. If a person gets infected, what is the magnitude of the infection and how long will it last? Could the infection lead to death?
3. What do we know about the safety and effectiveness of the drugs and vaccines? What are potential side effects and has the safety of the drugs and vaccination been empirically tested taking into account the pressures of the crisis? How has safety been tested and how can we ensure that safety has not been compromised as a result of the pressures of the crisis? How do the risks of side effects and the long-term effects of the vaccine compare to the risks from the disease?

Henrich and Heide (2011) identified a four-step approach in how people want to access this information. First it was determined that it would be helpful to have mainstream media serve as a conduit for information to come directly from lead health officials and experts. It was also determined how certain websites which are part of mainstream media and/or perceived as authoritative sources of information should also publish links to these sites as well as to other official health agency Web sites (regional or national). Second a utility value of centralizing all pandemic information so that it can be more easily located was identified. Third, employing a dissemination plan involving family doctors and where health agencies email critical information as it becomes available, would also be helpful as family physicians have been found to be highly trusted source for medical information by the general public. Finally, a fourth strategy that was identified was to persuade individuals comprising alternative subpopulations, to become more open to new drugs and vaccination by using alternative healthcare providers, like naturopaths and homeopaths to create a dissemination network.

### HOW SHOULD WE COMMUNICATE DURING A PANDEMIC?

#### Case Study: The Unite Arab Emeritus

In their qualitative analysis of two government run digital platforms in the United Arab Emirates, Radwan and Mousa (2020) discuss how different communication strategies were used during different phases of the pandemic.

For example, in their study the researchers discussed how in the quarantine phase motivating health and behavior change was the focus. For this reason communication comprised giving people information about the disease and in so doing raising awareness about the disease. In the coexistence phase, communication focused more on highlighting the importance of adhering to health measures and dealt more with information about health precaution information to safeguard against non-compliant attitudes. As the researchers note, the UAE government's communications used a number of strategies to inform and convince the public about what they needed to know as well as provided the public with reassurance that their government was doing its best to protect them. This included strategies that helped to correct misinformation by reducing ambiguity and clarifying information.

## What Is Risk Communication?

Risk communication involves disseminating information about health risks and is a specialized communication process which helps the public to better understand how to most effectively save lives during times of infections and disease threats and involves adapting attitudes and behaviors that may help them against risks. It has also been identified as a tool for guiding citizens during times of infectious and disease threats and is an interactive process of communication that aims to raise awareness during risks and disasters (Radwan & Mousa, 2020). We are defining risk communications as exchanges of information about health and/or environmental risks between interested parties (Covello et al., 1986).

The main goal of risk communication is to help communities to discuss social and environmental risks and from this, create mutual understanding and acceptance about procedures for keeping the community safe. In risk communication activities like situation analysis, assessing information, developing strategies, creating messages, integration, and coordination are important steps that help officials to build effective communication plans (Dickmann et al., 2016; Infanti et al., 2023).

## Identifying Communication Gaps: A Mental Models Approach

Within the context of disaster management, a mental models approach can help us to better understand what people already know about flash flood risks and responses, as well as help in the process of identification of critical gaps in their knowledge that might be addressed through improved risk communication (Lazrus et al., 2016). **Mental models** may be defined as a mental image or a verbal description that represents a real entity. They are not necessarily correct but rather substitutes in our thinking for the real system that is represented (Forrester, 1961).

Data from 26 interviews of mental models employed during a flash flood in Colorado, USA, were analyzed in Lazrus et al.'s (2016) study to better understand the public's perceptions of flash flood risks and mitigation. The study found that the majority of those interviewed displayed some incomplete understandings as well as misconceptions about factors of flash flood development and exposure which the researchers believed may have led to ineffective warning decisions during an actual flash flood. These included significant misunderstandings about how quickly a threat can evolve (flash floods), its speed of dispersion, and the best responses when the threat is forthcoming, as well as the locations and times that comprised the greatest risk. The study also mentioned the value of situational awareness and environmental cues, which helped to provide recommendations for ways to improve risk communication, to help people quickly recognize and understand threats, gather needed information, and make informed decisions in complex, rapidly evolving extreme threats such as flash floods.

## The Evolution of Trust during COVID-19

So let us begin by exploring what is meant by trust. Jiang (2022) argue that social trust requires confidence in other people, with the belief that "when required, people will display logical behavior in their interactions with others that are reciprocally beneficial" (Welch et al., 2005, as cited in Jiang, 2022).

But what happens during a pandemic when people are required to have faith or trust in the government? Do they perceive the government to behave in a manner that is beneficial for their citizens? In such a context, interaction between government and the public may not be reciprocal in its true sense, as the citizens of a country are recipients of whatever benefits the government bestows on them during a crisis level event. Another consideration are definitions of trust that highlight the importance of the development of trustworthiness from repeated interactions (Kanagaretnam et al., 2010) and yet, often natural disasters such as the COVID-19 pandemic are fraught with unpredictability, where there is often little time to prepare, and government policy on management of such an event changes frequently, which, in turn, depends on an ever-changing context. In such conditions, how does social trust develop?

## How the Development of Trust Has Been Impacted in Various Domains That Have Been Impacted by the COVID-19 Pandemic

Fell (2020) discusses how trust development has changed after the pandemic in multiple domains within society including interpersonal relationships, social behaviors, technology, and interactions with institutions and information. For this reason she urges us to consider a holistic understanding of trust to fully appreciate its formation in multiple contexts. Indeed, structural changes in society that have resulted from the COVID-19 pandemic raise the question of what the impacts of these changes are on how we communicate.

## The Root of COVID-19 Uncertainty: Situational Awareness

During a disaster event, such as a pandemic, there is ongoing and eminent danger with a lot of information to navigate through. The COVID-19 pandemic has drawn attention to the need for good situational awareness (Iskander & Bianchi, 2021). A general definition of scientific situational awareness, or awareness of the scientific information environment, may comprise searching for publication of new findings and sharing relevant references within organizations or emergency response structures (Iskander et al., 2017).

To trace the root of the concept, situational awareness originated in Human Factors (specifically in piloting). The main components of the term are arguably relevant in the context of how to survive during emergency events:

> Most simply put, SA is knowing what is going on around you. Inherent in this definition is a notion of what is important. SA is most frequently defined in operational terms. While someone not engaged in a task or objective might

> have awareness (e.g., someone sitting under a tree idly enjoying nature), this class of individuals has been largely outside the scope of human factors design efforts. Rather, we have been concerned mostly with people who need SA for specific reasons. For a given operator, therefore, SA is defined in terms of the goals and decision tasks for that job. The pilot does not need to know everything (e.g., the co-pilot's shoe size and spouse's name), but does need to know a great deal of information related to the goal of safely flying the aircraft. A surgeon has just as great a need for situation awareness; however, the things she needs to know about will be quite different, dependent on a different set of goals and decision tasks
>
> *(Endsley et al., 2000, p. 1).*

Bouzidi et al. (2022) discuss how they developed a model for predicting policy-relevant situational awareness. Specifically, Bouzidi and colleagues (2022) proposed an ad hoc real-time managing emergency model comprising elements of deep learning, artificial intelligence technologies, situational awareness, education, and damage assessment. The model was developed to permit monitoring of a disaster, inform the community about one's present state, send messages to get help and allows the user to write content informally, without any syntax, logic, noisy, containing spelling errors, abbreviations, etc., which of course is well suited to a crisis situation. The authors of the model claim to have made improvements to their original managing disaster model and evaluated it in the context of the COVID-19 virus with promising results.

## What Did We Know About Situational Awareness Prior to COVID-19?

Social media can be helpful in gathering information about an ever-changing situation, as in the case of a pandemic, in real-time. Employing data from Weibo and Twitter to explore what tweets contributed toward situational awareness and which did not, Sen et al. (2015) concluded the following:

> Typically, only a small fraction of these tweets contribute to situational awareness, while the majority merely reflect the sentiment or opinion of people. Real-time extraction of tweets that contribute to situational awareness is especially important for relief operations when time is critical. However, automatically differentiating such tweets from those that reflect opinion / sentiment is a non-trivial challenge, mainly because of the very small size of tweets and the informal way in which tweets are written (frequent use of emoticons, abbreviations, and so on). This study applies Natural Language Processing (NLP) techniques to address this challenge.
>
> *(p. 1)*

Espousing the value of social media analysis, Karami et al. (2017) proposed an analytical framework: which they refer to as Twitter Situational Awareness (TwiSA). This framework employs sentiment analysis and topic modeling to create improved SA for disaster preparedness, response, and recovery. The developers of this real-time crisis management plan claim a benefit of TwiSA is in helping disaster management teams to identify the public's concerns in a speedy way. Karami et al. (2017) also point out that their proposed framework can be used not only during a natural disaster but also as a post-event methodology review capability for future disaster risk reduction. We will now turn our attention to the significance of social media within the context of pandemics.

## The Role of Social Media in Promoting Situational Awareness during a Pandemic

It has been considered that social media are considered an effective communication platform during all phases of the disaster management life cycle (Abedin et al., 2014). Different types of information are needed for different purposes during the various stages of a disaster event. For example, during preparedness, information may be needed on how to handle the disaster while during the response phase, information about action-related tasks may be sought (Vongkusolkit & Huang, 2021).

With vast amounts of information online, Vongkusolkit and Huang (2021 argue for the need to quickly identify the most accurate and relevant information and then for a coding schema to separate information into different categories before they can be made actionable for good situational awareness. In their development of a framework of social media data for natural disaster analysis, Vongkusolkit and Huang (2021) conducted a comprehensive literature review of articles on this topic by employing. Google Scholar to search for scientific literature that used the terms 'social media,' 'natural hazard,' and 'situational awareness.' From an initial compilation of 493 articles, 92 manuscripts were selected that delineated various aspects of the social media use for natural disasters. Scholars such as Vongkusolkit and Huang (2021) have summarized key differences social media platforms offer compared to more traditional media as a means of gathering information. These are described below:

1 Convenience in assessing information and understanding people's emotions about this information. For example, compared to traditional news sources which have a general perspective of crises, people have been found to rely more on social media to get information on localized impact (Shklovski et al., 2010; cited in Vongkusolkit & Huang, 2021). In this way it is believed that the public uses social media to communicate and assess the damage and situation without having to deal with filtered information that has been censored.
2 Allowing participation in an interactive, decentralized, and large-scale discussion, for example, it has been stated by Al-Saggaf and Simmons (2015)

(cited in Vongkusolkit & Huang, 2021) suggest that social media may mediate a more decentralized discussion from minority groups of people who may not have much of a voice in public in the event of a disaster.

3 Insight to the situation from different perspectives and locations. In addition, they would also having other types of information about people's emotions, such as insight about people's personal emotions, feelings, opinions, and perspectives which arguably may help assist first responders in determining the level of damage and expediting recovery processes as this kind of information may help to narrow down where help is needed (Beigi et al., 2016; cited in Vongkusolkit & Huang, 2021). It was also argued that access to real-time insight and public perception toward a disaster that can be more effectively gathered from social media can provide additional information for sentiment analysis.
4 A more efficient and inexpensive way to receive real-time updates. Sutton et al. (2008 cited in Vongkusolkit & Huang, 2021) describe social media as less formal communications to the public compared to more traditional media that promotes more wide-scale interaction with the public given users are active participants in discussions rather than passive listeners and in so doing, provides additional information that may be helpful during a disaster event

**REFLECTION QUESTION:**

Do any of these ways of using information from social media, apply to how you searched for information during the COVID-19 pandemic? What strategy/strategies were most useful and why?

**DO WE NEED NEW COMMUNICATION STRATEGIES?**

Abrahams (2021) posed the following questions:

1 Do existing health risk communication tools, designed to meet short term needs of disease outbreaks, function effectively for an event as long and complex as a pandemic?
2 Given the interactive and dynamic nature of the internet, what do health communicators need to understand about communicating through this medium during a disaster event?
3 How are public health agencies and governments likely to effectively build trust in a post-trust society?
4 Considering the political, social, and economic nature of pandemics, in addition to being public health events, what are the key issues that communicators need to understand?

## Impacts on Communication in the Workplace

Post-pandemic virtual working arrangements have brought several challenges including, but not limited to reduced trust, disrupted communication, limited collaboration, lack of role clarity and lowered team performance (Mangla, 2021). Another issue, worthy of deeper discussion, is that the shift to virtual workplaces has necessitated different needs for workplace leaders. In a virtual context, team leaders are even more important in building trust among team members (Furumo et al., 2012, as cited in Mangla, 2021) given many times team members do not know each other, lack face to face interaction, and may even be from different time zones (Mangla, 2021). Cultural intelligence is an ability that enables a person to adapt themselves to better understanding other cultures, learning from ongoing interactions and gradually reshaping their thinking to other cultural perspectives (Thomas & Inkson, 2008). Cultural intelligence helps in fostering 'trust and understanding even among virtual teams (Mangla, 2021). In the context of a pandemic, cultural intelligence helps with adaptability in a world where we are often interacting with sometimes unknown parties from diverse backgrounds who may or may not be similar to ours.

## The Role of Good Leadership in Virtual Workplace Interactions

There is ample evidence that virtual teamwork has a negative impact on trust between coworkers (Breuer et al., 2016; Liao, 2017; Zolin, 2004, as cited in Zoonen et al., 2023), as well as shared goals (Gajendran & Harrison, 2007; cited in Zoonen, 2023) and shared contexts (Fell, 2020; Newman & Ford, 2021; cited in Zoonen et al., 2023) all of which are critical components of effective workplace communication. Arguably, the role of team leaders is different in virtual environments than in more traditional working environments of the past. Indeed, scholars have stated that the role of the virtual team leader is even more pivotal in building trust among team members (Furumo et al., 2012), with leader ensuring the clarity of goals, responsibilities and accountabilities for everyone in the team (Abudi, 2012; cited in Mangla, 2021).

## Key Lessons

The goal of this chapter was to further our understanding of how communication breakdowns take place during a pandemic. In order to do this, we explored past studies where natural disasters have taken place and the public responses to these events to investigate if lessons learned could be gleaned from their findings.

This led to an exploration of how communication may take place during a pandemic. Some questions to ponder included how do we seek information, process it, and equip ourselves for good decision-making during a public health crisis? This necessitated an in-depth investigation of many critical components of communication including the formation of type of holistic trust which led to an overview of situational awareness. We also discussed risk communication and explored ways on making it more effective in the context of the pandemic and other natural events. The chapter concluded with some thoughts about how the COVID-19 pandemic has altered how communication takes place in the virtual workplace. We specifically explored how the role of the team leader has changed in such contexts and the impact on shared responsibilities, goals, and trust within virtual groups.

## Bibliography

Abedin, B., Babar, A., & Abbasi, A. (2014). Characterization of the use of social media in natural disasters: A systematic review. *2014 IEEE Fourth International Conference on Big Data and Cloud Computing*, Sydney, NSW, Australia, pp. 449–454. doi: 10.1109/BDCloud.2014.17.

Abraham, T. (2011). Lessons from the pandemic: The need for new tools for risk and outbreak communication. *Emerging Health Threats Journal*, *4*(1), 7160.

Abudi, G. (2012). Best practices for managing and developing virtual project teams. Paper presented at *PMI® Global Congress*, North America, Vancouver, British Columbia, Canada, 23 October 2012. Newtown Square, PA: PMI.

Al-Saggaf, Y., and Simmons, P. (2015). Social media in Saudi Arabia: Exploring its use during two natural disasters. *Technological Forecasting and Social Change* 95(June), 3–15. doi: 10.1016/j.techfore.2014.08.013

Beigi, G., Hu, X., Maciejewski, R., & Liu, H. (2016). An overview of sentiment analysis in social media and its applications in disaster relief. In W. Pedrycz & S.-M. Chen (Eds.,), *Sentiment analysis and ontology engineering: An environment of computational intelligence* (pp. 313–340). Studies in Computational Intelligence. Cham: Springer International Publishing. doi: 10.1007/ 978-3-319-30319-2_13

Bouzidi, Z., Amad, M., & Boudries, A. (2022). Enhancing warning, situational awareness, assessment and education in managing emergency: Case study of COVID-19. *SN Computer Science*, *3*(6), 454.

Braithwaite, J., Clay-Williams, R., Vecellio, E., Marks, D., Hooper, T., Westbrook, M. et al. (2016). The basis of clinical tribalism, hierarchy and sterotyping: A laboratory controlled teamwork experiment. *BMJ Open, 6*, e012467. doi: 10.1136/bmjopen-2016-012467

Breuer, C., Hüffmeier, J., & Hertel, G. (2016). Does trust matter more in virtual teams? A meta-analysis of trust and team effectiveness considering virtuality and documentation as moderators. *Journal of Applied Psychology*, *101*(8), 1151. doi: 10.1037/apl0000113

Clark, D. (2020). Travel restrictions to remain in place as coronavirus precaution [Press release]. Retrieved on October 30, 2023 from www.beehive.govt.nz/release/travel-restrictions-remain-place-coronavirus-precaution.

Covello, V. T., Slovic, P., & Von Winterfeldt, D. (1986). Risk communication: A review of the literature.

De Bruin, Y. B., Lequarre, A. S., McCourt, J., Clevestig, P., Pigazzani, F., Jeddi, M. Z., … & Goulart, M. (2020). Initial impacts of global risk mitigation measures taken during the combatting of the COVID-19 pandemic. *Safety Science*, *128*, 104773.

Dickmann, J., Klappstein, J., Hahn, M., Appenrodt, N., Bloecher, H. L., Werber, K., & Sailer, A. (2016, May). Automotive radar the key technology for autonomous driving:

From detection and ranging to environmental understanding. In *2016 IEEE Radar Conference (RadarConf)* (pp. 1–6). IEEE.

Endsley, M. R., & Garland, D. J. (2000). Theoretical underpinnings of situation awareness: A critical review. *Situation Awareness Analysis and Measurement, 1*(1), 3–21.

Fell, L. (2020). Trust and COVID-19: Implications for interpersonal, workplace, institutional, and information-based trust. *Digital Government: Research and Practice* 2, 1, Article 10 (November 2020), 5 pages. doi: 10.1145/3428472

Forrester, J. (1961). *Industrial dynamics*. Cambridge, MA: Productivity Press.

Furumo, K., de Pillis, E., & Buxton, M. (2012). The impact of leadership on participation and trust in virtual teams. In *Proceedings of the 50th Annual Conference on Computers and People Research*, SIGMIS CPR, Milwaukee, Wisconsin, USA, 31 May–2 June 2012, pp. 123–126.

Gajendran, R. S., & Harrison, D. A. (2007). The good, the bad, and the unknown about telecommuting: Meta-analysis of psychological mediators and individual consequences. *Journal of Applied Psychology, 92*(6), 1524–1541. doi: 10.1037/0021-9010.92.6.1524

Ganesh, R., Salonen, B. R., Bhuiyan, M. N., Bierle, D. M., Moehnke, D., Haddad, T. C., … & Hurt, R. T. (2021). Managing patients in the COVID-19 pandemic: A virtual multidisciplinary approach. *Mayo Clinic Proceedings: Innovations, Quality & Outcomes, 5*(1), 118–126.

Hall, P. (2005). Interprofessional teamwork: Professional cultures as barriers. *Journal of Interprofessional Care, 19*, 188–196.

Henrich, N., & Holmes, B. (2011). Communicating during a pandemic: Information the public wants about the disease and new vaccines and drugs. *Health Promotion Practice, 12*(4), 610–619.

Infanti, A., Starcevic, V., Schimmenti, A., Khazaal, Y., Karila, L., Giardina, A., Flayelle, M., Hedayatzadeh Razavi, S. B., Baggio, S., Vögele, C., & Billieux, J. (2023). Predictors of Cyberchondria During the COVID-19 Pandemic: Cross-sectional Study Using Supervised Machine Learning. *JMIR Formative Research, 7*, e42206. doi: 10.2196/42206

Iskander, J. K., & Bianchi, K. M. (2021). Changes in the scientific information environment during the COVID-19 pandemic: The importance of scientific situational awareness in responding to the infodemic. *Health Security, 19*(1), 82–87.

Iskander, J., Rose, D. A., & Ghiya, N. D. (2017). Science in emergency response at CDC: Structure and functions. *American Journal of Public Health, 107*(suppl 2), S122–S125.

Jiang, S. (2022). The roles of worry, social media information overload, and social media fatigue in hindering health fact-checking. *Social Media+ Society, 8*(3), 1–12. doi: 10.1177/20563051221113070.

Kanagaretnam, K., Mestelman, S., Nainar, S. K., & Shehata, M. (2010). Trust and reciprocity with transparency and repeated interactions. *Journal of Business Research, 63*(3), 241–247.

Karami, A., Shah, V., Vaezi, R., & Bansal, A. (2020). Twitter speaks: A case of national disaster situational awareness. *Journal of Information Science, 46*(3), 313–324. doi: 10.1177/0165551519828620

Lazrus, H., Morss, R. E., Demuth, J. L., Lazo, J. K., & Bostrom, A. (2016). "Know what to do if you encounter a flash flood": Mental models analysis for improving flash flood risk communication and public decision making. *Risk Analysis, 36*(2), 411–427.

Liao, C. (2017). Leadership in virtual teams: A multilevel perspective. *Human Resource Management Review, 27*(4), 648–659. doi: 10.1016/j.hrmr.2016.12.010

Madhav, N., Oppenheim, B., Gallivan, M., Mulembakani, P., Rubin, E., & Wolfe, N. (2018). Pandemics: Risks, impacts, and mitigation. In Dean T. Jamison, Hellen Gelband, Susan Horton, Prabhat Jha, Ramanan Laxminarayan, Charles N. Mock, and Rachel Nugent (Eds.), *The International Bank for Reconstruction and Development*. Washington (DC): The World Bank.

Mangla, N. (2021). Working in a pandemic and post-pandemic period–cultural intelligence is the key. *International Journal of Cross Cultural Management, 21*(1), 53–69.

Newman, S. A., & Ford, R. C. (2021). Five steps to leading your team in the virtual COVID-19 workplace. *Organizational Dynamics, 50*(1), 100802.

Radwan, A. F., & Mousa, S. A. (2020). Government communication strategies during coronavirus pandemic: United Arab Emirates lessons. *Journal of Health Management, 22*(4), 516–527.

Rogers, L., De Brún, A., & McAuliffe, E. (2023). Exploring healthcare staff narratives to gain an in-depth understanding of changing multidisciplinary team power dynamics during the COVID-19 pandemic. *BMC Health Services Research, 23*(1), 419.

Schimmenti, A., Billieux, J., & Starcevic, V. (2020). The four horsemen of fear: An integrated model of understanding fear experiences during the COVID-19 pandemic. *Clinical Neuropsychiatry, 17*(2), 41.

Seale, H., McLaws, M. L., Van, D., Crimmins, J., &MacIntyre, C. R. (2011). University communication strategies during a pandemic—were the messages received? *Journal of Public Health Management and Practice, 17*(1), E29–E32.

Seddighi, H. (2020). COVID-19 as a natural disaster: Focusing on vulnerability and exposure for response. Retrieved on November 10, 2023 from COVID-19 as a Natural Disaster: Focusing on Exposure and Vulnerability for Response | Disaster Medicine and Public Health Preparedness | Cambridge Core

Sen, A., Rudra, K., & Ghosh, S. (2015, January). Extracting situational awareness from microblogs during disaster events. In *2015 7th International Conference on Communication Systems and Networks (COMSNETS)* (pp. 1–6). IEEE.

Shklovski, I., Burke, M., Kiesler, S., & Kraut, R. (2010). Technology adoption and use in the aftermath of hurricane Katrina in New Orleans. *American Behavioral Scientist, 53*(8), 1228–1246. doi: 10.1177/0002764209356252.

Sutton, J., Palen, L., & Shklovski, I. (2008). Backchannels on the front lines: Emergent uses of Social Media in the 2007 Southern California Wildfires, *9. Proceedings of the 5th International ISCRAM Conference*, May 4–7: Washington, D.C., USA.

Thomas, D., & Inkson, K. (2008). *Cultural intelligence: People skills for global business*. US: Berrett-Koehler.

Tompkins, E. L., Lemos, M. C., & Boyd, E. (2008). A less disastrous disaster: Managing response to climate-driven hazards in the Cayman Islands and NE Brazil. *Global Environmental Change, 18*(4), 736–745.

van Zoonen, W., Sivunen, A. E., & Blomqvist, K. (2023). Out of sight–Out of trust? An analysis of the mediating role of communication frequency and quality in the relationship between workplace isolation and trust. *European Management Journal*. doi: 10.1016/j.emj.2023.04.006

Vongkusolkit, J., & Huang, Q. (2021). Situational awareness extraction: A comprehensive review of social media data classification during natural hazards. *Annals of GIS, 27*(1), 5–28.

Welch, M. R., Rivera, R. E., Conway, B. P., Yonkoski, J., Lupton, P. M., & Giancola, R. (2005). Determinants and consequences of social trust. *Social Inquiry, 75*, 453–473.

Weller, J., Boyd, M., & Cumin, D. (2014). Teams, tribes and patient safety: overcoming barriers to effective teamwork in healthcare. *Postgraduate Medical Journal, 89*(1061), 149–154.

"Worldometer." (2023). Retrieved on June 16, 2023, from: https://www.worldometers.info/coronavirus/coronavirus-death-toll/

Zolin, R., Hinds, R., Fruchter, R., & Levitt, R. E. (2004). Interpersonal trust in cross-functional, geographically distributed work: A longitudinal study. *Information and Organization, 14*(1), 1–26.

## Glossary of Key Terms and Concepts

**Cultural Intelligence** is an ability that enables a person to adapt themselves to better understanding other cultures, learning from ongoing interactions and gradually reshaping their thinking to other cultural perspectives (Thomas & Inkson, 2008).

**Mental Models** is a mental image or a verbal description that represents a real entity. They are not necessarily correct but rather substitutes in our thinking for the real system that is represented (Forrester, 1961).

**Risk Communication** defining risk communications as exchanges of information about health and/or environmental risks between interested parties (Covello et al., 1986).

**Situational Awareness** refers to all information that is accessible and can be integrated into a coherent and comprehensive understanding to assess and cope with a given situation, when required (Sarter & Woods, 1991).

**Twitter Situational Awareness (TwiSA)** is a framework which employs sentiment analysis and topic modeling to create improved SA for disaster preparedness, response, and recovery (Karami et al., 2017).

## Discussion Questions

1 Given the shift to more virtual workplaces during the COVID-19 pandemic, what impact has this had on the role of team leaders on promoting effective communication? Please provide specific examples as they relate to promoting group trust between team members.
2 How can we re-build trust in a post-trust society? Please explain.
3 Describe how cultural intelligence can foster greater trust and understanding in the post pandemic workplace.
4 Please watch the YouTube video 'How technology during the pandemic has forever changed our work, community and government' at: https://www.youtube.com/watch?app=desktop&v=B0Zmht9XS_Y

# 2

# THE DANGERS OF THE INFODEMIC

## The Spreading of False Information About the COVID-19 Virus

### Key Lessons

- Define what is meant by the COVID-19 infodemic
- Discuss the various types of misinformation in the infodemic
- Discuss the role heuristics might play in people's propensity to spread misinformation
- Discuss why social media can be particularly dangerous in the spreading of misinformation

### Introduction

In this chapter we explore various types of misinformation that were present in the COVID-19 pandemic. We will discuss primary ways that misinformation can spread and people who may be more susceptible to becoming influenced by misinformation. After discussing ways of stopping the spread of misinformation, we conclude the chapter with an Infodemic Management Framework that is rooted in empirical studies.

The WHO has given infodemiology additional credence in scholarly writings, by formally acknowledging it as an emerging scientific field as well as a critical area of practice, during a pandemic (Eysenbach, 2020). Misinformation is a malignant force in our global world, enabling one false idea to spread instantly too many vulnerable ears (Nelson et al., 2020). During the early stages of a pandemic especially, it is critical that authentic fact-based information about self-care is disseminated as quickly and efficiently as possible; the lives of millions of people world-wide are contingent upon doing so. The danger of

DOI: 10.4324/9781003394983-2

widespread misinformation, especially during a public health crisis, is that it undermines collective sense making and collective action (West & Bergstrom, 2020). Indeed, given that misinformation is fast growing, and has reached crisis proportions, the spreading of misinformation about the severe acute respiratory syndrome coronavirus 2 (SARS-CoV-2) COVID-19 virus has been deemed a serious threat to public health (Basol et al., 2021; Roozenbeek et al., 2020; West & Bergstrom, 2020).

We begin this chapter with an overview of what constitutes various types of misinformation. We will then explore certain key questions concerning how to identify misinformation from authentic information about public health messages. This leads to a discussion of different types of misinformation in various forms of media and how we process this information.

With the spread of misinformation on the rise, we turn our attention to learning more about ways of controlling this spread including studies on digital intelligence listening reports which have been used to educate infodemic management activities. After this, we explore who are more susceptible to misinformation and how this may impact compliance to health measures implemented during the COVID-19 pandemic. Finally, we conclude this chapter with a discussion on how to safeguard against the spread of misinformation.

## Types of Incorrect Information and How We Process It

Let us define various types of incorrect information.

*Disinformation*: spreading untrue or false information with bad intent (Naeem & Boulos, 2021).

*Malinformation*: reconfigured or otherwise altered true information (Brennen et al., 2020).

*Misinformation*: refers to cases where people's beliefs in factual matters are not supported by clear evidence and/or expert opinion (Naeem & Boulos, 2021).

## Exploring Real-World Consequences of Fake News

A study conducted by Greene and Murphy (2021) using a sample size of 3,746 participants did not find providing a general warning about the dangers of online misinformation to result in notable behavioral response to the fake stories. This finding held, irrespective of whether the warning was framed in positive or negative terms. From this, the researchers concluded that generic warnings about online misinformation, which are typically used by governments and social media companies, are unlikely to be effective.

Given most people had considerably more time available to consume news since the COVID-19 lockdowns (Alvarez-Risco et al., 2020), the question is raised: how did they manage this plethora of information and what was being attended to more? In a study conducted by Ahmed (2020) 15 media diaries of university students in the United Arab Emirates were analyzed too better understand how individuals accessed and made sense of news during the early stages of COVID-19. The study found that news was consumed mainly on smart phones and laptops and that the total time spent on news relating to COVID-19 for the one week observational period varied from 23 minutes to just over 16 hours. It was also found that many participants shared the news due to a sense of social responsibility. The researchers noted a rise in news sharing after COVID-19 and that the average amount of sharing in their study ranged from some participants who did not share any news to 'heavy sharers' who shared approximately 80% of the news they consumed. Analyses of social media diaries revealed that some sharing was done of number of cases without sharing a link to the news source, while at other times participants reported calling up family members to watch the news with them, hence accessing COVID-19 news was a shared experience.

Ahmed's (2020) study also found participants made an informed decision about whether the news seemed believable. The study also found that social media was not associated with levels of mistrust or perceived misinformation in the media diaries. This finding is in line with other studies cited by the researchers (Bawden & Robinson, 2020; Savolainen, 2007). What is noteworthy, however, is that Ahmed (2020) referred to studies such as Newman et al.'s (2019) research, which found that 29% of survey respondents reported deciding not to share a news article where veracity of the information was doubtful (35% USA, 61% Brazil, 40% Taiwan, and 13% Netherlands), the study was not conducted during COVID-19 and hence does not reflect sharing of false information during the pandemic.

> Reflection: *Have you ever spread false information about COVID-19 without intending to do so? What may have been the consequences of doing so? Now that you are aware of the consequences are you more careful to check and re-check online information about the virus?*

## Types, Sources and Claims of COVID-19 Misinformation

Some of the most well-known sources of information about the dangers of the coronavirus are mobile applications, artificial-intelligence based chat boxes, electronic resources, video-based lectures, and social media trolling (Ali & Bhatti, 2020). The general consensus is that while social media sites are most frequently used as information sources, scientific information remains the most trusted as well as the strongest influencer of perceived personal and societal-level risk (Entradas, 2021; Shearer & Mitchell, 2021).

Some scholars argue that the spreading of fake news or other misinformation will never cease completely due to the nature of the confirmation bias

(Prasetya & Murata, 2020). In the field of psychology, the confirmation bias is defined as seeking or interpreting evidence in a manner that favors existing beliefs, expectations, or a pre-hypothesis (Nickerson, 1998).

But what are the types, sources, and major claims of misinformation about COVID-19? The International Fact-Checking Network (IFCN) and Google Fact Checking Tools were used by Brennen et al. (2020) to analyze information about whether the coronavirus was rated to be either false or misleading by professional fact-checkers. The study found that the number of fact-checks increased more than 900% from January to March in 2020; given the limited resources of these fact-checkers, the researchers speculated that this statistic is actually higher in reality. While only 38% of the information in this sample was found to be completely fabricated, 59% of the misinformation was manipulated in such a way where existing and often true information was altered in some manner as to become misleading. Although the study found that most of the misinformation came from the population at large, and that misinformation from prominent and public figures comprised 20% of the claims, these claims accounted for 69% of total social media engagement. The study also found significant variation in social media platforms in terms of posts rated to be false or given warnings.

Cotter et al. (2022) have found evidence that even when prominent social media sites claim to conduct fact-checking, doing so does not necessarily result in significantly decreasing the magnification and circulation of false and otherwise misleading information about the coronavirus online. In their study, the researchers conducted a thematic analysis of documents published by Facebook, Twitter, and YouTube regarding what platforms claimed they did, in addition to what the platforms actually did in reality. The results of the study found evidence that the platforms focused their attention mainly on the visibility of COVID-19 mis/disinformation on their sites and that there was considerable ambiguity regarding policies and practices.

## Who/What are the Primary Sources of Spreading the Misinformation?

In their analysis of media-generated misinformation during the COVID-19 pandemic, Evanega et al. (2020) found over 1 million articles were found to be covering, fact checking or in other ways repeating misinformation that was believed to have had a significant impact on the public's perception of the pandemic. Given that the overall bulk of misinformation came from powerful world stage actors, such as the US President, this study highlights the role of the media in disseminating misinformation through their choices in who and what to cover without proper verification the accuracy of the claims made.

## The Complexity of Sharing Behavior: What Studies Say

Anastasiades et al. (2021) offer an insightful explanation of potential reasons why we may share misinformation. First, they note that sharing behavior does not necessarily imply that the person sharing information believes in the accuracy of the information they are about to share (Pennycook et al., 2021) and that indeed, intention to share is a far more forceful driver of sharing behavior than the accuracy of the information (Pennycook et al., 2018). According to the work of Pennycook and Rand (2021) there may be at least three possible explanations for the disconnect between accuracy of information perceptions and sharing behavior: preference-based account, the confusion-based account, and the inattention-based account. For the preference-based account political identity or moral viewpoints may be given greater importance over accuracy and truth. From this perspective, even when people know information is not accurate, they may still decide to share it because of their political or moral ideology and in certain situations because it is interesting. According to the confusion-based account, people may believe misinformation is true and therefore share it. From the perspective of the inattention-based account while most people prefer to only share accurate information, they may not do so as a result of the attention economy (referring to how we have limited attention to devote to any given thing). In this case, posts on social media often compete for user attention and provide distractions which slow down analytic thinking processes (Salari et al., 2020) and misinformation is posted with the desire to capture as much attention as possible and garnering likes, sharing and other responses.

## The Complexity of Sharing Behavior: Potential Anthropological Routes

There is some evidence that we are more inclined to share negative news information as the potential costs of negative information outweigh the potential benefits of positive information (Soroka, 2023). Also, in threatening environments, where there is a lot of unpredictability, people often employ mental shortcuts called heuristics to help process vast amounts of information quickly. In the case of the COVID-19 pandemic, it believed that the source heuristic defined as people's propensity to believe in information supplied by politicians and other elites, who espouse congruent beliefs (Gallanger et al., 2021), may have played a role in the spread of misinformation.

When encountering new information about COVID-19 ask yourself:

> Reflection: *Am I simply accepting this information as true?*
> *Do I believe this information because it somehow makes me feel good to believe it?*

## Differences in Prevalence and Sources of Misinformation across Countries

In Al-Zaman's (2020) study, over 9,500 pieces of misinformation from 138 countries were analyzed to investigate the sources and prevalence of misinformation in different countries. The study found that the countries most impacted by misinformation were India (15.94%), the US (9.74%), Brazil (8.57%), and Spain (8.03%). The study also found that the largest amount of misinformation was produced by social media (84.94%) with Facebook producing 66.87% of the misinformation among all social media platforms. India was found to produce the largest amount of social media misinformation (18.07%) which the researchers attributed to the country's higher rate of Internet use, increasing social media consumption and lack of Internet literacy.

### DO SOME PEOPLE AVOID INFORMATION DURING THE COVID-19 PANDEMIC?

An intriguing study by Song et al. (2020) guided by the stimulus-organism response theory which posits that individuals' emotional responses can be influenced by sensory factors in our environment, which, in turn, can lead to responses of avoidance or approach behaviors, was conducted in China during the COVID-19 pandemic. The study found that information avoidance resulted in reluctance to engage in preventative behaviors during the COVID-19 pandemic. The results of the study suggest that devoting energy to process information overload and/or information perceived to be threatening may trigger a set of negative psychological states such as anxiety, sadness, and cognitive dissonance leading to avoidance of health information.

### *Misinformation from Scientific Journals*

While the credibility of online information has long been questioned, it is generally assumed that scientific information, particularly that taken from scientific, peer reviewed journals is highly credible. In this regard, we also need to consider some of the inherent biases in the peer review process itself. As has been pointed out by West and Bergstrom (2020) science features an analogous filtering process wherein significant results have a higher likelihood of being published than studies with findings that do not reach statistical significance. This publication bias may present a false sense of things.

## Misinformation from Traditional/Mass Media

According to the head of Public Health Emergencies at UNICEF, Carlos Navarro a lot of incorrect information is spreading through traditional mass media:

> [o]ften, they pick the most extreme pictures they can find... There is overkill on the use of [personal protective equipment] and that tends to be the photos that are published everywhere, in all major newspapers and TV...that is, in fact, sending the wrong message.
>
> *(Zarocostas, 2020, p. 676)*

Other researchers have found similar results. For example, in their study which compared misinformation about the COVID-19 pandemic in 19 Canadian news articles to a large corpus of Twitter Tweets, Bridgman et al. (2020) found that traditional news media is more likely to cover and encourage preventative measures for the pandemic than social media.

### *Misinformation from Social Media*

To better understand how misinformation about the coronavirus was spread in Iran, Bastani and Bahrami (2020) conducted a qualitative study to explore the most commonly used social media sites in this country. The study identified cultural factors, demand pressure for information during the crisis, to contribute to the ease in which information dissemination can take place across social networks. According to the researchers, some of the implications of the dissemination of misinformation regarding the disease included psychosocial; economic; health status; health system and ethical factors.

### *Misinformation about COVID19 on Twitter*

Twitter has become ingrained in the public's mind as an information source with over 100,000 tweets are sent using the #COVID19 hashtag (www.symplur.com) a statistic that is growing at an alarming rate as the pandemic continues. However, despite its unique advantage in enabling interaction with experts in a given field compared to other social media platforms, the veracity of Twitter tweets may be questioned as the information is not peer reviewed or necessarily scientifically credible.

Using the Buzzsuma analytic tool, Obiala et al. (2021) analyzed the 30 most highly shared articles about COVID-19 prevention in April 2020; and then classified them according to accuracy and then further classified them by number of shares, topic and sharing platform. The study found that the top 30 articles about coronavirus prevention were shared 4,904, and shared 160 times and with 96.8%

of all shares through Facebook in one month. Eighty percent of the articles were found to be accurate, however they accounted for only 64% of shares, therefore the most shared articles were found to be inaccurate.

Some scholars have speculated that the plethora of unclear, ambiguous and inaccurate information during COVID-19 led to information overload which, in turn, increased anxieties about one's health as well as misinformation sharing (Laato et al., 2020). For this reason, it has been speculated that many have turned to social media which amplified the spread of news through the sharing of links, both authentic news and fake news about the coronavirus (Islam et al., 2020). Ku et al.'s (2019) study found that one third of adolescents reported social media to be their primary news source. Chadwick and Vaccari (2019) found that over 40% of people reported sharing news online said they had shared misinformation.

Social media fatigue may be defined as a number of emotional responses to activities on social networking sites including tiredness, burnout, exhaustion, frustration as well as apathetic feelings toward real world communication (Zheng & Ling, 2021). There is ample evidence to suggest a relationship between social media fatigue and the sharing of misinformation on social media (Islam et al., 2020; Jiang, 2022). The two theories that are believed to make sense of what may exacerbate social media fatigue (SMF) are the cognitive load theory (CLT) and the stressor-strain-outcome model. CLT posits that SMF can be predicted by varies types of overload such as information, communication, system feature, social, and connection overload (Islam et al., 2020).

## Exploration of Misinformation about COVID19 on YouTube

Röchert et al.'s (2020) study explored structural features of YouTube videos and their comments to better understand the level of informational congruity associated with misinformation on COVID-19 and how this changed with the passing of time. The data for this study was gathered from January to March 2020. It is noteworthy how this may contrast with other social media platforms such as Twitter and Facebook, which have a different form of structure for comments (for example in the case of Facebook, account holder can censor comments to only friends or however they wish and while technically the same for YouTube, in the latter, comments are typically made by strangers, hence less of a social repercussion if one commenter openly challenges another commenter). Röchert et al.'s (2020) study found that nodes (defined as either individual users or channels) which spread misinformation were usually integrated in heterogeneous discussion networks. The study found that in the majority of cases this involved content other than misinformation and it was noted that this pattern remained stable over time.

Using keywords 'coronavirus' and 'COVID-19' Li et al. (2020) conducted a YouTube search in March 2020 in which they analyzed the top 75 viewed videos. Of 150 videos screened, comprising 257,804,146 views, 27.5% of the videos were found to contain non-factual information, totaling 62,042,609 views. In a later study by Li et al. (2022) in which a search on YouTube in July 2021 was conducted using keywords 'COVID-19 vaccine' on a cleared-cache web browser, after a search sorted by 'views,' the top 150 most-viewed videos were collected and analyzed. The study found that more than 10% of YouTube's most viewed videos on COVID-19 vaccines, comprising 18 million views, did not match information from the WHO or the Centers for Disease Control and Prevention.

Suter et al.'s (2022) study analyzed comments about videos about the pandemic from four popular YouTube channels during 16-month duration. Results of their study suggest that fake news statistically garnered more likes, and that once fake information was introduced into online discussions this led to a spiraling effect of comments based on misinformation.

### *Misinformation about COVID19 on TikTok*

TikTok is a social media platform that has become globally recognized as an entertainment platform for viral video-sharing (Southwick et al., 2021). van Kampen et al. (2022) explored the content of the top 100 TikTok trending with the hashtag #covidvaccine on TikTok. The videos analyzed in their study comprised 62 000 followers with a median number of plays of 1,700,000 and with median shares of 9,224. Of these videos, 14.7% of TikTok included HCPs, from these 80% could be verified via social media or other methods of regulatory body search. All of the HCP-created TikTok supported vaccine use, and more than 80% of all TikTok content explored in this study supported vaccine use.

Southwick et al. (2021) explored the content of 750 TikTok videos with the hashtag #coronavirus with health-related content posted from January to March 2020. The study attempted to explore how TikTok videos posted during the initial months of the COVID pandemic changed over time as more cases developed. The videos were coded to assess content, misinformation, and public sentiment; videos were also assessed on frequency of being shared as a gauge of measuring their power to engage. The study found that TikTok videos posted in January to February 2020 had less shares and comments than videos posted in March 2020. However, the study also found that the proportion of shares and comments for "misleading and incorrect information" featured in videos decreased with the passing of time.

### *Misinformation on Instagram*

Quinn et al. (2021) conducted a study analyzing the top ten English Instagram posts. The study was conducted every day for ten days with the hashtag #hoax

(April 21–30th, 2020). It was found that for the first day, that #government lies was the most frequent additional hashtag on #hoax posts and that #plandemic, which refers to the false claim that SARS-CoV-2 was created and spread in a planned manner, was the second most common hashtag resulting in a total of 100 posts per hashtag. According to the study, general mistrust and conspiracy theories were the two main themes among the Instagram posts. These findings are consistent with a study conducted by Georgiou et al. (2020) which found that COVID-19-related beliefs were strongly linked with underlying beliefs in conspiracy theories.

### *What Works?*

In Seo et al.'s (2020) review of studies on correcting misinformation (Bode & Vraga, 2018; Pennycook et al., 2018; Seo et al., 2019, 2021; Vraga & Bode, 2017), it was concluded that most effective way to correct misinformation is of a complex nature where a 'best method' is too difficult to identify. The researchers investigated correction from different users on social media such as fact checking websites as well as the frequency of correction in three online experiments. In this set of studies, participants were evaluated for perceived accuracy and willingness to share in terms of real and fake news of COVID-19, respectively. The study found participants' perceived accuracy rating on the COVID-19 fake news across all experiments was effectively reduced by a single correction from the health organizations

## Digital Fact Checkers in the Era of COVID-19

Fact checkers have been around since the twentieth century when the validity of assertions was increasingly questioned with the advent of the information age. Scholars have argued that fact-checkers play a fundamental role in understanding how information flows, why mistakes are made, and how to counteract them (Seaton et al., 2020). Fact-checking efforts to curb the spread of misinformation about the coronavirus have been considered one of the most promising solutions to counter the growth of fake news (Ceron et al., 2021).

## Digital Intelligence Listening Reports

The WHO infodemic management pillar has increased its digital resources In order to better understand social media data use and understand how these data are shared with countries on a weekly basis, the WHO infodemic management pillar has raised its digital resources. The purpose of these resources has been to better inform countries about the information needs of their citizens and provide them with the information they request.

These weekly digital listening reports, distributed by the WHO, have reached policy-makers, health authorities, field staff and partners who lead and support infodemic management activities (WHO, 2021). The purpose of these reports was to offer weekly information updates on various COVID-19 categories that indicate infodemic challenges that need to be addressed. Better understanding of public social media posts, for example, are believed to provide insights into the kinds of emotions people are expressing, which, in turn, can help to guide efforts in how to respond effectively (WHO, 2021). Further, by becoming more aware of emerging narratives and how quickly they are spreading, this data can help health authorities better understand how the public may be impacted. Consequently, this information can, in turn, inform help authorities better understand the types of messages they would need to distribute to lessen the spread of false information. Finally, a better understanding of what types of questions people are asking online, may help us better identify the location of online information sources that are not garnering public trust. To answer those questions health authorities can work more efficiently to deliver and display the empirically based health information needed to counteract conspiracy theories and prevent misinformation from having a chance to multiply (WHO, 2021).

## Contact Tracing: Protection vs. Privacy Considerations

A number of governments around the world have adopted mobile tracking technologies to implement rapid contact tracing. This raises the issue of privacy, as the effectiveness of these technologies is to a great extent dependent on the public's willingness to adopt them. But how is the public weighing their health benefits with concerns over privacy and security?

A study by Garrett et al. (2021) found that while there was initially widespread acceptance of such tracking technologies, a widespread intention-behavior gap was observed between the Australian public's stated attitudes and actual uptake of such devices. Similar concerns have been identified by studies conducted in the US (Ioannou & Tussyadiah, 2021), while other studies also in the US have found a smaller percentage of respondents support government encouragement of citizens to download and use contact tracing apps compared with other surveillance measures (Zhang et al., 2020). Other studies suggest socio-political contexts may be influencing these public attitudes toward tracking technologies during the pandemic. For example, Zhang et al. (2020) found that while acceptance of contact tracing apps is higher in China than in the US or Germany, public acceptance of digital contact tracing is more contingent upon the belief that the apps are perceived as effective in lowering infection rates and providing health information than concerns about privacy.

## Who Is More Susceptible to Misinformation?

Roozenbeek et al. (2020) conducted an international study comprising five national samples from the UK (*n* = 1050 and *n* = 1,150), Ireland (*n* = 700), the USA (*n* = 700), Spain (*n* = 700), and Mexico (*n* = 700), where predictors of belief in the most common statements about the virus that contain misinformation were explored. The study found that greater exposure to information about the virus on social media was associated with higher susceptibility to misinformation. The researchers theorize that misinformation via social media may be more persuasive to some, given the amplifying role (albeit unsubstantiated) of social consensus. This study also found that participants who self-identified as a member of a minority group were more susceptible to misinformation about the virus in all the countries that were surveyed, except the UK. The researchers cite the results of other studies (Freeman et al. 2022; Goertzel, 1994; van Prooijen et al., 2018) which postulate that marginalized groups are more likely to believe in conspiracy theories given that they are more likely to exhibit lower levels of education, income, as well as psychological well-being.

## Link between Susceptibility to Misinformation and Reluctance to Comply with Health Guidelines and Vaccine Hesitancy

In their cross-national survey where samples were taken from the US, Spain, Mexico, the UK, and Ireland, Roozenbeek et al. (2020) explored the role of misinformation about the COVID-19 virus in predicting important health behaviors. Specifically, the study found that susceptibility to misinformation was linked to a decrease in likelihood to get vaccinated along with recommending vaccination to loved ones such as family and friends, and that this effect was found to be consistent across all countries except Spain. It appears that type of media exposure also has an impact on compliance behavior. Bridgman et al. (2020) found that individuals more exposed to news media were associated with fewer misperceptions and more social distancing compliance while the opposite was true regarding exposure to social media exposure which was associated with more misperceptions and less social distancing compliance.

## Inoculation Based Interventions against the Infodemic: Does It Work?

In two separate studies, each with a sample size of over 1,700 respondents, Basol et al. (2021) assessed the efficacy of two 'prebunking' interventions which had the goal of improving people's ability to spot manipulation techniques commonly used in COVID-19 misinformation. The studies used survey materials in English, French and German and it was found that the intervention which comprised a five-minute browser game: increased how manipulative misinformation about COVID-19 was perceived to be. The first intervention, Go Viral!, is a novel and freely available five-minute choice-based browser game similar in design to other 'fake news' games such as Bad News and Harmony Square. The researchers created Go Viral! (www.goviralgame.com) in collaboration with the UK Cabinet Office and DROG with support from the WHO and the United Nations' Verified Campaign to expose three manipulation techniques commonly used in COVID-19 misinformation, which the authors list as fear mongering, using fake experts, and spreading conspiracy theories. The researchers point out that this scenario relies on two common techniques used in online misinformation: impersonation and the fake expert technique. Results of the study found evidence for improved confidence in their ability to find misinformation and reduced self-reported willingness to share misinformation with others. In the second manipulation, the researchers found that reading real-world info graphics from UNESCO improved the ability and confidence of respondents to find COVID-19 misinformation.

However, some researchers warn against blind adherence to the powers of inoculation-based interventions that attempt to change susceptibility to belief in misinformation about the COVID-19 virus. For example, Van der linden (2022) argue that targeting false claims by debunking them, a common strategy in combating vaccine misinformation, might actually worsen the negative effects of misinformation. Van der linden (2022) further explain that because corrections directly contradict misinformation, this process can actually trigger the "continued influence effect," (Van der linden, 2022, p. 2) in which individuals continue to recall misinformation even when acknowledging the correction. The corrections can then trigger psychological resistance, especially when corrections are perceived as attacking important values and ideologies that hold meaning for the individual and align with the misinformation.

## The Role of Strategic Partnerships in Proper Dissemination of Authentic Information

It has been argued that the dissemination of valid information about public health messages rests on the careful collaboration of multiple stakeholders such as the mass media, healthcare organization, community-based organizations and other important stakeholders, and that the dissemination should be launched from common platforms (Tasnim et al., 2020).

## Themes of Different Types of Misinformation

From January 1 to May 26, 2020, over 1.1 million individual articles (total 1,116,952) mentioning COVID-19 misinformation was published in English-language traditional media outlets, representing just under 3% of the overall COVID-19 conversation (total 38,713,161 articles) during this timeframe. A study conducted by Evanega et al. (2020) identified five different subsections within the overall COVID-19 misinformation conversation. The study found that the misinformation categories comprised misinformation conspiracies, Trump mentions, and infodemic topics, fact-checking, and Trump only.

The results of this study found that former President Donald Trump was the source of 37.9% of the misinformation identified in the study.

## How to Encourage Searchers to Find Timely and Accurate Information

In order to understand searching style, the WHO and Google, collaborated in the creation of an online public service announcement on COVID-19, in the form of search ads. The WHO conducted a study employing 71 text ads comprising four COVID-19 topics: COVID-19 (general), vaccines that were COVID-19 specific, vaccines (general), and masks. The study was conducted in early 2020 using a multi-disciplinary team to design these experimental ads and included different message frames such as descriptive, gain, and loss frames as well as appeals to values and reasons for using the vaccine. The experimental WHO text ads had views of 13 million which lead to 1.4 million click-throughs to the WHO website. The study found a wide gap between the most effective and least effective messages. For messages on COVID-19, the best performing framings were found to be more than twice as effective as the worst performing framings. Specifically, gain-framed or 'health affirming' messages were found to perform better than loss-framed or 'illness detecting' messages in the mask and vaccine topics. The researchers note, however, that across topics, countries and demographic factors had a moderating effect on these results, so that a given frame might work better in one language or a certain country (Pattison et al., 2022).

## How to Stop the Spread of Misinformation

Scholars have suggested a number of ways to combat the spread of misinformation. For example, Tasnim et al. (2020) have suggested four ways in which this can be done. First, they argue, frontline healthcare providers need to be prepared or otherwise trained with the most up to date and accurate scientific research finding. They should be ready to use this information during the process of direct care-giving and communicate it to patients with whom they are interacting directly. Coming from frontline health-care providers, patients are more likely to trust and act upon this information given its source.

Second, Tasnim et al. (2020) suggest we should acknowledge the critical role that mass media, community organizations, support groups, and civil society role play in the spread of accurate information. They argue that it may be necessary to build strategic partnerships at both local as well as international levels, in which offline and online resources may be connected and thereby coordinated manner in a manner such that validated information is communicated across platforms in greater breadth.

Third, Tasnim et al. (2020) argue that ultimately all hoaxes and rumors should be removed from the Internet which will enable the public to better build awareness of the COVID-19 virus from scientifically validated information they can find online. Finally, Tasnim et al. (2020) argue that more should be done to effectively bring those spreading misinformation including online portals and personnel producing and/or playing a part in the propagation of inaccurate information about the coronavirus, to justice. This process may be expedited with more training of local and national regulatory authorities who would be better equipped to address these issues within their respective jurisdictions.

Based on the work of Haciyakupoglu et al. (2018) on how to counter fake news, Dash et al. (2021) propose a three-level approach for handling the infodemic that would be of particular service to low and middle-income countries. The first step (pre-emptive measures) in this approach comprises limiting the spread of false information by developing clear definitions of terms relevant to the infodemic. The authors argue that the value of doing so would allow countries to choose the agencies required to manage the infodemic in a manner where roles would be clarified and communication strategies enhanced. Knowledge sharing would potentially take place, in this first step, through the establishment of regional as well as global collaborations, even comprising governmental as well as nongovernmental agencies.

In the second step (immediate measures) surveillance should be established, and the public should be educated. One way the public may be educated is through summaries of scientific evidence that should be made accessible to all and should use clear jargon-free language, so the public is aware of the true facts of the pandemic. In this stage, Dash et al. (2020) argue that the public needs to be monitored, and that the information that is synthesized from this surveillance should be used to inform policy-making decisions. They suggest that digital technologies may be used to conduct fact checking and detect rumors during this surveillance.

Finally, in the third step (long term measures), Dash et al. (2020) argue for the need to develop curriculum for the management of fake news. This is the time to promote health literacy and create public health awareness campaigns. This argument is also advocated by the work of Sun et al. (2022) who state that the effectiveness of such public health awareness campaigns may be maximized if conducted via video-based platforms:

> [C]ompared to text-based platforms, video-based social media such as TikTok have the power to vividly present what is going on at grassroots levels. The

> videos analyzed in the present study captured diverse, immediate, broad, and vivid scenes about local communities and residents. It is quite common for viewers to identify videos that are close to them in terms of both physical and psychological distance. Research has shown that socially immediate videos are more likely to influence people, both cognitively and affectively.
>
> *(p. 12)*

Similar to the work of Dash et al. (2020), Gunther Eysenbach, a pioneer in the field of infodemiolgy, theorizes that there are 'four pillars' of infodemic management comprising how information is monitored, building eHealth Literacy and science literacy capacity, encouraging peer-review and fact-checking, as well as ensuring accurate and timely knowledge translation. Ultimately, regardless of what approach is taken to combat the spreading of misinformation about the COVID-19 virus, Naeem and Boulos (2021) caution that given the complexity of the COVID-19 infodemic, it is highly unlikely that any one approach will be fully effective. Instead Naeem and Boulos (2021) suggest the advantages of a mixed, interdependent approach, where the best of many strategies can be combined, such as learning-based approaches, checklists, myth-busters, fact-checkers, and health-literacy guidelines.

## Infodemic Management Framework

An analysis team comprising policy makers, representatives from the media, private sector organizations and others from related professional and scientific disciplines brainstormed a total of 594 suggestions. These resulted in a set of 50 proposed actions for a framework for managing infodemics in health emergencies; which were developed into the following six policy implications to consider (Tangcharoensathien et al., 2020):

1 Interventions and messages should be empirically based, and must be presented in a manner which is easily understandable for the public so that informed decisions on how to protect oneself in a health emergency can be made.
2 Knowledge should be translated into messages that result in actionable behavior-change. These messages should be clear and easily understood by and accessible to individuals around the world.
3 Governments should involve key communities to ensure their concerns and information needs are understood. This way, important health messages can be better tailored to meet the needs of the audiences they represent.
4 All sectors should be involved in the creation of strategic partnerships, such as individuals from technology sectors, academia, and civil society.

5 Health authorities should ensure that these actions are based on reliable information which helps to clarify understanding of how misinformation circulates as well as changes within various communities.
6 Infodemic management approaches are improved through empirically based methods and should inform risk mitigation.

## Key Lessons

The spreading of false information about the coronavirus is a serious problem that needs attention at the world level. This chapter has overviewed the results of a number of studies on types of misinformation about the COVID-19 pandemic and how this information has spread particularly on social media. We also explored factors that make certain individuals more susceptible to being persuaded by misinformation. This was followed by a review of digital fact finders as well as digital listening devices and how they can be employed to curb the spread of the virus. The chapter concluded with some best measure practices on how to curb the spread of misinformation.

## References

Anastasiades, E., Argyrides, M., & Mousoulidou, M. (2021). Misinformation about COVID-19: psychological insights. *Encyclopedia, 1*(4), 1200–1214.

Ahmed, S. T. (2020). Managing news overload (MNO): The COVID-19 infodemic. *Information, 11*(8), 375.

Ali, M. Y., & Bhatti, R. (2020). COVID-19 (coronavirus) pandemic: Information sources channels for the public health awareness. *Asia Pacific Journal of Public Health, 32*(4), 168–169.

Alvarez-Risco, A., Mejia, C. R., Delgado-Zegarra, J., Del-Aguila-Arcentales, S., Arce-Esquivel, A. A., Valladares-Garrido, M. J.,... & Yáñez, J. A. (2020). The Peru approach against the COVID-19 infodemic: Insights and strategies. *The American Journal of Tropical Medicine and Hygiene, 103*(2), 583.

Al-Zaman, M. S. (2022). Prevalence and source analysis of COVID-19 misinformation in 138 countries. *IFLA Journal, 48*(1), 189–204.

Basol, M., Roozenbeek, J., Berriche, M., Uenal, F., McClanahan, W. P., & Linden, S. V. D. (2021). Towards psychological herd immunity: Cross-cultural evidence for two prebunking interventions against COVID-19 misinformation. *Big Data & Society, 8*(1), 20539517211013868.

Bastani, P., & Bahrami, M. A. (2020). COVID-19 related misinformation on social media: A qualitative study from Iran. *Journal of Medical Internet Research*. Advance online publication. doi: 10.2196/18932.

Bawden, D., & Robinson, L. (2020). *Information overload: An introduction*. Oxford, UK: Oxford University Press. Available online: https://oxfordre.com/politics/view/10.1093/acrefore/9780190228637.001.0001/ acrefore-9780190228637-e-1360?rskey=pGstwF&result=1#acrefore-9780190228637 -e-1360-div2-2

Bode, L., & Vraga, E. K. (2018). See something, say something: Correction of global health misinformation on social media. *Health Communication, 33*(9), 1131–1140.

Brennen, J. S., Simon, F. M., Howard, P. N., & Nielsen, R. K. (2020). *Types, sources, and claims of COVID-19 misinformation* (Doctoral dissertation, University of Oxford).

Bridgman, A., Merkley, E., Loewen, P. J., Owen, T., Ruths, D., Teichmann, L., & Zhilin, O. (2020). The causes and consequences of COVID-19 misperceptions: Understanding the role of news and social media. *Harvard Kennedy School Misinformation Review, 1*(3). formatted_causes_consequences_bridgman-et-al4.pdf (harvard.edu)

Ceron, W., Gruszynski Sanseverino, G., de-Lima-Santos, M. F., & Quiles, M. G. (2021). COVID-19 fake news diffusion across Latin America. *Social Network Analysis and Mining, 11*(1), 47.

Chadwick, A., & Vaccari, C. (2019). News sharing on UK Social Media: Misinformation, disinformation, and correction. Online Civic Culture Centre, Loughborough University. https://www.lboro.ac.uk/research/online-civic-culture-centre/news-events/articles/o3c-1-survey-report-news-sharing-misinformation

Cotter, K., DeCook, J. R., & Kanthawala, S. (2022). Fact-checking the crisis: COVID-19, infodemics, and the platformization of truth. *Social Media+ Society, 8*(1). doi: 10.1177/20563051211069048

Dash, S., Parray, A. A., De Freitas, L., *et al.* (2021). Combating the COVID-19 infodemic: A three-level approach for low and middle-income countries. *BMJ Global Health, 6*, e004671. doi: 10.1136/bmjgh-2020–004671

Dentith, M. (2013). Have you heard?: The rumor as reliable. In M. Dentith (Ed.), *Rumor and communication in asia in the internet age* (pp. 46–60). Routledge.

van Der Linden, S., Roozenbeek, J., & Compton, J. (2020). Inoculating against fake news about COVID-19. *Frontiers in Psychology, 11*, 566790. doi: 10.3389/fpsyg.2020.566790.

DiFonzo, N., Robinson, N. M., Suls, J. M., & Rini, C. (2012). Rumors about cancer: Content, sources, coping, transmission, and belief. *Journal of Health Communication, 17*(9), 1099–1115.

Entradas, M. (2021). In science we trust: The effects of information sources on COVID-19 risk perceptions. *Health Communication*, 37(14), 1715–1723. doi: 10.1080/10410236.2021.1914915

Evanega, S., Lynas, M., Adams, J., Smolenyak, K., & Insights, C. G. (2020). Coronavirus misinformation: Quantifying sources and themes in the COVID-19 'infodemic'. *JMIR Preprints, 19*(10), 2020.

Eysenbach, G. (2002). Infodemiology: The epidemiology of (mis)information. *American Journal of Medicine, 113*(9), 763–765.

Eysenbach, G. (2003). SARS and population health technology. *Journal of Medical Internet Research, 5*(2), e14.

Eysenbach, G. (2006). Infodemiology: Tracking flu-related searches on the web for syndromic surveillance. *AMIA Annual Symposium Proceedings*, 244–248.

Eysenbach, G. (2009). Infodemiology and infoveillance: Framework for an emerging set of public health informatics methods to analyze search, communication and publication behavior on the Internet. *Journal of Medical Internet Research, 11*(1), e11.

Eysenbach, G. (2020). How to fight an infodemic: The four pillars of infomedic management. *Journal of Medical Internet Research, 22*(6), e21820. doi: 10.2196/21820

Freeman, D., Waite, F., Rosebrock L., Petit, A., Causierm C., East A., ... Lambe, S. (2022). Coronavirus conspiracy beliefs, mistrust, and compliance with government guidelines in England. *Psychological Medicine, 52*(2), 251–263.

Gallagher, M. W., Smith, L. J., Richardson, A. L., D'Souza, J. M., & Long, L. J. (2021). Examining the longitudinal effects and potential mechanisms of hope on COVID-19 stress, anxiety, and well-being. *Cognitive Behaviour Therapy, 50*(3), 234–245.

Gallagher, R. J., Doroshenko, L., Shugars, S., Lazer, D., & Foucault Welles, B. (2021). Sustained online amplification of COVID-19 elites in the United States. *Social Media+ Society, 7*(2), 1–16, doi: 10.1177/20563051211024957.

Garrett, P. M., White, J. P., Lewandowsky, S., Kashima, Y., Perfors, A., Little, D. R.,... & Dennis, S. (2021). The acceptability and uptake of smartphone tracking for COVID-19 in Australia. *PLoS One, 16*(1), e0244827.

Georgiou, N., Delfabbro, P., & Balzan, R. (2020). COVID-19-related conspiracy beliefs and their relationship with perceived stress and pre-existing conspiracy beliefs. *Personality and Individual Differences, 166*, 110201.

Ginsberg, J., Mohebbi, M. H., Patel, R. S., Brammer, L., Smolinski, M. S., & Brilliant, L. (2009). Detecting influenza epidemics using search engine query data. *Nature, 457*(7232), 1012–1014.

Goertzel, T. (1994). Belief in conspiracy theories. *Politcal Psychology, 15*, 731–742. doi: 10.2307/3791630.

Greene, C. M., & Murphy, G. (2021). Quantifying the effects of fake news on behavior: Evidence from a study of COVID-19 misinformation. *Journal of Experimental Psychology: Applied, 27*(4), 773.

Haciyakupoglu, G., Hui, J. Y., & Suguna, V. S. (2018). Countering fake news a survey of recent global initiatives. Singapore. https://www.rsis.edu.sg/ wp- content/uploads/2018/03/PR180416_Countering-Fake-News.pdf

Ioannou, A., & Tussyadiah, I. (2021). Privacy and surveillance attitudes during health crises: Acceptance of surveillance and privacy protection behaviours. *Technology in Society, 67*, 101774.

Islam, A. N., Laato, S., Talukder, S., & Sutinen, E. (2020). Misinformation sharing and social media fatigue during COVID-19: An affordance and cognitive load perspective. *Technological Forecasting and Social Change, 159*, 120201.

Jiang, S. (2022). The roles of worry, social media information overload, and social media fatigue in hindering health fact-checking. *Social Media+ Society, 8*(3), 1–12. doi: 10.1177/20563051221113070.

van Kampen, K., Laski, J., Herman, G., & Chan, T. M. (2022). Investigating COVID-19 vaccine communication and misinformation on tiktok: Cross-sectional study. *JMIR Infodemiology, 2*(2), e38316.

Ku K. Y. L., Kong Q., Song Y., Deng L., Kang Y., & Hu A. (2019). What predicts adolescents' critical thinking about real-life news? The roles of social media news consumption and news media literacy. *Think. Ski. Creat.* 33:100570. doi: 10.1016/J.TSC.2019.05.004

Laato, S., Islam, A. N., Islam, M. N., & Whelan, E. (2020). What drives unverified information sharing and cyberchondria during the COVID-19 pandemic? *European Journal of Information Systems, 29*(3), 288–305.

Laato, S., Islam, A. N., & Laine, T. H. (2020). Did location-based games motivate players to socialize during COVID-19? *Telematics and Informatics, 54*, 101458.

Li, H. O. Y., Bailey, A., Huynh, D., & Chan, J. (2020). YouTube as a source of information on COVID-19: A pandemic of misinformation? *BMJ Global Health, 5*(5), e002604.

Li, H. O. Y., Pastukhova, E., Brandts-Longtin, O., Tan, M. G., & Kirchhof, M. G. (2022). YouTube as a source of misinformation on COVID-19 vaccination: A systematic analysis. *BMJ Global Health*, *7*(3), e008334.

Naeem, B. S., & Boulos, M. N. K. (2021). COVID-19 misinformation online and health literacy: A brief overview. *International Journal of Environmental Research and Public Health*, *18*(15), 8091.

Nelson, T., Kagan, N., Critchlow, C., Hillard, A., & Hsu, A. (2020). The danger of misinformation in the COVID-19 crisis. *Missouri Medicine*, *117*(6), 510.

Newman, N., Fletcher, R., Kalogeropoulos, A., & Nielsen, R. K. (2019). *Reuters Institute Digital News Report 2019*. Oxford, UK: Reuters Institute for the Study of Journalism.

Nickerson, R. S. (1998). Confirmation bias: A ubiquitous phenomenon in many guises. *Review of General Psychology*, *2*(2), 175–220.

Obiała, J., Obiała, K., Mańczak, M., Owoc, J., & Olszewski, R. (2021). COVID-19 misinformation: Accuracy of articles about coronavirus prevention mostly shared on social media. *Health Policy and Technology*, *10*(1), 182–186.

Pattison, A. B., Reinfelde, M., Chang, H., Chowdhury, M., Cohen, E., Malahy, S., O'Connor, K., Mehdi Sellami, M., Smith, K. L., Stanton, C. Y., Voets, B., & Wei, H. G.(2022). Finding the facts in an infodemic: Framing effective COVID-19 messages to connect people to authoritative content. *BMJ Global Health*. doi: 10.1136/bmjgh-2021–007582

Pennycook, G., Cannon, T. D., & Rand, D. G. (2018). Prior exposure increases perceived accuracy of fake news. *Journal of Experimental Psychology: General*, *147*(12), 1865–1880.

Pennycook, G., McPhetres, J., Zhang, Y., Lu, J. G., & Rand, D. G. (2020). Fighting COVID-19 misinformation on social media: Experimental evidence for a scalable accuracy-nudge intervention. *Psychological Science, 31*, 770–780.

Pennycook, G., & Rand, D. G. (2021). The psychology of fake news. *Trends in Cognitive Sciences*, *25*(5), 388–402.

Prasetya, H. A., & Murata, T. (2020). A model of opinion and propagation structure polarization in social media. *Computational Social Networks*, *7*(1), 1–35. doi: 10.1186/s40649- 019–0076-z URL https://link.springer.com/articles/10.1186/s40649-019-0076-z

Quinn, E. K., Fazel, S. S., & Peters, C. E. (2021). The Instagram infodemic: Cobranding of conspiracy theories, coronavirus disease 2019 and authority-questioning beliefs. *Cyberpsychology, Behavior, and Social Networking*, *24*(8), 573–577.

Röchert, D., Neubaum, G., Ross, B., Brachten, F., & Stieglitz, S. (2020). Opinion-based homogeneity on YouTube: Combining sentiment and social network analysis. *Computational Communication Research, 2*(1), 81–108.

Roozenbeek, J., Schneider, C. R., Dryhurst, S., Kerr, J., Freeman, A. L., Recchia, G., … & Van Der Linden, S. (2020). Susceptibility to misinformation about COVID-19 around the world. *Royal Society Open Science*, *7*(10), 201199.

Salari, N., Hosseinian-Far, A., Jalali, R., Vaisi-Raygani, A., Rasoulpoor, S., Mohammadi, M., Rasoulpoor, S., & Khaledi-Paveh, B. (2020). Prevalence of stress, anxiety, depression among the general population during the COVID-19 pandemic: A systematic review and meta-analysis. *Global Health, 16*, 57.

Savolainen, R. (2007). Filtering and withdrawing: Strategies for coping with information overload in everyday contexts. *Journal of Information Science*, *33*, 611–621.

Seaton, J., Sippitt, A., & Worthy, B. (2020). Fact checking and information in the age of covid. *The Political Quarterly, 91*(3), 578–584.
Seo, H., Xiong, A., & Lee, D. (2019). Trust it or not: Effects of machine-learning warnings in helping individuals mitigate misinformation. In *Proceedings of the 10th ACM conference on web science* (pp. 265–274).
Seo, H., Xiong, A., Lee, S., & Lee, D. (2021). (In) effectiveness of accumulated correction on COVID-19 misinformation. In *Proceedings of technology, mind & society.* https://tmb.apaopen.org/pub/ss8t2ayg/release/1
Seo, H., Xiong, A., Lee, S., & Lee, D. (2022, May). If you have a reliable source, say something: Effects of correction comments on COVID-19 misinformation. In *Proceedings of the international AAAI conference on web and social media* (Vol. 16, pp. 896–907).
Shearer, E., & Mitchell, (2021). *A news use across social media platforms in 2020.* Washington, DC: Pew Research Center.
Soon, C., & Goh, S. (2018). Fake news, false information and more: Countering human biases. *Institute of Policy Studies (IPS) Working Papers, 31.*
Song, S., Yao, X., & Wen, N. (2021). What motivates Chinese consumers to avoid information about the COVID-19 pandemic?: The perspective of the stimulus-organism-response model. *Information Processing & Management, 58*(1), 102407.
Soroka, S. (2023). 'Why do we pay more attention to negative news than to positive news?'
Retrieved on September 5, 2023 from: https://blogs.lse.ac.uk/politicsandpolicy/ why-is-there-no-good-news/#Author
Southwick, L., Guntuku, S. C., Klinger, E. V., Seltzer, E., McCalpin, H. J., & Merchant, R. M. (2021). Characterizing COVID-19 content posted to TikTok: Public sentiment and response during the first phase of the COVID-19 pandemic. *Journal of Adolescent Health, 69*(2), 234–241.
Sun, S., Liu, Z., Zhai, Y., & Wang, F. (2022). COVID-19 vaccines on TikTok: A big- data analysis of entangled discourses. *International Journal of Environmental Research and Public Health, 19*(20), 13287.
Suter, V., Shahrezaye, M., & Meckel, M. (2022). COVID-19 induced misinformation on YouTube: An analysis of user commentary. *Frontiers in Political Science, 4*, 26.
Tangcharoensathien, V., Calleja, N., Nguyen, T., Purnat, T., D'Agostino, M., Garcia-Saiso, S., … & Briand, S. (2020). Framework for managing the COVID-19 infodemic: Methods and results of an online, crowd sourced WHO technical consultation. *Journal of Medical Internet Research, 22*(6), e19659.
Tasnim, S., Hossain, M., & Mazumder, H. (2020). Impact of rumours and misinformation on COVID-19 in social media. *Journal of Preventive Medicine and Public Health, 53*, 171–174.
Tolia, V., Renin Singh, R., Deshpande, S., Dave, A., & Rathod, R. M. (2022). Understanding factors to COVID-19 vaccine adoption in Gujarat, India. *International Journal of Environmental Research and Public Health, 19*(5), 2707.
Van der Linden, S. (2022). Misinformation: susceptibility, spread, and interventions to immunize the public. *Nature Medicine, 28*(3), 460–467.
van Prooijen, J.-W., Staman, J., & Krouwel, A. P. M. (2018). Increased conspiracy beliefs among ethnic and Muslim minorities. *Applied Cognitive Psychology, 32*, 661–667.

doi: 10.1002/acp.3442. Vraga, E. K., & Bode, L. (2017). Using expert sources to correct health misinformation in social media. *Science Communication, 39*(5), 621–645.
Vraga, E. K., & Bode, L. (2021). Addressing COVID-19 misinformation on social media preemptively and responsively. *Emerging Infectious Diseases*, 27(2), 396.
West, J. D., & Bergstrom, C. T. (2021). Misinformation in and about science. *Proceedings of the National Academy of Sciences, 118*(15), e1912444117.
World Health Organization. (2021). Infodemic management: An overview of infodemic management during COVID-19, January 2020–May 2021. 9789240035966-eng.pdf
Zarocostas, J. (2020). How to fight an infodemic. *The Lancet, 395*(10225), 676.
Zhang, B., Kreps, S., McMurry, N., & McCain, R. M. (2020). Americans' perceptions of p privacy and surveillance in the COVID-19 pandemic. *PLos One, 15*(12), e0242652.
Zheng, H., & Ling, R. (2021). Drivers of social media fatigue: A systematic review. *Telematics and Informatics, 64*, 101696.

## Glossary of Key Terms and Concepts

**Confirmation Bias** as seeking or interpreting evidence in a manner that favors existing beliefs, expectations, or a pre-hypothesis (Nickerson, 1998).

**Continued Influence Effect** in this process individuals continue to retrieve misinformation from memory even when acknowledging the correction; the corrections can then trigger psychological resistance, especially when corrections are perceived as attacking salient values and ideologies with which misinformation can resonate (Soon & Goh, 2018).

**Disinformation** spreading untrue or false information with bad intent (Naeem & Boulos, 2021).

**Health literacy** health literacy has been defined as the individuals' capacity to obtain, process, and understand basic health information and services needed to make appropriate health decisions (Alvarez-Risco et al., 2020).

**Infodemiology** defined as an emerging research discipline and methodology" which attempts to identify the determinants and distribution of health information and misinformation. Infodemiology is believed to be of assistance to health professionals and patients in guiding them to high quality online health information (Eysenbach, 2020).

**Malinformation** reconfigured or otherwise altered true information (Brennan et al., 2020).

**Misinformation** cases in which people's beliefs in factual matters are not supported by clear evidence and expert opinion (Naeem & Boulos, 2021).

**Rumour** an act of communication containing unverified or false information and can serve as a way for a group of people to make sense of uncertainty; the hearer must have some belief in this information (Dentith, 2013).

**Source Heuristic** people's propensity to believe in information supplied by politicians and other elites, who espouse congruent beliefs (Gallanger et al., 2021).

## Discussion Questions

1 In your opinion, what are some dangers to society if the spread of misinformation about the coronavirus goes unchecked? Explain.
2 Can you think of some reasons that make conspiracy theories appealing? Explain.
3 Why do you think some people are more prone to believing misinformation about the coronavirus than others? Explain.
4 Explain why sharing misinformation is a complex issue and not just about wanting to educate others?
5 In the context of the study that analyzed comments about the contents of the pandemic on YouTube, explain how political polarization may increase the spread of misinformation?
6 Discuss the three manipulation techniques for spreading misinformation about the COVID-19 virus identified by the GoViral campaign?
7 Please visit https://www.youtube.com/watch?v=n029n44DFWI Why are CTs appealing
8 In a group of 3 to 4 people, discuss how you would design a social media campaign to help stop the spread of fake information about COVID-19. What tool(s) might you apply and what would be your primary message(s)?

# 3

# TRUST IN THE GOVERNMENT DURING THE COVID-19 PANDEMIC AND HOW TO BE A GOOD LEADER

## Chapter Learning Objectives

- Describe the importance of institutional trust during a pandemic
- Explain the concept of the paradox of trust in a pandemic
- Describe some of the factors that influence trust in heads of state during a crisis such as the pandemic
- Discuss Cognitive Appraisal Theory
- Discuss Affective Intelligence Theory
- Discuss the main elements of good communication during a crisis event

## Introduction

During a pandemic, governments play a significant role in communicating expert health advice to the public as well as mandating that the public follow certain behavioral guidelines to safeguard against further spread of the virus (Suhay et al., 2022). Thus, a better understanding of the role of institutional trust in pandemic control is crucial for the development of meaningful policy applications (Stefaniak et al., 2022). It has often been assumed that greater trust in the government will encourage the citizens of a nation to be more compliant with health policies designed to protect their well-being, but the coronavirus pandemic has challenged this assumption. While some studies suggest this is true (Saechang et al., 2021; Wong & Jensen, 2020), other studies suggest higher political trust, defined as confidence in as well as public support for essential political institutions such as the government and the legislature (Newton et al., 2018), is associated with decreased compliance with public health policies, especially during a public health crisis (Trent et al., 2022; Woelfert & Kunst, 2020).

DOI: 10.4324/9781003394983-3

Given that the concept of trust has traditionally been reported to be elusive (Santos, 2021; McCune, 1998) and multi-dimensional (Corazzini, 1977; Gefen, 2002; Hirvi et al., 2021) the global experience of the coronavirus pandemic makes it even more important to understand how the pandemic has impacted trust (Devine et al., 2021). In its most basic form, trust may be understood to be an agent's willingness to accept vulnerability in an interaction with the belief that this vulnerability will not be exploited (Rotter, 1967). **Social trust** refers to trust in a generalized other where the trusting party does not have any individual- or context-specific information about this generalized other (Özcan & Bjørnskov, 2011). It has been suggested that in the case of **institutional trust**, which refers to trust in government institutions, the people of a nation might use different criteria to evaluate how to trust different institutions (Fisher et al., 2010, cited in Devine et al., 2021). The public might make decisions to trust institutions in one of two ways: "either pragmatically or strategically in terms of the perceived delivery record of the institution, or about the moral capacity of its leaders to do the right thing, or about the checks and balances in place to make sure that those leaders behave appropriately" (Devine et al., 2021, p. 275).

As researchers we need to clarify how do we measure institutional trust: should we stipulate it is a pragmatic process (are leaders doing what they promised, are they delivering etc.) or affective (are leaders acting ethically with compassion etc.)? Research suggests this issue is quite complex. For example, Liu et al.'s (2020) study suggests that a number of factors such as the nature of a country's government system as well as institutional ethos can impact the public's trust in their government. Other studies suggest that trust, especially during a pandemic, may change over time (Six et al., 2023).

Given that information from a plethora of sources, including people's perception of the trustworthiness of these sources, will ultimately influence how people understand and respond to a public health crisis (Nielson et al., 2020), this chapter will explore the role of institutional trust in impacting the public's compliance behaviors during the COVID-19 pandemic. Questions of interest include: what are some of the antecedents of trust? How do we define trust? Does trust in the government necessarily result in greater adherence to government issued safety rules and policies? And what is the role of communication in establishing trust during a large-scale world disaster?

## The Role of Communication in Establishing Trust During a Pandemic

### *Why We Seek Information during a Crisis and How We Process it*

Griffin et al. (2004) explain that certain psychological processes take place when seeking and processing information during a crisis event once individuals have sought timely information typically from a variety of sources. They explain that after receiving information, two sets of remedial processes occur. In the first phase, individuals can observe the behavior of others, and in this phase, mediated information can be employed to reduce tension and anxiety. Sense-making can occur at this time through hearing the experiences of others. In the second phase, information is believed to facilitate more specific remedial responses. It is believed that a person's ability to take action during a crisis enables a feeling of empowerment such that they feel they have some control over their situation. There are ample studies that suggest the importance of crisis messages promoting a sense of self-efficacy (Seeger et al., 2003; Witte, 1994).

### *Importance of Point to Point and Whole Picture Perspectives in Trust*

It has been argued that unpredictable situations such as pandemics require individuals and organizations to have the ability to both to receive trusted information, and this information should originate from a central source, from where the whole picture can be seen and understood. In the same vein, point-by-point information is also needed. Indeed, it has been argued that individuals and groups need access to both of these systems in order to reduce the likelihood of panic (Glass & Schoch-Spana, 2002; Surowiecki, 2004).

Until recently, only governments in most countries had the ability to see at a glance their entire communications sector of both point-to-point and point-to-multipoint perspectives so they would be in a unique position to understand how each agency and industry could play a role in resilience communication (Longstaff & Yang, 2008). **Situational awareness** is defined as "the perception of the elements in the environment within a volume of time and space, the comprehension of their meaning and the projection of their status in the near future" (Endsley, 1995, p. 36). Currently there is a growing body of research on the role of situation awareness during the Coronavirus-19 pandemic within the contexts of tele-health services (Dixit et al., 2020), decisions to travel (Naseer et al., 2021), and mathematical modeling (Adiga et al., 2020) to name a few.

### *Importance of Trust between Health Officials and the Public*

As stated earlier, pandemics by nature are unstable and unpredictable. Further, given that the trust the public typically has in its government is based on social contracts being met, the suspension of civil liberties being breached during lockdowns, may have negative implications on mutual trust (Thomas, 1998). The combination of these changes arguably produces an even more challenging context to build trust public health disasters. The public's trust in its government has also been found to be contingent upon a number of factors including the nature of its legal system which influences the quality, capability, and effectiveness of welfare services, and which, in turn, impacts a government's responsiveness to a health emergency, as well as its corresponding institutional ethos and degree of accountability (Liu et al., 2022).

So how do we build trust between health officials and the public? Perhaps the most difficult and complex area of concern is ensuring that emergency communications can be trusted by the public. At the very least, government agencies need to provide clear and ongoing communication with the public which will help to build trust. For example, clear communications regarding how proposed actions will be mandated can help the public feel more in control and better plan for their safety in times of crisis (Long Staff & Young, 2008).

## The Role of Institutional Trust During A Pandemic

As researchers we need to clarify how we measure institutional trust: should we stipulate it is a pragmatic process (are leaders doing what they promised, are they delivering etc.) or an affective process (are leaders acting ethically with compassion etc.)? Research suggests this issue is quite complex. For example, Liu et al.'s (2020) study suggests that public trust can be contingent and vary depending on the nature of a country's government system as well as its corresponding institutional ethos and its degree of accountability (Liu et al., 2020).

There is no denying the important role of trust in the government during crisis events, as in the case of the populations of the DACH countries trust in its government being one of the highest in the world, and the impact of this on pandemic policy effectiveness (Desson et al., 2020; Turi & Virag, 2021). Trust cannot be established on the first day of a disaster (Longstaff & Yang, 2008). Based on this consideration, how does one establish trust in one's government during a pandemic?

### *Trust in the Government and the Head of State*

In their content analysis of 233 viral tweets (defined as having 500 likes or more) of the G7 leaders, Rufai and Bunce (2020) found 82.8% were informative, 9.4% were morale boosting, and 6.9% were political. Given that 28.6% of the informative tweets provided links to official government resources, the researchers interpreted this as a positive finding to suggest the mass spread of authoritative information about the coronavirus by world leaders (Rufai & Bunce, 2020).

There is ample evidence that suggests a relation between citizens' satisfaction with the public sector and trust in their government (Boateng & Cox, 2016; Cooper et al., 2008; Grimmelikhuijsen & Knies, 2017; Mizrahi et al., 2019; Van de Walle & Bouckaert, 2003; Vigoda-Gadot & Mizrahi, 2014). Other factors that have been linked to trust in the government during a pandemic include quality of communication, closely following the news, and confidence in the vaccine (Quinn et al., 2013) as well as transparent and clear government communication and successful pandemic management (Kye & Hwang, 2020). In their analysis of PM Arden's leadership during the pandemic, McGuire notes how referring to her country as a team of 5 million, New Zealand Prime Minister Jacinda Ardern convinced her citizens to establish new social norms. Her speeches to the public, McGuire observed, comprised various discursive devices, images of social solidarity, and information that explained the concepts of responsibility and success

Kim and Kreps (2020) underscored the pivotal role of government communication in stabilizing society. The authors further highlighted the importance of effective government communication in informing key stakeholders such as first responders, health officials, law enforcement and the general public how to safeguard against threats during these emergencies, as ineffective government communication may lead to a chaotic society where fear and uncertainty prevail. Along this line, Kim and Kreps (2020) also discuss the negative ramifications of disseminating incorrect, inconsistent, and contradictory information between federal and state presentations of important health data for the public in the government. They cite an almost 30% discrepancy between number of positive cases of COVID-19 reported for the state of Louisiana on April 3, 2020 by the Center for Disease Control and Prevention's Coronavirus Cases Last Updates website (6,424 cases) and the Louisiana State Office of the Public Health (9,150) which also is believed to have undermined public trust in the government and in so doing, increased fear and confusion about health risks concerning the COVID-19 virus.

Scholars have found that the public's trust in its government is somewhat contingent on the government's ability to meet public expectations. This, in turn, is dependent on or varies in relation to the nature of a country's governance system, its corresponding institutional ethos, and degree of accountability (Lin & Liu 2022). In their review of the literature of trust within the context of the coronavirus pandemic, Devine et al. (2021) have attempted to understand the dynamics of trust, specifically, how it hinders and facilitates policy decisions. Given its multi-dimensional nature, the question put forth is whether trust in one's government should be conceptualized as a pragmatic assessment of how well an institution governs as in their record of delivery or instead be conceptualized as the moral capacity of a leader to do the right thing (Devine et al., 2021). Another important question is: should we assume trust in the government will result in greater compliance with safety measures?

### *The Complexity of Political Trust during a Pandemic*

Devine et al. (2021) argue that trust may have a double-edged nature. First, on the basis of US-based studies, trust can increase non-compliance if trusted actors/sources encourage non-compliant behavior. Second, risk perception of the virus may decrease as trust in the government increases. Other studies have found similar results. For example, Saechang et al.'s (2021) cross-sectional study conducted during the coronavirus outbreak (February to March of 2020) in Thailand found a strong positive relationship between respondents' trust in the government and compliance with safety measures to protect against the spread of the virus.

Employing social media tracking and online focus groups, Wong and Jensen (2020) found opposite results in their study administered in Singapore between January and April 2020. The researchers noted that too much public trust in the government might in fact result in less compliance with safety measures during a public health crisis as people believing strongly in their government's competence may then underestimate the risks of the virus. Specifically, Wong and Jensen (2020) describe the concept of 'the paradox of trust' during a pandemic. While risk management research advocates trust in public authorities as an important and effective component of risk management in a pandemic, the primary responsibility of risk management is not always centralized. For this reason public trust in government authorities may lead the public to underestimate risks leading to reduced belief in the importance of complying to safety precautions against the spread of the virus (such as vaccinating and/or complying to social distancing measures).

### *Trust in State vs. Federal Governments*

Further adding to the complex nature of trust during a disaster event, such as the COVID-19 pandemic, is that political systems vary: while there is centralized decision-making in some countries, in other countries there is shared decision-making between the federal government and state governments. This means that in certain cases shared decision-making occurs between different government bodies where each government agency may not have all information at the same time. Further, research suggests that public trust may not be uniformly distributed across all government agencies. For example, a US-based study conducted on 2,615 Americans in October 2020 found that the more people trusted in their state/local governments, the more likely they maintained physical distancing and wore face masks while the opposite was found for trust in the federal government, in that the more Americans trusted the federal government, the less likely they were to maintain physical distancing or wear face masks in public (Li et al., 2022). The study found a positive association between trust in the state/local governments as COVID-19 information sources with physical distancing and mask-wearing, while trust in the federal government as a COVID-19 information source was negatively associated with wearing masks and with physical distancing, which suggests the different roles that state/local governments and the federal government played in mobilizing Americans to comply with preventive measures.

Bickham and Francis (2021) conducted a survey which examined whether the public's perceptions of government credibility, trust in government, as well as message exposure, influenced their adherence to information from the government regarding COVID-19 virus testing, stay at home orders, and social distancing measures. Guided by **Source Credibility theory** (which posits a relationship between sources that are considered with high regard and the likelihood for people to agree with those sources) and **Situational Crisis Communication theory** (which highlights the importance of effective communication, or the lack thereof, in impacting people's perceptions in a crisis, the study attempted to identify response strategies for crisis management). The survey used in this study investigated communication preferences during the pandemic and whether credibility perceptions differed according to the level of government (local, state and federal). The study found that message exposure influenced respondents' perceived credibility of and trust in government officials during and after the stay-at-home order and that respondents reported higher levels of trust in local and state levels of government compared to the federal government level.

## Cognitive Appraisal Theory and the COVID-19 Pandemic

**Cognitive Appraisal theory** is based on the assumption that individuals' beliefs influence how they respond to different stressful events. In order to explore the role of emotions in shaping responses to crisis events, Miocevic (2021) conducted a study that explored high level managers' cognitive appraisal of the COVID-19 pandemic by means of a survey of 155 top managers of Croatian SMEs. The findings revealed that being emotionally charged impacted managers' proactivity such that managers with positive emotions were more likely to invest whereas managers charged with negative emotions were more likely to divest during the pandemic, as a response to the economic crisis. Using a sample size of 980 working adults in Pakistan a wide variety of professions, Ali et al. (2021) administered the Stress Appraisal Measure to assess the cognitive stress appraisal of the COVID-19 situation being the anticipatory stressor. These measures consisted of 28 items with five points Likert scale and consisted of seven subscales: threat, challenge, centrality, control by self, control by others, uncontrollability, and stressfulness. The results revealed that threat, centrality, and stressfulness appraisal, as well as avoidant emotional coping, were significant positive predictors of stress during the lockdown of COVID-19 in Pakistan.

The pandemic has exacerbated cognitive load for certain professions, and this is certainly the case for frontline workers. For example, in the case of registered nurses in the Emergency Department (EDRNs) the pandemic has meant a number of additional new roles including triaging patients to determine the order of treatment as well as providing emergency care for high-risk patients within a strict timeline; indeed it is no surprise that with the pandemic there has been an association of higher levels of anxiety, depression, and burnout (Lasalvia et al., 2021). Lin et al.'s (2023) scoping review of studies exploring stress-related cognitive appraisal of EDRNs during the COVID-19 pandemic found a positive association between stress-coping capabilities and confidence in confronting the COVID-19 outbreak.

### Affective Theory of Intelligence and the COVID-19 Pandemic

The **theory of affective intelligence** posits the existence of two basic decision strategies: one that is based on rational calculations and the other that is more affective-based that is appropriate as a short-cut of sorts for different situations. The reason for the alternative strategies is that rational decision-making can require a lot of time and effort which is not always something we have, so quicker decision-making strategies may be more practical, especially for familiar and/or recurring choice situations (MacKuen et al., 2007). Studies have found that good emotional intelligence (EI) has contributed toward greater organizational resilience (Dhoopar et al., 2022; Guillén et al., 2022) which positively impacted workplace productivity (Dhoopar et al., 2022).

### The Different Role of Interpersonal Trust and Institutional Trust

It appears that institutional trust and interpersonal trust may play different roles in emergency situations such as the COVID-19 pandemic. For example, in a set of studies comprising behavioral experiments, and agent-based modeling Lou et al. (2022) found institutional trust was associated with lower COVID-19 fatality rates and a higher willingness to get tested, whereas interpersonal trust was a better predictor of how quickly COVID-19 was controlled in the early stages of the pandemic as well as the public's willingness to comply with norms that would help to prevent the spread of the virus.

> Reflection Question: *Can you think of some examples of interpersonal trust in your own life as well as institutional trust. How may have the COVID-19 pandemic altered either of these?*

### Key Lessons

Trust has always been an elusive concept, and contextualizing it within the pandemic, makes it even more so. In this chapter we have provided an overview of the role of communication in the establishment of trust during a pandemic. Given that trust typically develops over time, and the nature of emergency events such as the pandemic is that much action has to take place immediately before trust can be established, we need to ensure that there is ongoing and clear communication among first responders, various health agencies, the media and the public for trust to be established with time. In order to process vast amounts of information as efficiently as possible, it is also imperative that we have clear understanding of point-by-point information, as well as situation awareness of the current status of the virus.

This chapter has also presented ample evidence that institutional trust, especially during times of uncertainty such as a pandemic, is a complex concept that is not understood easily. There is a lack of consensus in the existing literature regarding the processes that lies behind the development of the public's trust in its government. It may be that we base our decision to trust our political leaders based on their record of timely delivery of promises made or it may be that we place more trust in government leaders based on their compliance with ethical leadership. Irrespective of how institutional trust is formed, ultimately, trust in one's government does not necessarily ensure compliance with government issued safety measures to safeguard oneself during a public health crisis.

Undoubtedly the COVID-19 pandemic has altered our conceptions of trust in its many forms. There is much future work that can be done to explore how new conceptions of trust have impacted how we communicate in our post-pandemic world.

## Bibliography

Adiga, A., Dubhashi, D., Lewis, B., Marathe, M., Venkatramanan, S., & Vullikanti, A. (2020). Mathematical models for covid-19 pandemic: A comparative analysis. *Journal of the Indian Institute of Science, 100*(4), 793–807.

Ali, A., Khan, A. A., Abbas, S., Khan, A. S., & Ullah, E. (2021). Cognitive appraisal, coping, stress and fear contracting Covid-19 in working people in Pakistan. *Journal of Rational- Emotive & Cognitive-Behavior Therapy, 40*(4), 663–682. doi: 10.1007/s10942-021-00433-z

Beilstein, C. M., Lehmann, L. E., Braun, M., Urman, R. D., Luedi, M. M., & Stüber, F. (2021). Leadership in a time of crisis: Lessons learned from a pandemic. *Best Practice & Research Clinical Anaesthesiology, 35*(3), 405–414.

Bickham, S. B., & Francis, D. B. (2021). The public's perceptions of government officials' communication in the wake of the COVID-19 pandemic. *Journal of Creative Communications, 16*(2), 190–202.

Boateng, J., & Cox III, R. W. (2016). Exploring the trust question in the midst of public management reforms. *Public Personnel Management, 45*(3), 239–263.

Coombs, W. T. (2007). Protecting organization reputations during a crisis: The development and application of situational crisis communication theory. *Corporate Reputation Review, 10*, 163–176.

Cooper, C. A., Knotts, H. G., & Brennan, K. M. (2008). The importance of trust in government for public administration: The case of zoning. *Public Administration Review, 68*(3), 459–468.

Corazzini, J. G. (1977). Trust as a complex multi-dimensional construct. *Psychological Reports, 40*(1), 75–80.

Devine, D., Gaskell, J., Jennings, W. & Stoker, G. (2021). Trust and the coronavirus pandemic: What are the consequences for and of trust? An early review of the literature. *Political Science Review, 19*(2), 274–285.

Desson, Z., Lambertz, L., Peters, J. W., Falkenbach, M., & Kauer, L. (2020). Europe's Covid-19 outliers: German, Austrian and Swiss policy responses during the early stages of the 2020 pandemic. *Health Policy and Technology, 9*(4), 405–418.

Dhoopar, A., Sihag, P., Kumar, A., & Suhag, A. K. (2022). Organizational resilience and employee performance in COVID-19 pandemic: The mediating effect of emotional intelligence. *International Journal of Organizational Analysis, 30*(1), 130–155.

Dixit, R. A., Hurst, S. H., Adams, K. T., Boxley, C., Lysen-Hendershot, K., Bennett, S. S., Booker, E., & Ratwani, R. M. (2020). Rapid development of visualization dashboards to enhance situation awareness of COVID-19 telehealth initiatives at a multihospital healthcare system. *Journal of the American Medical Informatics Association, 27*(9), pp. 1456–1461.

Ellsworth, P. C. (1991). Some implications of cognitive appraisal theories of emotion. In K. T. Strongman (Ed.), *International Review of Studies on Emotion* (vol. 1, pp. 143–161). New York: Wiley.

Endsley, M. R. (1995). Toward a theory of situation awareness in dynamic systems. *Human Factors, 37*, 32–64.

Fisher, J., Van Heerde, J., & Tucker, A. (2010). Does one trust judgement fit all? Linking theory and empirics. *The British Journal of Politics and International Relations, 12*(2), 161–188.

Gefen, D. (2002). Reflections on the dimensions of trust and trustworthiness among online consumers. *ACM Special Interest Group on Management Information Systems, 33*(3), 38–53.

Glass, T. A., & Schoch-Spana, M. (2002). Bioterrorism and the people: How to vaccinate a city against panic. *Clinical Infectious Diseases, 34*(2), 217–223.

Griffin, R. J., Neuwirth, K., Dunwoody, S., & Giese, J. (2004). Information sufficiency and risk communication. *Media Psychology, 6*(1), 23–61.

Grimmelikhuijsen, S., & Knies, E. (2017). Validating a scale for citizen trust in government organizations. *International Review of Administrative Sciences, 83*(3), 583–601.

Guillén, M. E., Tirado, D. M., & Sánchez, A. R. (2022). The impact of COVID-19 on university students and competences in education for sustainable development: Emotional intelligence, resilience and engagement. *Journal of Cleaner Production, 380*, 135057.

Hirvi, S. K., Laulainen, S., & Taskinen, H. (2021). Trust as a multidimensional phenomenon in LMX relationships. *Journal of Health Organization and Management, 35*(1), 17–33.

Kim, D. K. D., & Kreps, G. L. (2020). An analysis of government communication in the United States during the COVID-19 pandemic: Recommendations for effective government health risk communication. *World Medical & Health Policy, 12*(4), 398–412.

Kye, B., & Hwang, S. J. (2020). Social trust in the midst of pandemic crisis: Implications from COVID-19 of South Korea. *Research in Social Stratification and Mobility, 68*, 100523.

Lasalvia, A., Amaddeo, F., Porru, S., Carta, A., Tardivo, S., Bovo, C., Ruggeri, M., & Bonetto, C. (2021). Levels of burn-out among healthcare workers during the COVID-19 pandemic and their associated factors: A cross-sectional study in a tertiary hospital of a highly burdened area of north-East Italy. *BMJ Open, 11*(1), e045127. doi: 10.1136/bmjopen-2020–045127

Li, H., Chen, B., Chen, Z., Shi, L., & Su, D. (2022). Americans' trust in COVID-19 information from governmental sources in the Trump era: Individuals' adoption of preventive measures, and health implications. *Health Communication, 37*(12), 1552–1561.

Lin, C. H., Siao, S. F., Lin, Y. J., Hsin, P. H., Shelley, M., & Lee, Y. H. (2023). Cognitive appraisals and coping strategies of registered nurses in the emergency department combating COVID-19: A scoping review. *Journal of Nursing Scholarship, 55*(1), 79–96.

Lin, Z., & Liu, H. (2022). A national study of racial–ethnic differences in COVID-19 concerns among older Americans: Evidence from the Health and Retirement Study. *The Journals of Gerontology: Series B, 77*(7), e134–e141.

Liu, J., Shahab, Y., & Hoque, H. (2022). Government response measures and public trust during the COVID-19 pandemic: Evidence from around the world. *British Journal of Management, 33*(2), 571–602.

Longstaff, P. H., &Yang, S. U. (2008). Communication management and trust: Their role in building resilience to "surprises" such as natural disasters, pandemic flu, and terrorism. *Ecology and Society, 13*(1), Art 3.

Lou, et al. (2022). Different roles of interpersonal trust and institutional trust in COVID-19 pandemic control. *Social Science and Medicine* (1982), *293*, 114677. doi: 10.1016/j.socscimed.2021.114677

Lowry, P. B., Wilson, D. W., & Haig, W. L. (2014). A picture is worth a thousand words: Source credibility theory applied to logo and website design for heightened credibility and consumer trust. *International Journal of Human-Computer Interaction, 30*(1), 63–93.

MacKuen, M., Marcus, G. E., Neuman, W. R., & Keele, L. (2007). The third way: The theory of affective intelligence and American democracy. In George E. Marcus, W. Russell Neuman, and Michael MacKuen (Eds.), *The affect effect: Dynamics of emotion in political thinking and behavior* (pp. 124–151). doi: 10.7208/chicago/9780226574431.003.0006

McCune, J. C. (1998). That elusive thing called trust. *Management Review, 87*(7), 10.

Miocevic, D. (2021). Investigating strategic responses of SMEs during COVID-19 pandemic: A cognitive appraisal perspective. *BRQ Business Research Quarterly, 26*(4), 313–326. doi: 10.1177/23409444211005779

Mizrahi, S., Eran, V.-G., & Nissim, C. (2019). Drivers of trust in emergency organizations networks: The role of readiness, threat perceptions and participation in decision making. *Public Management Review*. doi: 10.1080/14719037.2019.1674367.

Mizrahi, S., Vigoda-Gadot, E., & Cohen, N. (2021). How well do they manage a crisis? The government's effectiveness during the Covid-19 pandemic. *Public Administration Review, 81*(6), 1120–1130.

Naseer, K., Qazi, J., Qazi, A, Avulgah, B. K., Tahir, R., Rasheed, R. A., Khan, S. K., Khan, B. A Zeeshan, M., Humayun, M. A. & Naseem, U. (2021). Travel behavior prediction amid COVID-19 underlaying situational awareness theory and health belief model. *Behaviour & Information Technology*. doi: 10. 0144929X2021.1984579.

Newton, K., Stolle, D., & Zmerli, S. (2018). Social and political trust. In Eric M. Uslaner (Ed.), *The Oxford Handbook of Social and Political Trust* (pp. 961–976). New York: Oxford University Press.

Nielsen, M., & Levkovich, N. (2020). COVID-19 and mental health in America: Crisis and opportunity? *Families, Systems, & Health, 38*(4), 482.

Özcan, B., & Bjørnskov, C. (2011). Social trust and human development. *The Journal of Socio-Economics*, *40*(6), 753–762.

Quinn, S. C., Parmer, J., Freimuth, V. S., Hilyard, K. M., Musa, D., & Kim, K. H. (2013). Exploring communication, trust in government, and vaccination intention later in the 2009 H1N1 pandemic: Results of a national survey. *Biosecurity and Bioterrorism: Biodefense Strategy, Practice, and Science*, *11*(2), 96–106.

Rotter, J. B. (1967). A new scale for the measurement of interpersonal trust. *Journal of Personality, 35*(4), 651–665.

Rufai, and Bunce. (2020). World leaders' usage of Twitter in response to the COVID-19 pandemic: A content analysis, *Journal of Public Health, 42*(3), 510–516.

Saechang, O., Yu, J. & Li, Y. (2021). Public trust and policy compliance during the COVID19 Pandemic: The role of professional trust, *Healthcare, 9,* 151. doi: 10.3390/healthcare9020151

Santos, A. M. S. (2021). Violence, rumor, and elusive trust in Mocímboa da Praia, Mozambique. *Social Analysis*, *65*(3), 44–66.

Seeger, M. W., Sellnow, T. L., & Ulmer, R. R. (2003). *Communication and organizational crisis*. Bloomsbury Academic.

Six, F., De Vadder, S., Glavina, M., Verhoest, K., & Pepermans, K. (2023). What drives compliance with COVID-19 measures over time? Explaining changing impacts with goal framing theory. *Regulation & Governance*, *17*(1), 3–21.

Spence, P. R., Lachlan, K. A., & Griffin, D. R. (2007). Crisis communication, race, and natural disasters. *Journal of Black Studies, 37*(4), 539–554.

Stefaniak, A., Wohl, M. J., & Elgar, F. J. (2022). Commentary on "Different roles of interpersonal trust and institutional trust in COVID-19 pandemic control". *Social Science & Medicine*, *299*, 114765.

Suhay, E., Soni, A., Persico, C., & Marcotte, D. E. (2022). Americans' Trust in Government and Health Behaviors During the COVID-19 Pandemic. *RSF: The Russell Sage Foundation Journal of the Social Sciences*, *8*(8), 221–244.

Surowiecki, J. (2004). *The wisdom of crowds: Why the many are smarter than the few and how collective wisdom shapes business, economies, societies, and nations*. Doubleday & Co.: NY.

Thomas, C. W. (1998). 'Maintaining and restoring public trust in government agencies and their employees', *Administration & Society*, *30*, 166–193.

Trent, M., Seale, H., Chughtai, A. A., Salmon, D., & MacIntyre, C. R. (2022). Trust in government, intention to vaccinate and COVID-19 vaccine hesitancy: A comparative survey of five large cities in the United States, United Kingdom, and Australia. *Vaccine*, *40*(17), 2498–2505.

Van de Walle, S., & Geert, B. (2003). Public service performance and trust in government: The problem of causality. *International Journal of Public Administration, 26*(8), 891–913.

Vigoda-Gadot, E., & Mizrahi, S. (2014). *Managing Democracies in Turbulent Times*. New York: Springer.

Weick, K. (1995). *Sensemaking in Organizations*. Thousand Oaks, CA: Sage.

Witte, K. (1994). Generating effective risk messages: How scary should your risk communication be? In B. Burleson (Ed.), *Communication Yearbook*, 18 (pp. 229–254). Thousand Oaks, CA: Sage.

Woelfert, F. S., & Kunst, J. R. (2020). How political and social trust can impact social distancing practices during COVID-19 in unexpected ways. *Frontiers in Psychology*, *11*, 572966.

Wong, C. M. L., & Jensen, O. (2020). The paradox of trust: Perceived risk and public compliance during the COVID-19 pandemic in Singapore, *Journal of Risk Research*, *23*(7–8), 1021–1030.

## Glossary of Key Terms and Concepts

**Affective Intelligence Theory** posits the existence of two basic decision strategies: one that is based on rational calculations and the other that is more affective-based, which are appropriate as a short-cut of sorts for different situations. The reason for the alternative strategies is rational decision-making can require a lot of time and effort which is not always something we have, so quicker decision-making strategies may be more practical especially for familiar and/or recurring choice situations (MacKuen et al., 2007).

**Cognitive Appraisal Theory** posits that emotions are the resultants of a set of appraisals. is based on the assumption that individuals' beliefs influence how they respond to different stressful events (Ellsworth, 1991).

**Institutional trust** refers to trust in government institutions

**Interpersonal trust** refers to trust between people.

**Paradox of trust** refers to the double-edged nature of trust during a pandemic where some studies have found that too much trust in the government might cause the public to underestimate current risks of contracting the virus (Wong & Jensen, 2020).

**Political trust** refers to confidence in as well as public support for essential political institutions such as the government and the legislature (Newton et al., 2018).

**Situational Crisis Communication theory** highlights the importance of effective communication, or the lack thereof, in impacting people's perceptions in a crisis. The theory assumes the public's perception of an organization is threatened by a crisis (Coombs, 2007).

**Social trust** refers to trust in a generalized other where the trusting party does not have any individual or context specific information about this generalized other (Özcan & Bjørnskov, 2011).

**Source Credibility theory** posits a relationship between sources that are considered with high regard (perceived to be credible) and the likelihood for people to agree with those sources (Lowry et al., 2014).

## Discussion Questions

1 Describe the various components of institutional trust during times of uncertainty. Is it an affective or cognitive process – please explain.
2 Why is point-by-point understanding and holistic understanding both important during crisis events?
3 Does high institutional trust necessarily result in greater compliance with government measures? Please explain.
4 What roles might interpersonal trust and institutional trust in public compliance with government measures according to Lou et al.'s (2022) study? Please explain.
5 You have just been hired by the PMO to advise The new Prime Minister. She is newly elected and is now managing the COVID-19 pandemic. In her public briefings, she is doing her best and being as empathetic as possible, and in trying to become popular is attempting to display adaptability by changing policies without necessarily explaining why she is doing this. Public surveys reveal that the public is confused about her inconsistencies and losing trust in the new Prime Minister.

  As the adviser to the PM, make three recommendations on how she can improve her popularity ratings.

# 4

# PANDEMIC COMPLIANCE, NON-COMPLIANCE

## A Review of Theories and Empirical Studies

### Chapter Learning Objectives

- Define what is a conspiracy theory
- Describe the five elements of conspiracy theories
- Explain what is meant by the information-action ratio in the context of the COVID-19 pandemic
- Discuss some of the key drivers of getting vaccinated
- Discuss some of the motivators to comply with the non-pharmaceutical industry NPIs
- Describe how compliance behavior may change over time
- Explain what is meant by 'the COVID-19 pandemic is a slow-creeping crisis'
- Discuss how risk perception is related to compliance with preventative health behaviors during the COVID-19 pandemic

### Introduction

In an ideal world, authentic health information on measures about how to contain the COVID-19 virus is dispersed quickly and efficiently and is subsequently processed by people world-wide who implement these guidelines for their own and others' safety. Information is of little use if it does not lead to action, especially during times of crisis. Indeed, during times of public health emergencies, one of the most important assets a country will have is its access to information, which will make contribute to making its citizens more resilient (Longstaff & Young, 2008). Misinformation, however, is not always the primary cause for vaccine hesitancy (Bates et al., 2022).

DOI: 10.4324/9781003394983-4

**Vaccine hesitancy** has been described as a multifaceted phenomenon comprising the existence of many factors such as psychological, cognitive, cultural and socio-demographic aspects which contribute toward the reluctance to vaccinate (Sallam, 2021). Vaccine hesitancy refers to a delay in acceptance or refusal of safe vaccines irrespective of whether vaccination services are available (MacDonald, 2015). In their systematic review of literature on vaccine hesitancy, Larson et al. (2014) conclude that some of the limitations of the current research include, (1) the complex nature of vaccine hesitancy is not easily understood as it is driven by a variety of context-specific factors, (2) the majority of studies on vaccine hesitancy were conducted in industrialized countries, and (3) that frameworks used as determinants of vaccine hesitancy are in large part taken from classic models which do not adequately account for contextual influences.

In this chapter we will review the nature of vaccine hesitancy and how the way messages are framed can impact vaccine hesitancy. We will then explore various theories of misinformation to further our understanding of how they have contributed toward vaccine hesitancy and other non-compliant behaviors during the pandemic. This will be followed by an overview of the empirical literature regarding various potential causes of vaccine hesitancy, motivators to get vaccinated as well as drivers of NPI (non-pharmaceutical intervention) compliance. We will then discuss some theoretical models from the health literature that may provide insight regarding why some people chose to comply with preventative health measures during a pandemic while others do not. The chapter will conclude with a discussion on how to best incorporate empirical findings into more effective vaccination campaigns.

## What Do People Know About Vaccination?

In an attempt to understand vaccine hesitancy of patients at the emergency department of a hospital, Gentsch et al. (2022) conducted a study on 65 adults to elicit the perspectives on COVID-19 vaccination concerns and potential approaches that might increase their vaccine acceptance. The study found that trust played a significant role for patients in promoting vaccine acceptance and that trusted messengers of information included healthcare providers as well as family or friends.

## What Motivates People to Share Vaccine Information?

A study by Bradshaw (2023) of vaccine advertisements on Facebook identified five emerging that motivated vaccine accepting mothers to share information: information about the sponsor, image selection, spokesperson, wording, and attitude homophily. The researchers noted that their study showed that choice of advertising platform plays an important role in effectively promoting vaccines on social media.

## The Dynamic Nature of 'Vaccine Hesitancy'

Duong et al. (2022) explored four types of attitudes toward vaccines: acceptance, conditional acceptance, hesitancy and anti-vaccination in Vietnamese professions of differing socio-economic variables. Participant from each of these professions varied in vaccination status, chronic underlying health conditions and geographical locations. The study found that participants' willingness to accept a vaccine was not static; instead, it was contingent upon various factors such as the quality of the vaccine manufacturing as well as perceived risk of acquiring the infection due to the existence of other health conditions. These findings are consistent with previous research on vaccine hesitancy previous research (Ruiz & Bell, 2021).

## Framing of COVID-19 Preventative Healthcare Messages

### *Loss/Gain Frames of COVID-19 Messages and Intention to Comply with Healthcare Measures*

According to Gantiva et al. (2021) gain-framed health messages were more effective in increasing intentions to comply with self-care measures, as well as increasing message strength and motivating more self-care behavior in others. In their study, 319 participants were presented with an unforced choice task where they selected the message they believed to be more effective in promoting health preventative behaviors from COVID-19 messages that were either gain or loss-framed. The findings of this study suggested that health messages that were gain-framed were judged to be stronger and increased individuals' intention to adhere to self-care behaviors.

### HOW WOULD PEOPLE DESIGN MESSAGES PROMOTING VACCINATION?

In this case study we explore potential incentives to getting vaccinated. Schmidtke et al. (2022) conducted an intriguing workshop where behavioral science and design thinking theory were jointly applied and where members of the public, immunizers, and public health specialists were brought together to co-design/revise behavioral messages promoting getting vaccinated. A narrative analysis was conducted to identify themes related to vaccine hesitancy and found which included 'treatment trade-offs' such as taking the vaccine now to avoid taking medications later and/or to avoid ongoing environmental contamination at a future time. Another theme that emerged was 'embodiment of freedom, which outlined pleasurable activities that would be possible after becoming vaccinated. Incentives also included 'self-serving perspectives, as well as meaningful relationships (how others would be benefited from the person's vaccination).

### *The Role of Motivational Interviewing*

Several studies suggest the technique of motivational interviewing which has been described as a framework that helps motivate behavior change from a patient-centered perspective, as a method for healthcare providers to reduce vaccine hesitancy (Boness et al., 2022). **Motivational interviewing** is believed to communicate support to the patient and thereby deepen rapport, and improve receptivity to information being shared (Breckenridge et al., 2022).

### *Pandemic Fatigue – What Is It?*

**Pandemic fatigue** is understood to be an expected and natural reaction to the prolonged nature of the COVID-19 pandemic and the associated inconvenience and hardship which poses a serious threat to efforts to control the spread of the virus (WHO, 2020). In Pandemic Fatigue: Reinvigorating the Public to Prevent COVID-19, the WHO proposes four key strategies for governments to re-motivate public support to adhere to compliance measures. They include devoting time and energy toward understanding people, allowing people to live their lives while reducing probability of contracting the virus, acknowledging and finding solutions for the various challenges that the public is experiencing and engaging people as part of the solution.

Test yourself: *Drawing on the results of studies in the fields of psychology and communication, how would you engage people as part of the solution?*

## Conspiracy Theories and Other Theories of Misinformation

**Conspiracy Theories** comprise the perception that a number of people are banded together in order to achieve a hidden goal which is perceived to be unlawful or malevolent and do so in secret agreement (Proojien, 2018). **Conspiracy beliefs** regarding dangers specific to public health are rampant and widespread (Oliver & Wood, 2014). They include the following five elements: patterns, agency, coalitions, hostility and continued secrecy (Proojien, 2018). The danger of conspiracy beliefs is that they can lead people to ignore or otherwise disregard appropriate health-related behaviors (Jolley & Douglas, 2014),and in so doing, endangering the lives of people world-wide. By better understanding questions such as why certain people have a greater propensity to believe in conspiracy theories and misinformation about COVID-19 and *why* they hold such beliefs, we can better inform strategies to mitigate the harmful effects of the beliefs (Uscinski et al., 2020).

## *Conspiracy Theories and How Information Spreads on Social Media*

Theocharis et al.'s (2021) study employing online survey data from 17 countries, suggests that conspiracy theories spread differently across various social media platforms. Specifically, the researchers noted that their study suggested a complex relational structure between a technological tool and the user which might enable or constrain behavioral outcomes in a given context. In particular, they found Twitter was the sole platform to have a negative effect on Conspiracy theories compared to Facebook, YouTube and Messenger services that had a positive effect on Conspiracy theories. While a given platform's features may be the reason for this finding, the researchers note that users' particular characteristics or motivations to use a given social media platform may be at the root of this finding.

## *What Makes People Believe in Conspiracy Theories? – A Potentially Evolutionary Root*

In their survey of 2023 American adults in March of 2020, Uscinski et al. (2020) found that strong predictors of belief in COVID-19 conspiracy beliefs included denialism, defined as a psychological predisposition to reject expert, authoritative information, conspiracy thinking, and partisan motivations.

Prooijen and Vugt (2018) discuss a potentially evolutionary basis for our belief in conspiracy theories. For example, they argue that illusory pattern perceptions may be a result of the human tendency to make sense which could make us more vulnerable to believing in conspiracy theories. Specifically, if we consider that the human mind, when attempting to establish true causal relationships between people and events, typically seeks evidence for existing patterns because doing so is indispensable for survival. However, doing so may of course result in false positives, or finding patterns that do not exist, leading to various kinds of seemingly irrational beliefs.

Hartman et al.'s (2021) study extends the exploration of the potential evolutionary roots in predisposing us to believe in conspiracy theories as they argue that certain psychological variables may give certain individuals greater sensitivity to certain types of threats. For example, people who score on right-wing authoritarianism (RWA) generally believe the world is an inherently threatening place and where dissident and dangerous out-groups are to blame (Hartman et al., 2021).

In order to better understand the evolution of conspiracy theories, let us explore the work of Hartman et al.'s (2021) longitudinal study, which used survey data from two waves of life during the lockdown in the United Kingdom. The study explored factors associated with belief in three conspiracy theories that speculate about the origin of the COVID-19 virus, namely that it (1) its source of origin was in a meat market in Wuhan, China; (2) was developed in a lab in Wuhan, China; and (3) was caused by 5G mobile networks. The findings of the study suggested that political-psychological predispositions were strongly associated with belief in Conspiracy theories about the virus. Other predictors of belief in Conspiracy theories found in this study included anxiety about the pandemic, a lack of trust in scientists, information from social networks/media, ethnocentrism or fanatic beliefs as well as an intolerance of uncertainty and social dominance orientation.

### *Higher Order Beliefs at the Root of the Belief in CT*

Miller et al. (2020) attempted to explore higher order beliefs that may be at the root of the tendency to believe in conspiracy theories. The goals of their study were: (1) to assess whether COVID-19 CTs comprise a monological belief system and (2) to examine whether personal uncertainty connects CT beliefs together. Ultimately the results of the study provided strong support for the theory that COVID-19 CTs form a monological belief system. More specifically, in addition to finding that the CTs were highly correlated, the study also found that a large majority of individuals believe more than one and that mutually contradictory CTs were positively related to one another. The study also found that, this belief system was more constrained for individuals who were currently experiencing a great deal of uncertainty in their lives. The researchers noted two limitations of their research. First, of the study was unable to include the full variety of COVID-19 CTs that were in existence during the time the study took place. Second, the researchers acknowledged that it was possible that some of the CT responses represented expressive responding such as demand characteristics, rather than true beliefs (Schaffner & Luks, 2018).

#### *Health Literacy as a Moderator for Belief in Conspiracy Theories*

In order to explore health literacy in Japan, Cheng and Nishikawa (2022) conducted a path and cluster analyses on survey data collected from 1,488 adults from this country. Their study found that while health literacy reduced people's belief about COVID-19 and vaccination misinformation, it had no direct effect on their belief in COVID-19 conspiracy theories. The researchers noted that although high health literacy does not provide assurance of a low level of belief in conspiracy theories, low health literacy was associated with high susceptibility to both misinformation and conspiracy theories. This finding provides credence for why it is important to promote health literacy as much as possible.

### *Religious Misinformation Theories*

Despite the societal role of religion in providing contentment and a sense of security throughout human civilization, they can also simultaneously play a productive and counterproductive role in shaping people's behavior during any global disaster, epidemic or pandemic (Barua et al., 2020). Bronstein et al. (2019) set of two online studies comprising over 900 participants, found that dogmatic individuals as well as religious fundamentalists were more likely to believe false news and information, and this is due to a tendency to engage in less analytic and less actively open-minded thinking.

In a set of two large scale studies panel data was collected: four times in Israel and five times in Japan from March to June 2020, to explore the association between religious faith and intention to become vaccinated. It should be noted that most of Israel's population is monotheistic while the majority of people in Japan are unaffiliated with any particular religion (Lahav et al., 2022). The study found that people with strong religious beliefs are less likely to get vaccinated than those who self-report as less religious.

### *What Makes People Believe in Religious Theories Debunking COVID-19*

Given the massive destruction the COVID-19 pandemic has caused, scholars have argued that in such a context, engagement with religious practices may give people a sense of control over the situation, (Kowalczyk et al., 2020).

Bronstein et al. (2019) conducted two online studies with over 900 participants. The study found that dogmatic individuals and religious fundamentalists were more likely to believe false news. As the researchers found that these relationships could in large part be explained by analytic cognitive style, it was suggested that increasing analytic and actively open-minded thinking might help to reduce belief in fake news.

## Ethnic Minorities and Vaccine Hesitancy

During the pandemic, ethnic minorities have dealt with a number of barriers to receiving culturally tailored medical treatment, which, in turn, may have resulted in receiving biased health communication which may have impacted ethnic minority groups' perceptions of vaccine hesitancy (Zhou et al., 2022). To better understand cultural nuances that may have impacted cultural hesitancy and also understand preferred feature and suggestions for culturally tailored messages about the COVID-19 vaccine, Zhou's interview of ethnic minority groups in the US found a preference for encouraging messages that emphasized the concept of hope and care for others. A unique cultural finding for African American participants in this study was reporting that witnessing others take the vaccine would encourage them to do so as well (Zhou et al., 2022). Interestingly, the study found that ethnic minorities were open to vaccine information being delivered in various innovative platforms such as through chat box interventions but expressed a dislike for long or otherwise overly complicated information about the COVID-19 vaccine.

### *Racial Disparities Regarding Intention to Obtain COVID-19 Vaccination*

There is also some evidence to suggest that a combination of affective and cognitive factors may play a role in observed lack of acceptance of the COVID-19 vaccine when it comes to racial disparities. McLaren (2021) for example, found racial differences in beliefs about the vaccine such as its health benefits impacted trust in the vaccine and the widespread distrust of many Black Americans in the medical system also impacted vaccine uptake.

## How Do People Decide if a Claim Is an Opinion or Fact?

In their exploration of the process by which people label unsubstantiated claims as either opinion or facts, Brotherton and Son (2021) attempted to identify how the process of meta-cognitive belief-categorization takes place; they do so in the context of mundane claims, contentious political issues, and conspiracy theories (Brotherton & Son, 2021). Brotherton and Son (2020), for example, conducted two studies that attempted to explore how claims are categorized as fact, opinion or a blend of the two in the context of being a mundane claim, a contentious political issue or a part of a conspiracy theory. The findings of this study suggest that that there is a greater chance of a claim being labeled to be factual if a person subjectively agrees with the content of the claim. The study further found that conspiracy theories appear to be categorized somewhere between fact and opinion.

## Understanding Health Risks and Taking Action

Employing thematic analysis of interview data from 15 male and 15 female participants in Norway, Berg et al. (2022) investigated how people make use of mental models to make sense of scientific information and apply it to their lives and behavior in the context of COVID-19 The study was not able to identify uniformity in how people use mental models to process information about scientific information about COVID-19 related health risks. For example, the study found that while certain individuals expressed a preference for understanding *why* certain behavior and activities were considered high risk, other individual preferred clearer more simple messages where it was very easy to understand *what* to do and *how* to protect themselves. Similarly, information about health consequences produced panic in certain participants while bringing more awareness to other participants.

In Table 4.1, we present some key differences between COVID-19 public health risk information published on the Norwegian Institute of Public Health website (NIPH) compared to how the public perceived and acted upon this information from Berg et al.'s (2020) study (Table 4.2).

Findings from Berg et al.'s (2020) thematic analysis are instructive for several reasons. First, there are some serious perception issues that interfere with the public's ability to correct information about pandemic-related safety. Some examples include risk associated with the virus, how likely the virus is to be transmitted. Second, if basic safety information on how to prevent virus transmission is not understood correctly, it is reasonable to assume this will impact health preventative behaviors. Clearly these are important lessons for those framing important health messages regarding the COVID-19 pandemic.

## What Factors Influence the Information-Action Ratio?

The spread of misinformation plays a large role in global vaccine hesitancy, which highlights the need for clear communication of scientific data about vaccines, and the dissemination of this information with minimal delay (Rausch et al., 2021). Indeed, it has been argued that the success of vaccination strategies rests in coordinated action between multiple stakeholders such as public health authorities, healthcare practitioners, and the media and that a "one size-fits-all" strategy is no longer effective (Rausch et al., 2021).

## Drivers of Vaccine Hesitancy and Social Distancing

Vaccine hesitancy was considered one of WHO's (World Health Organization) top ten global health threats in 2019 and clearly presents a serious threat to the containment of the virus on a global level (Crawshaw et al., 2021). Barriers to vaccination include fears over vaccine safety, side effects, and the rapid development of the vaccine (Associated Press-University of Chicago National Opinion Research Center, 2020; Fisher et al., 2020). Numerous drivers of vaccine hesitancy have been identified in the literature including media and social media, personal beliefs, immunity misconception, previous COVID-19 infection, and suspicions about novel vaccines and the local availability (Riad et al., 2021), lack of trust in the government, healthcare, or pharmaceutical companies, rushed development, fear of side effects, history of medical mistreatment, and a perception of low risk of disease (Sekimitsu et al., 2022); socio-economic factors (Riad et al., 2021), political beliefs (Kennedy, 2019) as well as misinformation and distrust in the vaccine (Webb et al., 2021). As in the case of vaccination, social distancing policies have also become a key measure in reducing the spread of the COVID-19 pandemic around the world (Woelfert & Kunst, 2020).

**TABLE 4.1** Comparison of COVID-19 Health Information from Experts and Layperson

| *NIPH Messages* | *Public Perceptions, Actions and Ways of Learning* |
|---|---|
| Virus transmission modes<br>Relevant transmission modes:<br>• Droplets<br>• Air<br>• Contact | Not consistently mentioned:<br>• Droplets<br>• Air<br>• Or/and contact<br>Also mentioned:<br>• Food<br>• Clothes<br>• Feces |
| Dominant transmission route<br>• Droplet transmission most likely/significant<br>• Airborne transmission and contact transmission exist but are nonsignificant | • Most participants did not separate between (less) probable routes of transmission<br>• Belief in a number of equally important ways of transmission |
| Symptomatic, asymptomatic, presymptomatic spread<br>• Can be infected with and transmit SARS-CoV-2 virus without developing COVID-19<br>• Can be symptomatic carriers with COVID-19<br>• People with COVID-19 are most contagious for one to two days before the onset of symptoms and in the first days after the onset of symptoms | • Emphasized symptomatic transmission<br>• Being sick without symptoms not mentioned by most but emphasized as vital to understand why you should keep distance and quarantine |
| Terminology<br>• Terminology used on website: contact transmission, droplet transmission, airborne transmission | • Terms understood differently and not used by most of the participants<br>• Talked about transmission in relations to behaviors for how transmission occurred:<br>• Spitting<br>• Hugging<br>• Kissing<br>• Touching<br>• talking |
| *Virus survival*<br>• The virus can survive on surfaces from a few hours to several days<br>• Depends on the amount of virus, temperature, sunlight, and humidity<br>• The role that virus survival on surfaces plays in causing infection in humans is uncertain and constantly changing<br>• Poorly ventilated rooms increase the concentration of particles containing the virus | • Acted on evidence from informal sources, e.g., three-day survival on surfaces<br>• Few mentioned wind, climate and ventilation affected virus spread<br>• Many participants sought more information about how far droplets spread and how long they could survive in the air |

(*Continued*)

**TABLE 4.1** (Continued)

| *NIPH Messages* | *Public Perceptions, Actions and Ways of Learning* |
|---|---|
| *Basic infection prevention measures*<br>• Maintain social distancing, have fewer contacts, maintain hand hygiene and cough etiquette and use of face masks when not able to keep a distance | • All participants were informed about the main mitigation measures<br>• Some participants wanted to understand *why* certain behavior and activities were considered high risk, others preferred simple, clear messages explaining *what* to do and *how* to protect themselves<br>• Some sought informal sources to better comprehend the *why*<br>• Easily accessible, up-to-date online information<br>• Need someone to explain and interpret restrictions<br>• Sometimes enacting mitigation measures was a symbolic action |
| *Safe distance*<br>• The amount of virus exposed at distances of more 1–2 m would rarely be sufficient to cause infection<br>• Mainly infected within 1–2 m reach from infected person<br>• Keep one meter of distance<br>• The greater that the distance that you keep is, the less that the probability is that you will be exposed to infection | • None of the participants talked in terms of probabilities<br>• One of the participants misunderstood the 1-m rule as a clear boundary between safe and unsafe distances<br>• Did not understand why 1 m and not 2 m |
| *Risky activities*<br>• Risky activities due to increased expulsion of aerosols and/or being close to others are<br>  • Pubs<br>  • Traveling<br>  • Exercise centers<br>  • Poorly ventilated rooms | • Increased risk of being physically close to others was well understood<br>• Difficulty in understand why some activities were not allowed<br>• Some participants wanted information about risky situations/localizations |
| *Protecting others*<br>• The virus is possibly deadly for the oldest and some groups of people with chronic disease | All participants understood their collective responsibility to protect others |
| Contagiousness<br>• The R-number is how many persons that one corona infected person infects further<br>• A person infected with the coronavirus infects an average of 2–3 others, while one person with the flu infects 1–2 others | • COVID-19 contagiousness was underestimated by all of the participants<br>• To comprehend the contagiousness of the virus, they had to understand that this disease was not influenza |

(*Continued*)

**TABLE 4.1** (Continued)

| *NIPH Messages* | *Public Perceptions, Actions and Ways of Learning* |
|---|---|
| *Control of the spread*<br>• The *R*-value was communicated in terms of numbers, but exponential growth was not explained to the public | • The R-number was perceived as a good indicator regarding the control of the spread but otherwise was often misunderstood<br>• No participant understood exponential growth correctly |
| *Consequences of the pandemic*<br>• NIPH communicated the health effects for the individual | • After one year with pandemic restrictions, most emphasized secondary consequences (e.g., economy, mental health)<br>• Information about health consequences produced panic in some interviewees and awareness in others<br>• There were daily trade-offs between social life and the risk of becoming ill |

*Source*: Adapted from Berg et al. (2020).

**TABLE 4.2** Summary of Berg et al.'s (2020) Thematic Analyses Results

**FOCUS TOPIC: THEMATIC ANALYSIS OF HOW MENTAL MODELS ARE USED TO UNDERSTAND AND ACT UPON PANDEMIC HEALTH RISK INFORMATION**

Berg et al.'s (2022) qualitative exploration of how people perceive and act upon health risk information about the pandemic provides much insight regarding why compliance with COVID-19 preventative healthcare measures may not be taking place even when the public is not intending to non-comply and put themselves and others at additional risk.

In their study, Berg et al. (2020) explored the following three areas: virus transmission, risk mitigation and consequences of COVID-19; excerpts of interest from each of these themes will be discussed in detail in the sections below

**Theme 1: Virus Transmission.**

Comprehending Modes of Virus Transmission. Some participants were confused regarding what they perceived to be the government's contradictory information about the health risk:

*"You do not have to have contact through body fluids to get it, so you do not have to drink from the same water bottle to get it. You can get it through*

*breathing the same air. If you are infected, you exhale corona particles, and then I can breathe in and be infected that way. But now I am very insecure. This is where I have actually gotten mixed messages (No.9, Female, 19 years old)" (Berg et al., 202, p. 3).*

*Understanding Terms Differently*. Some participants understood terms differently from the formal NIHP definitions. Furthermore, some participants had difficulty distinguishing between droplet and airborne transmission. When the media used these terms, both consisted of droplets traveling through the air, which lead to further confusion of what the terms meant.

*Acting on Certain Evidence*. Some participants suggested that more specific information was needed in order to apply the advice to daily life; when they needed this information, some participants reported searching for this information from nongovernmental and informal sources, despite its scientific uncertainty. As the researchers note: "One man avoided touching metal surfaces; one woman started disinfecting her mobile phone after watching a YouTube video that depicted contact transmission" (Berg et al., 2020, p. 5).

*it...I think it can be transmitted through food. I feel insecure when grocery shopping.*

Theme 2: Risk Mitigation
Affecting exposure to risk
Learning about mitigation in different ways
Being driven by symbolic values
Theme 3: Consequences of COVID-19
Building Situational Awareness

## Theme 2: Risk Mitigation

*Affecting exposure to risk*. All participants were cognizant that they needed to maintain a 1 meter distance from others to minimize their risk of exposure to the coronavirus. Notwithstanding, this 'generic advice' was not sufficient for participants to make daily life decisions. Some participants suggested that receiving more specific information about risk activities, infection locations, level of risk (high risk vs. low risk), if an outbreak was confined to a specific social environment, and whether it was under control could help participants make better decisions:

*Learning about mitigation in different ways*. Health risk information related to COVID-19 was sometimes perceived as confusing, complicated, rapidly changing, and variably practiced across regions. One source of dissatisfaction was that given that the NIPH communicated *what* mitigation measures people should follow, participants expressed the need to comprehend both the *what, why,* and *how* of COVID-19 mitigation and expressed a variety of ways of learning about this topic.

*Being driven by symbolic values.* Understanding the importance of social distancing and hand washing was not always considered sufficient for the participants to protect themselves from the virus. Instead, participants' daily decision-making to reduce exposure to risk was at times reported to be driven by symbolic values rather than a lack of knowledge.

### Theme 3: Consequences of COVID-19

*Building Situational Awareness.* Some participants reported difficulty understanding the contagiousness of the virus because they lacked generic knowledge of the virus. As the researchers noted:

"Half of the participants expressed that the basic reproduction number (*R*-value), which was repeatedly communicated in the media, helped them to build situational awareness about the risk of losing control of the outbreak; however, they complained of a lack of knowledge of the full meaning of the *R*-value. Some misunderstood the term as a correlation coefficient or the number of people [re-infected] with COVID-19. The term "exponential growth" was perceived as a difficult concept to comprehend, and the participants stated that communications about the rapid spread of the virus and its consequences were more important than the use of the actual scientific term "exponential growth" (Berg et al., 2020, p. 8).

*Perceiving personal health consequences differently.* There was some variability in how participants perceived communications regarding individual health consequences and the disease itself. While some participants sought to know more about the disease and its long-term health consequences; others reported that this type of information elicited fear and excessive worry.

*Emphasizing secondary consequences* Some participants reported being tired of living under restrictive stay at home measures and expressed struggling with loneliness, isolation, and a loss of freedom. Participants also expressed being worried about personal and financial consequences due to the loss of income and jobs and the impact of this on the social lives and mental health of children, elderly people, and students; they reported making trade-offs between social decisions and increasing their risk of exposure:

*"If I see people coughing, I turn away. I stay away from people who have even small symptoms of disease, even though I have to admit that I have had my grand children over for visit with symptoms. I think it's just a little cold. It is a qualified choice I make then. I understand that I am exposing myself to risk. When the minister of health said we should not be with grandchildren, I thought that I cannot stand a year without cuddling with my grandchildren (No. 2, Female, 67 years old)" (Berg et al., 2020, p. 9).*

In a large-scale longitudinal study comprising representative surveys for 12 countries over the period from March to December 2020, Algan et al. (2021) found a major driving force behind individual support for and compliance with NPIs and for favorable attitudes toward vaccination was trusting scientists. In their study of 2013 Black Americans, Sekimitsu et al. (2022) found that having more opportunities once a person was vaccinated as well as having family and friends that were vaccinated to be motivators likely to increase COVID-19 vaccine uptake.

Barriers to social distancing is also problematic and a number of factors have been argued to increase this behavior such as lived environment, beliefs about consequences of non-compliance, influence of others, practical support, and trust in government (Burton et al., 2022). In an intriguing set of three studies (two conducted in the UK and the third, an online survey, conducted across 65 countries), Woelfert and Kunst (2020) found mixed effects of political trust on compliance behavior during the COVID-19 pandemic. In the first study no main effect was found for political trust on social distancing. In the second study, the researchers increased individual-level political trust experimentally in order to test its potential effects on social distancing. The findings of this second study suggested that the intervention increased political trust, but no effect on social distancing intentions were identified. The third study tested whether political and social trust at the national level would be related to social distancing behavior as well as to increases in rates of COVID-19 cases and mortality rates. The results of this third study found that there was a negative association between political trust and social distancing during the first wave of the pandemic, though this finding was not identified for the second wave of the pandemic. The researchers discuss this in the context of a previous study conducted in Singapore by Wong and Jensen (2022) that found similar results and suggested that high levels of political trust may result in low perceived risk from the virus.

In their study comprising over 2,000 online participants employing self-report measures of social distancing as well as simulations comprising graphical depictions mirroring multiple real-world scenarios of social distancing, Fazio et al. (2020) found belief systems were related to compliance with social distancing directives. Specifically, the researchers found that recognition of true statements about the COVID virus and rejection of misinformation about the virus, each correlated with social distancing. As the researchers anticipated, self-beliefs relating to interpersonal compassion *and* concern for others' vulnerability to the virus were also associated with more social distancing. The study also found believing in conspiracy theories to be a predictor of less social distancing behavior.

Kooistra and Rooij's (2020) review of 45 studies with data about compliance behavior during the first wave of the pandemic (searches included data from March 1 to June 30, 2020) found that a combination of variables influenced compliance behavior, including people's fear of the virus, psychosocial factors, institutional variables, and situational variables. Examples of psychosocial factors in this study included impulsivity, self-efficacy, and negative emotions, institutional variables included knowledge of the virus, how people felt about the mitigation measures as well as their belief in Conspiracy theories and situational variables included the chance or opportunity to violate rules as well as the capacity to obey them.

### *Personality and Compliance Behavior*

A number of researchers have noted personality variables to be a predictor of compliance behavior with social distancing measures. For example, Kooistra and van Rooij's (2020) systematic review of 45 studies on compliance with pandemic rules found that personality traits such as fear of the virus, psychosocial factors (including impulsivity, negative emotions, self-efficacy, and social norms), institutional variables (including attitudes toward the mitigation measures, belief in conspiracy theories, and knowledge of the virus), and situational nine variables (capacity to obey and opportunity to violate the rules) significantly impacted compliance behavior during the first wave of the COVID-19 pandemic. Other researchers have identified certain general personality traits to predict compliance behavior. In a study conducted in Germany with over 1,500 respondents, Twardawski et al. (2021) found evidence for the existence of what they termed 'the three pillars of individuals' engagement in physical distancing anxiety, pro-sociality, and rule compliance.' And yet some researchers have found few if any variables to correlate with compliance behavior. Harper et al. (2021), for example, noted that only fear of the virus was a significant predictor of compliance behavior and noteworthy in this study was that politically relevant variables were not. Lachowicz-Tabaczek and Kozłowska (2021) conducted a set of studies which attempted to identify a context-specific personality variable enabling a robust prediction of compliance with COVID-19 pandemic measures. The researchers conducted two studies and in the first the researchers analyzed the specificity of the current pandemic and proposed a concept and a measure of individual differences in the sense of responsibility for collective health (SRCH). The researchers operationalized this concept to reflect a person's others-oriented approach to the pandemic which included an individual's concern for collective health and the feeling of obligation to stop the spreading of the virus in one's social environment to the best of one's ability. The results of this first study confirmed SRCH as the strongest predictor of the acceptance of pandemic-related restrictions.

In the second study, the researchers compared the ability of SRCH to predict increased hygiene and social distancing with that of pandemic-related worries and narcissistic traits, as well as personal values comprising social responsibility, all of which were treated as others-oriented personality trait. The results revealed that SRCH explained most of the variance in social distancing, whereas pandemic-related worries which predicted most of the variance in hygiene practices.

But what happens when people are not others-oriented? Will they be motivated to comply with pandemic measures? In the sections to follow we will explore this after which we will turn our attention to reviewing more general theoretical frameworks that discuss motivators of practicing health preventative measures.

### *Building Trust and Threats to Trust during COVID-19*

> "Surgical training and culture highlight the importance of the physical examination, of the power of touch, to determine diagnosis and treatment plans and to solidify the doctor–patient relationship...The doctor–patient relationship hinges on mutual respect and trust... Medicine, like life, is a series of choices and trade-offs, and decisions are always made in the context of current societal norms... Practicing medicine in the unprecedented times of the current COVID-19 pandemic has changed the way doctors interact with their patients"
>
> (Rosen et al., 2020).

There is ample evidence to suggest trust takes time to build (Galford & Drapeau, 2003; Hautsch et al., 2018; McKinney & Berube, 2018), particularly in the field of healthcare (Dubé et al., 2021). Traditionally trust between clinicians and their patients have been built through clinicians' respect of patients' knowledge, perspectives, and lived experience and inviting patients into a dialog where both parties actively participate (Baker, 2020). How does this inform the building of trust during the COVID-19 pandemic? A pandemic is a crisis event; there is little time to build dialog between healthcare providers and patients. Further, beliefs related to information sharing are largely anchored by people's predispositions and preexisting attitudes. In the context of the COVID-19 pandemic, however, given that people lacked strong preexisting attitudes or knowledge of the disease (Trust source article) it is difficult to understand compliance behavior in adhering to preventative health measures to reduce the risk of being infected and/or infecting others. In the section to follow, we will explore a number of theoretical frameworks and empirical studies that delve into factors motivating compliance with preventative health measures.

## Compliance With Vaccination and Preventative Health Measures

The COVID-19 pandemic can be characterized as a slow-burning or creeping crisis, with unclear beginnings and ends that may undercut the legitimacy of many public institutions (Boin et al., 2020).

For this reason, it is important to examine theoretical frameworks which may help us better understand what may influence the public's willingness to comply with preventative health measures. What are some of the factors that may motivate people to adopt preventative health measures? These are the questions that will guide the studies reviewed in the sections to follow.

### *Theoretical Frameworks*

In their overview of the mental models approach to risk communication Berg et al. (2020) explain how is founded on the tendency of people to think about a given phenomenon in a certain way, despite the availability of new information. Citing the anchoring bias which posits that people filter new information based on alignment with pre-existing understandings, beliefs and values, there appears to be evidence that in the case of pandemics such as the COVID-19 pandemic, people have a tendency to understand it based on pre-existing mental models of what a pandemic is like, instead of relying more on new, available information.

### *Health Compliance Behavior: Driven by Affect or Cognition?*

In their review of attitudinal and demographic determinants of protective behaviors during crisis events, Bish and Michie (2010) argue that health protective behavior during a pandemic may be categorized into the following three categories: preventive, avoidant, and management of disease behaviors. But what drives these health protective behaviors? Founded on studies in clinical and physiological psychology, Loewenstein et al. (2001) postulate 'the risk-as-feelings hypothesis,' which suggests that emotional or affective reactions drive behavior when we make choices under risky and/or uncertain conditions. Using a snowball sampling technique within a longitudinal two-wave design, Kowalski and Black (2021) explored both cognitive and affective contributors to the frequency with which respondents engaged in protective health behaviors related to the COVID-19 crisis. The results of their study found that younger females were more likely to comply with protective health behaviors which is consistent with similar findings about engagement in self-protective health behaviors in the context of SARS.

The two predominant theories of the role of emotions in influencing our attitudes and decision-making during COVID-19 are cognitive appraisal theory and affective intelligence theory (AIT) (Eberhardt & Ling, 2021).

### *Cognitive Theories of Preventative Health Behaviors*

According to cognitive theories, people make decisions based on an evaluation of various alternatives or choices; a calculus is then used to arrive at a decision. Here, cognition precedes emotion and risk perception is a significant driver of adopting preventative health behaviors.

### *Protection Motivation Theory and COVID-19*

A famous cognitive theory of health behavior is Protection-Motivation Theory (PMT), which posits that a person's willingness to begin a health-promoting behavior or to end a health-compromising behavior is motivated by perceived vulnerability to the health threat, perceived severity of the health threat, outcome efficaciousness of behaviors that would reduce the health threat, and self-efficacy (Rogers & Prentice-Dunn, 1997). It has been argued that when employed to predict health-protective behaviors, people who will be most likely to engage in recommended COVID-19 protective behaviors would be people who believe the virus is serious, that recommended behaviors will have a significant impact in reducing risk of contracting the virus, that they are capable of following risk-reducing recommendations and that their vulnerability to the virus is high (Kowalski & Black, 2021). On the other hand, if risk is perceived to be low, the disease not perceived to be overly serious. Conversely, those who believe their risk is low, that the disease is mild, and who do not believe that protective measures are not effective would have the lowest frequency of engaging in protective behaviors (Kowalski & Black, 2021).

Eberhardt and Ling (2021) performed a hierarchical multiple linear regression in three stages on the following PMT constructs – severity, susceptibility, maladaptive response costs, and self-efficacy on 382 online respondents in a survey conducted in the UK. The researchers found significant positive correlations between the preventive behaviors of COVID-19 and perceived vulnerability, perceived severity, response efficacy, self-efficacy, and protection motivation.

## ***Affective Theories of Preventative Health Behaviors***

In their analysis of the role of emotions and trust in the government during times of COVID-19, Eberhardt and Ling (2021). explain that affective intelligence theory (AIT) focus on the role of emotions during information processing. Arguably, crisis events may be considered to be complex situations in life, and emotional reactions enable flexible reactions to crises events. According to Eberhardt and Ling (2021):

> Depending on how a threat or dangerous situation is perceived, it may trigger different emotions, such as fear and anger. In particular, the appraisals of attribution and control are important in this regard. Fear is more likely to arise when the source of the threat is ambiguous and the individual does not perceive to be in control, resulting in harm-avoidance behavior. Anger, in contrast, is more likely to be evoked when someone is accountable and can be blamed for the threat and when the individual feels in control, resulting in actions targeted at removing the source of harm from her or his environment.
> *(p. 341)*

Citing studies that suggest fear and anger have separate impacts on political participation, Eberhardt and Ling (2021) argue that in consideration of studies that suggest that fear typically makes one more pessimistic, it should therefore increase risk-avoidance behavior such that fearful individuals should be more prone to support precautionary measures and follow/adhere to actions designed to prevent and protect citizens from the danger of the coronavirus.

### *The Health Belief Model*

The Health Belief Model (HBM) is considered to be one of the most widely used models for understanding hesitancy to vaccinate against COVID-19 (Chen et al., 2021; Gabriel et al., 2019; Mahmud et al., 2021; Shmueli, 2021; Zampetakis & Melas, 2021). According to the HBM, health-related behavior depends on the combination of different factors including perceived susceptibility, perceived severity, perceived benefits, perceived barriers, cues to action, and self-efficacy (Rosenstock, 1982).

The HBM is based on the concepts of threat and benefits and comprises the following four constructs which are believed to predict engagement with health protective behaviors: perceived susceptibility and severity (relating to threat) and perceived benefits and barriers (relating to benefit). According to this theory, behavior is a function of the degree to which people value a result and their evaluation of the expectation, that a certain action will lead to a given result.

Numerous studies have applied the Health Belief Model to better understand the COVID-19 pandemic (Mercadante & Law (2021); Christian et al., 2021; Wong et al., 2020). What is of specific interest to us is how does the Health Belief Model help us to better understand compliance with preventative health measures during the COVID-19 pandemic? Christian et al.'s (2021) research attempted to articulate the reasons behind the low level of compliance toward health protocols during the COVID-19 pandemic in Indonesia through the application of the theory of the Health Belief Model. Analyses using six components of the Health Belief Model showed that low compliance toward health protocols during the COVID-19 pandemic were the results of society's perception of a low chance of being infected by the coronavirus and perceiving it to be similar in seriousness to the common flu. Mercadante and Law (2021) found that Americans are less likely to make health decisions based on population threat of the virus, compared to perceived individual risks and benefits. In their study, the researchers analyzed 1,159 survey responses and found that perceived benefits (understood as the vaccination decreases the chance of infection and the vaccine will make people less worried) was the highest significant motivator to intention to take the managerial and or other professional occupations were also more likely to be willing to pay for the vaccine if needed.

## Empirical Findings

### Citizens' Perceptions of Government Effectiveness and Willingness to Cooperate

Employing data collected in Israel at two points in time, during the first peak of the COVID-19 crisis in late March 2020 and in October 2020 when Israel was exiting from a second lockdown, Mizrahi et al. (2021) explored factors relating to citizens' willingness to cooperate with government imposed measures to safeguard public health. The study found citizens focus on the short term and seek immediate results in terms of readiness and preparedness and that citizens 'willingness to cooperate with the government during crises situations are more strongly related to government's responsiveness and transparency, as well as the public's participation in decision-making.

### The Role of Emotion in Trust in the Government during COVID 19

Devine's (2024) discusses a term they call the "rally-round-the-flag "effect regarding various variables that influence trust in political institutions and actors during a crisis event. However, studies around the world suggest a mixed effect; for example, studies conducted in Spain suggest that people who personally experience COVID-19 or have a loved one with that experience have lower levels of political trust, whereas the implementation of lockdown measures increased trust in the government in other European countries (Bol et al., 2021). Other studies have found that lockdown measures resulted in different types of trust; for example, in the Netherlands lockdowns did not increase trust, whereas a study in Sweden shows government preventative measures resulted in increased trust in the government which, in turn, impacted interpersonal trust (Esaiasson et al., 2021).

### The Role of Risk Perception in the Adoption of Preventative Measures

Risk perception has been found to be a strong predictor of adoption of preventative health measures during the COVID-19 pandemic (Dryhurst et al., 2020; Ju et al., 2021). For example, employing a sample size of nearly 7000 respondents in ten countries across Europe, Asia, and America, Dryhurst et al. (2020) conducted what is believed to be the first international assessment of public risk perception of COVID-19. The results of this study found that when pooled across countries, personal experience with the virus, individualistic and pro-social values, learning about the virus from friends and family, trust in government, science, and healthcare professionals, personal knowledge of government strategy, as well as personal and collective efficacy were all significant predictors of risk perception. As predicted, risk perception was found to correlate significantly with reported adoption of preventative health behaviors in all ten countries examined in this study.

### *The Role of Ethnically Concordant Healthcare Provider-Recipient in Building Trust for Vaccine Acceptance*

Many studies suggest that some people who are reluctant to vaccinate would be more inclined to do so, if such messages were promoted by ethnically concordant spokespeople and/or healthcare providers (Kricorian & Turner, 2021). For example, in a recently survey of 1,950 US adults, African-American and Hispanic respondents reported being more willing to vaccinate if COVID-19 vaccine endorsements came from racially concordant healthcare professionals. These respondents further reported that they would also be motivated by receiving more information on the experiences of vaccine study participants who are of their own race and ethnicity (Kricorian & Turner, 2021).

### *Comparing Compliance Policies across Countries: No One Size Fits All*

The COVID-19 pandemic was managed differently by various countries in the world; with variation in timing and severity of implementation of boarder closures, lockdowns and mandates requiring hand sanitization and wearing face masks in public. Some countries were more lenient with restrictive measures and some had few and relied more on public obligation to do what was morally right to contain spread of the virus.

In order to better understand the role of beliefs, motivations, and policy measures on public health behaviors, van den Broek-Altenburg and Atherly (2021) compared two Dutch-speaking countries, the Netherlands and Flanders, Belgium, which were selected as they are linguistically and economically similar, but utilized different lockdown strategies during the early phases of the COVID-19 pandemic. When describing their study, the researchers noted communication differences, between the two countries comprising the perception of politeness. For example, tasks were more the focus within the Dutch cultural context, such that achievement and being effective were more valued skills compared to the Flemish focus on building relationships. The results of the study identified cultural differences in motivations for complying with social measures. For example, the impetus for the Flemish to engage in self-protecting behaviors was conformity as well as to protect the public and their families, compared to the Dutch were more likely to engage in these behaviors to protect themselves.

Kuiper et al. (2020) described the Dutch approach to contain the spread of the virus to focus more on moral appeals and self-discipline than physically repressive measures. Their study found mixed evidence for moral and social motivations to comply with personality factors such as impulsiveness mitigating the effectiveness of appeals on self-discipline.

The Swedish approach to management of the COVID-19 pandemic has been described as relaxed by many as there were no lockdowns as well as less regulation and more voluntary action expected of citizens and organizations than in other countries (Giritli Nygren & Olofsson, 2021). However, this approach may not have been successful given statistics based on the total population of the country, three times more people died from COVID-19 in Sweden compared to Germany, with even more alarming statistics comparing Sweden versus Taiwan (Jung et al., 2020).

Yet there is no strong evidence that strict and timely lockdowns can lower death tolls from the virus. For example, Bonardi et al. (2020) conducted a study employing a data set of 184 countries from December 31st, 2019, to May 4th, 2020, which considered data on when lockdowns were adopted, along with confirmed cases and deaths. The study found that reducing movements within countries was effective in developed economies – averting about 650,000 deaths – but not in developing ones, and that countries that acted more quickly progressed better. The study also found that closing borders has had no appreciable effect, even after 50 days had passed.

### *Compliance to COVID-19 Measures Over Time*

Guided by Lindenberg's Goal Framing Theory, Six et al. (2023) explored the impacts of time on social compliance behavior during the COVID-19 pandemic. **Lindenberg's Goal Framing Theory**, comprises three overarching goals: the normative goal (including variables pro-social behavior, trust in government, observed respect for rules and rule legitimacy), the hedonic goal (including variables fear and opportunities for fun and happiness), and the gain goal (including variable worsened income position). The researchers collected data during three different stages of the first months of the COVID-19 crisis in Flanders (Survey Wave 1, April 7; Survey Wave 2, April 28; Survey Wave 3, June 30). Wave 1 took place at the peak of infections, comprising a strict lockdown, as at the time it was not yet known whether the measures were working. During the second wave, the effectiveness of the lockdowns were clear as the infections and hospitalization rates were declining and the future relaxation of measures was announced. Finally, during the third wave, infections were at a comparatively low point and further suspension of the remaining lockdown measures were expected to take effect the very next day.

The results of the study found that the fear of the severity of the COVID-19 virus was significant during all three waves. In this study – fear (severity), observed respect for rules, and rule appropriateness were found to drive compliance through all three waves. During the first wave, the public's fear of the virus as well as respect for rules, impacted compliance more strongly than pro-social behavior. During the second and third waves it was found that respondents in this study had different motivations for compliance and this trend becomes more pronounced with time. Thus, in the third wave, different levels of compliance behavior are identified for different groups, such that more older people were found to comply compared to younger people; more women were complying compared to men; and more self-interested people were failing to comply compared to pro-social people.

## Key Lessons

This chapter overviewed theoretical and empirical literature on vaccine hesitancy. This led to exploring a number of questions including what is the nature of vaccine hesitancy, what leads to vaccine hesitancy and what role does misinformation play in promoting vaccine hesitancy? With the abundance of information at our disposal, how do we discriminate between fake and authentic information about the COVID 19 virus? In order to address this question, the chapter began with an overview of various theories of misinformation such as conspiracy and religion-based theories regarding the spread of the COVID-19 virus. We also learned how the strategic framing of messages designed to encourage vaccination influenced the persuasiveness of these messages. This led to an overview of affective and cognitive-based theories of health preventative behaviors.

The chapter drew heavily from the thematic analysis of Berg et al.'s (2022) study which provides a wealth of insights into understanding how COVID-19 health risk messages are misconstrued by the public. After reviewing literature on factors that motivate people to comply with COVID-19 NPIs, we discussed a number of motivators of non-compliance with self-protective measures by reviewing the literature on key drivers of compliant behavior during the pandemic. We also learned about how ethnic minorities may perceive health communication and certain biases they may have about the vaccine that may contribute toward vaccine hesitancy.

We briefly reviewed studies that suggest how to culturally tailor messages for minority populations to lower vaccine hesitancy among certain ethnic minority groups.

In the hopes of promoting a better understanding of compliance policies such that society can more effectively convince the public of their importance during global disaster events, the chapter then discussed how various compliance policies adopted by countries around the world, fared during the COVID-19 pandemic. The chapter concluded with a discussion of how compliance to health-preventative measures during COVID-19 changed with time.

## Bibliography

Algan, Y., Cohen, D., Davoine, E., Foucault, M., & Stantcheva, S. (2021). Trust in scientists in times of pandemic: Panel evidence from 12 countries. *Proceedings of the National Academy of Sciences*, *118*(40), e2108576118.

Associated Press-University of Chicago National Opinion Research Center. (2020). *Expectations for a COVID-19 vaccine*. https://apnorc.org/projects/expectations-for-a-covid-19- vaccine/

Baker, D. W. (2020). Trust in health care in the time of COVID-19. *JAMA, 324*(23), 2373–2375.

Barua, Z., Barua, S., Aktar, S., Kabir, N., & Li, M. (2020). Effects of misinformation on COVID-19 individual responses and recommendations for resilience of disastrous consequences of misinformation. *Progress in Disaster Science, 8*, 100119.

Bates, B. R., Villegas-Botero, A., Costales, J. A., Moncayo, A. L., Tami, A., Carvajal, A., & Grijalva, M. J. (2022). COVID-19 vaccine hesitancy in three Latin American countries: Reasons given for not becoming vaccinated in Colombia, Ecuador, and Venezuela. *Health Communication, 37*(12), 1465–1475.

Berg, S. H., Shortt, M. T., Thune, H., Røislien, J., O'Hara, J. K., Lungu, D. A., & Wiig, S. (2022). Differences in comprehending and acting on pandemic health risk information: A qualitative study using mental models. *BMC Public Health, 22*(1), 1–15.

Bish, A., & Michie, S. (2010). Demographic and attitudinal determinants of protective behaviours during a pandemic: A review. *British Journal of Health Psychology, 15*(4), 797–824. doi: 10.1348/135910710X485826

Boin, A., Ekengren, M., & Rhinard, M. (2020). Hiding in plain sight: Conceptualizing the creeping crisis. *Risk, Hazards & Crisis in Public Policy, 11*(2), 116–138.

Bol, D., Giani, M., Blais, A., & Loewen, P. J. (2021). The effect of COVID-19 lockdowns on political support: Some good news for democracy? *European Journal of Political Research, 60*(2), 497–505.

Bonardi, J. P., Gallea, Q., Kalanoski, D., & Lalive, R. (2020). Fast and local: How lockdown policies affect the spread and severity of covid-19. *Covid Economics, 23*, 325–351.

Boness, C. L., Nelson, M., & Douaihy, A. B. (2022). Motivational interviewing strategies for addressing covid-19 vaccine hesitancy. *The Journal of the American Board of Family Medicine, 35*(2), 420–426.

Bradshaw, A. S. (2023). To share or not to share: A framing analysis of paid vaccine advertisements on facebook during COVID-19 and pro-vaccine mothers' willingness to promote vaccines within their peer networks. *Journal of Current Issues & Research in Advertising, 44*(2), 142–168.

Breckenridge, L. A., Burns, D., & Nye, C. (2022). The use of motivational interviewing to overcome COVID-19 vaccine hesitancy in primary care settings. *Public Health Nursing, 39*(3), 618–623.

van den Broek-Altenburg, E., & Atherly, A. (2021). Adherence to COVID-19 policy measures: Behavioral insights from The Netherlands and Belgium. *PLoS One, 16*(5), e0250302.

Bronstein, M. V., Pennycook, G., Bear, A., Rand, D. G., & Cannon, T. D. (2019). Belief in fake news is associated with delusionality, dogmatism, religious fundamentalism, and reduced analytic thinking. *Journal of Applied Research in Memory and Cognition, 8*(1), 108–117. doi: 10.1037/h0101832

Brotherton, R. & Son, L. K. (2021). Metacognitive labelling of contentious claims: Facts, opinions, and consipiracy theories. *Frontiers in Psychology*. doi: 10.3389/fpsyg.2021.644657

Burton, A., McKinlay, A., Dawes, J., Roberts, A., Fynn, W., May, T., & Fancourt, D. (2022). Understanding barriers and facilitators to compliance with UK social distancing guidelines during the COVID-19 pandemic: A qualitative interview study. *Behaviour Change*, *40*(1), 30–50.

Champion, V. L., & Skinner, C. S. (2008). The health belief model. *Health Behavior and Health Education: Theory, Research, and Practice*, *4*, 45–65.

Chen, H., Li, X., Gao, J., Liu, X., Mao, Y., Wang, R., … & Dai, J. (2021). Health belief model perspective on the control of COVID-19 vaccine hesitancy and the promotion of vaccination in China: Web-based cross-sectional study. *Journal of Medical Internet Research*, *23*(9), e29329.

Cheng, J. W., & Nishikawa, M. (2022). Effects of health literacy in the fight against the COVID-19 infodemic: The case of Japan. *Health Communication*, *37*(12), 1520–1533.

Cheng, T., Horbay, B., Nocos, R., Lutes, L., & Lear, S. A. (2021). The role of tailored public health messaging to young adults during COVID-19:"There'sa lot of ambiguity around what it means to be safe". *PLoS One*, *16*(10), e0258121.

Chou, W. Y. S., & Budenz, A. (2020). Considering emotion in COVID-19 vaccine communication: Addressing vaccine hesitancy and fostering vaccine confidence. *Health Communication*, *35*(14), 1718–1722.

Christian, A. C. S. (2021). Public obedience to health protocols during Covid-19 pandemic in Indonesia: A perspective from health belief model theory. *Soshum: Jurnal-Sosial dan Humaniora*, *11*(2), 201–210.

Christian, D. D., McCarty, D. L., & Brown, C. L. (2021). Experiential education during the COVID-19 pandemic: A reflective process. *Journal of Constructivist Psychology*, 34(3), 264–277.

Crawshaw, A. F., Deal, A., Rustage, K., Forster, A. S., Campos-Matos, I., Vandrevala, T., & Hargreaves, S. (2021). What must be done to tackle vaccine hesitancy and barriers to COVID-19 vaccination in migrants? *Journal of Travel Medicine*, *28*(4), taab048.

Devine, D. (2024). Does political trust matter? A meta-analysis on the consequences of trust. *Political Behavior*, published online: 10 February 2024. https://doi.org/10.1007/s11109-024-09916-y

Dubé, E., Wilson, S., Gagnon, D., Deeks, S. L., & Dubey, V. (2021). "It takes time to build trust": A survey Ontario's school-based HPV immunization program ten years post-implementation. *Human Vaccines & Immunotherapeutics*, *17*(2), 451–456.

Duong, M. C., Nguyen, H. T., & Duong, M. (2022). Evaluating COVID-19 vaccine hesitancy: A qualitative study from Vietnam. *Diabetes & Metabolic Syndrome: Clinical Research & Reviews*, *16*(1), 102363.

Dryhurst, S., Schneider, C. R., Kerr, J., Alexandra L., J. Freeman, J., Recchia, G., van der Bles, A. M., Spiegelhalter, D., & van der Linden, S. (2020) Risk perceptions of COVID-19 around the world. *Journal of Risk Research*, *23*(7–8), 994–1006. doi: 10.1080/13669877.2020.1758193

Eberhardt, J., & Ling, J. (2021). Predicting COVID-19 vaccination intention using protection motivation theory and conspiracy beliefs. *Vaccine*, *39*(42), 6269–6275.

Esaiasson, P., Sohlberg, J., Ghersetti, M., & Johansson, B. (2021). How the coronavirus crisis affects citizen trust in institutions and in unknown others: Evidence from 'the Swedish experiment'. *European Journal of Political Research*, *60*(3), 748–760.

Fazio, R. H., Ruisch, B. C., Moore, C. A., Samayoa, J. A. G., Boggs, S. T., & Ladanyi, J. T. (2020). Who is (not) complying with the social distancing directive and why? Testing a general framework of compliance with multiple measures of social distancing. *medRxiv* 2020. doi: 10.1101/2020.10.26.20219634

Fisher, K., Bloomstone, B., Walder, J., Crawford, S., & Fouayzi, H. (2020, September 4). Attitudes toward a potential SARS-CoV-2 vaccine: A survey of U.S. adults. *Annals of Internal Medicine*, M20–3569. In Press. https://www.acpjournals.org/doi/full/10.7326/M20-3569.

Gabriel, E. H., Hoch, M. C., Cramer, R. J. (2019). Health belief model scale and theory of planned behavior scale to assess attitudes and perceptions of injury prevention program participation: An exploratory factor analysis. *Journal of Science and Medicine in Sport, 22*, 544–549.

Galford, R., & Drapeau, A. S. (2003). The enemies of trust. *Harvard Business Review, 81*(2), 88–95.

Gantiva, C., Jiménez-Leal, W., & Urriago-Rayo, J. (2021). Framing messages to deal with the COVID-19 crisis: The role of loss/gain frames and content. *Frontiers in Psychology, 12*, 568212.

Gentsch, A. T., Butler, J., O'Laughlin, K., Eucker, S. A., Chang, A., Duber, H., … & Rodriguez, R. M. (2022). Perspectives of COVID-19 vaccine–hesitant emergency department patients to inform messaging platforms to promote vaccine uptake. *Academic Emergency Medicine, 30*(1), 32–39.

Georgiou, N., Delfabbro, P., & Balzan, R. (2020). COVID-19-related conspiracy beliefs and their relationship with perceived stress and pre-existing conspiracy beliefs. *Personality and Individual Differences*, 166, 110201.

Giritli Nygren, K., & Olofsson, A. (2021). Swedish exceptionalism, herd immunity and the welfare state: A media analysis of struggles over the nature and legitimacy of the COVID-19 pandemic strategy in Sweden. *Current Sociology, 69*(4), 529–546.

Harper, C. A., Satchell, L. P., Fido, D., & Latzman, R. D. (2021). Functional fear predicts public health compliance in the COVID-19 pandemic. *International Journal of Mental Health and Addiction, 19*(5), 1875–1888.

Harper, T., Tomkinson, S., & Attwell, K. (2022). Communication is not a virus: COVID-19 Vaccine-Critical activity on Facebook and implications for the 'Infodemic' concept. *Journal of Health Communication, 27*(8), 563–573.

Hartman, T. K., Marshall, M., Stocks, T. V.A., McKay, R., Bennett, K., Butter, S., Miller, J. G., Hyland, P., Levita, L., Martinez, A. P., Mason, L., McBride, O., Murphy, J., Shevlin, M., Vallières, F. & Benta, R. P. (2021). Different conspiracy theories have different psychological and social determinants: Comparison of three theories about the origins of the COVID-19 virus in a representative sample of the UK Population. *Frontiers in Political Science.* doi: 10.3389/fpos.2021.642510

Hautsch, N., Scheuch, C., & Voigt, S. (2018). Building trust takes time: Limits to arbitrage in blockchain-based markets. *arXiv preprint arXiv:1812.00595.*

Ju, I., Ohs, J., Park, T., & Hinsley, A. (2021). Interpersonal communication influence on health-protective behaviors amid the COVID-19 crisis. *Health Communication.* doi: 10.1080/10410236.2021.1956038

Jolley, D., & Douglas, K. M. (2014). The effects of anti-vaccine conspiracy theories on vaccination intentions. *PLoS One, 9*(2), e89177.

Jung, F., Krieger, V., Hufert, F. T., & Küpper, J. H. (2020). Herd immunity or suppression strategy to combat COVID-19. *Clinical Hemorheology and Microcirculation, 75*(1), 13–17.

Kaine, G., Greenhalgh, S., & Wright, V. (2022). Compliance with Covid-19 measures: Evidence from New Zealand. *PLoS One, 17*(2), e0263376.

Kennedy, J. (2019). Populist politics and vaccine hesitancy in Western Europe: An analysis of national-level data. *The European Journal of Public Health, 29*(3), 512–516. doi: 10.1093/eurpub/ckz004

Kim, S. (2021). Searching for general model of conspiracy theories and its implication for public health policy: Analysis of the impacts of political, psychological, structural factors on conspiracy beliefs about the COVID-19 pandemic. *International Journal of Environmental Research and Public Health, 18*(1), 266. doi: 10.3390/ijerph18010266

Kooistra, E. B., & van Rooij, B. (2020). Pandemic compliance: A systematic review of influences on social distancing behaviour during the first wave of the COVID-19 outbreak. *Available at SSRN 3738047.*

Kowalczyk, O., Roszkowski, K., Montane, X., Pawliszak, W., Tylkowski, B., & Bajek, A. (2020). Religion and faith perception in a pandemic of COVID-19. *Journal of Religion and Health, 59*, 2671–2677.

Kowalski, R. M., & Black, K. J. (2021). Protection motivation and the COVID-19 virus. *Health Communication, 36*(1), 15–22.

Kricorian, K., & Turner, K. (2021). COVID-19 vaccine acceptance and beliefs among Black and Hispanic Americans. *PLoS One, 16*(8), e0256122.

Kuiper, M. E., de Bruijn, A. L., Reinders Folmer, C., Olthuis, E., Brownlee, M., Kooistra, E. B., … & Van Rooij, B. (2020). The intelligent lockdown: Compliance with COVID-19 mitigation measures in the Netherlands. *Amsterdam Law School Research Paper* (2020-20).

Lachowicz-Tabaczek, K., & Kozłowska, M. A. (2021). Being others-oriented during the pandemic: Individual differences in the sense of responsibility for collective health as a robust predictor of compliance with the COVID-19 containing measures. *Personality and Individual Differences*, 183, 111138.

Lahav, E., Shahrabani, S., Rosenboim, M. & Tsuitsu, Y. (2022). Is stronger religious faith associated with a greater willingness to take the COVID-19 vaccine? Evidence from Israel and Japan. *The European Journal of Health Economics, 23*, 687–703.

Larson, H. J., Jarrett, C., Eckersberger, E., Smith, D. M., & Paterson, P. (2014). Understanding vaccine hesitancy around vaccines and vaccination from a global perspective: A systematic review of published literature, 2007–2012. *Vaccine*, *32*(19), 2150–2159.

Lockyer, B., et al. (2020). Understanding COVID-19 misinformation and vaccine hesitancy in context: Findings from a qualitative study involving citizens in Bradford, UK. *Health Expectation, 24*(4), 1158–1167.

Loewenstein, G. F., Weber, E. U., Hsee, C. K., & Welch, N. (2001). Risk as feelings. *Psychological Bulletin, 127*(2), 267–286. doi: 10.1037/0033-2909.127.2.267

Longstaff, P. H. & Yang, S. U. (2008). Communication management and trust: Their role in building resilience to "surprises" such as natural disasters, pandemic flu, and *terrorism. Ecology and Society, 13*(1), 3.

MacDonald, N. E. (2015). Sage working group on vaccine hesitancy. Vaccine hesitancy: Definition, scope and determinants. *Vaccine*, *33*, 4161.

Mahindarathne, P. P. (2021). Assessing COVID-19 preventive behaviours using the health belief model: A Sri Lankan study. *Journal of Taibah University Medical Sciences*, *16*(6), 914–919.

Mahmud, I., Kabir, R., Rahman, M. A., Alradie-Mohamed, A., Vinnakota, D., & Al-Mohaimeed, A. (2021). The health belief model predicts intention to receive the COVID-19 vaccine in Saudi Arabia: Results from a cross-sectional survey. *Vaccines*, *9*(8), 864.

Mizrahi, S., Vigoda-Gadot, E., & Cohen, N. (2021). How well do they manage a crisis? The government's effectiveness during the Covid-19 pandemic. *Public Administration Review, 81*(6), 1120–1130.

McKinney, S. E., & Berube, C. (2018). Building trust and respect. *The Education Digest*, *83*(8), 55–59.

McLaren, J. (2021). Racial disparity in COVID-19 deaths: Seeking economic roots with census data. *The BE Journal of Economic Analysis & Policy, 21*(3), 897-919.

Mercadante, A. R., & Law, A. V. (2021). Will they, or Won't they? Examining patients' vaccine intention for flu and COVID-19 using the Health Belief Model. *Research in Social and Administrative Pharmacy, 17*(9), 1596–1605.

Miller, J. M. (2020). Do COVID-19 conspiracy theory beliefs form a monological belief system? *Canadian Journal of Political Science/Revue canadienne de science politique*, *53*(2), 319–326.

Oliver, E., & Wood, T. (2014). Medical conspiracy theories and health behaviors in the United States. *JAMA Internal Medicine, 174*(5), 817–818. doi: 10.1001/jamainternmed 190

Oltedal, S., Moen, B. E., Klempe, H., & Rundmo, T. (2004). Explaining risk perception: An evaluation of cultural theory. *Rotunde*, *85*(Apr), 1–33.

Prooijen, J. W. (2018). *The psychology of conspiracy theories*. Routledge.

van Prooijen, J. W., & Van Vugt, M. (2018). Conspiracy theories: Evolved functions and psychological mechanisms. *Perspectives on Psychological Science*, *13*(6), 770–788.

Rausch, C., Pitts, P. J., & le Louët, H. (2021). Vaccine hesitancy: When political miscommunication replaces scientific benefit/risk assessment. *Journal of Commercial Biotechnology*, *26*(3). doi: 10.5912/jcb1012

Riad, A., Abdulqader, H., Morgado, M., Domnori, S., Koščík, M., Mendes, J. J., ... & IADS- SCORE. (2021). Global prevalence and drivers of dental students' COVID-19 vaccine hesitancy. *Vaccines*, *9*(6), 566.

Robin, M. K., & Black, K. J. (2021). Protection Motivation and the COVID-19. *Virus, Health Communication, 36*(1), 15–22. doi: 10.1080/10410236.2020.1847448

Rogers, R. W., & Prentice-Dunn, S. (1997). Protection motivation theory. In D. S. Gochman (Ed.), *Handbook of health behavior research 1: Personal and social determinants* (pp. 113–132). Plenum Press.

Rosen, C. B., Joffe, S., & Kelz, R. R. (2020). COVID-19 moves medicine into a virtual space: A paradigm shift from touch to talk to establish trust. *Annals of Surgery*, *272*(2), e159.

Rosenstock, I. (1982).The health belief model and nutrition education. *Journal of the Academy of Nutrition and Dietetics, 43*, 184–192.

Ruiz, J. B., & Bell, R. A. (2021). Predictors of intention to vaccinate against COVID-19: Results of a nationwide survey. *Vaccine*, *39*(7), 1080–1086.

Sabahelzein, M. M., Hartigan-Go, K. & Larson, H. J. (2021). The politics of COVID-19 vaccination confidence. *Current Opinion in Immunology, 71*, 92–96.

Sallam, M. (2021). COVID-19 vaccine hesitancy worldwide: A concise systematic review of vaccine acceptance rates. *Vaccines*, *9*(2), 160. doi: 10.3390/vaccines9020160

Schaffner, B. F., & Luks, S. (2018). Misinformation or expressive responding? What an inauguration crowd can tell us about the source of political misinformation in surveys. *Public Opinion Quarterly*, *82*(1), 135–147. doi: 10.1093/poq/nfx042

Schmidtke, K. A., Skrybant, M., Kudrna, L., Russell, S., Ding, I. L., & Clarke, A. (2022). A workshop to co-design messages that may increase uptake of vaccines: A case study. *Vaccine*, *40*(37), 5407–5412.

Sekimitsu, S., Simon, J., Matsuuchi, M., Lindsley, M. J., Jalloh, U., Mabogurie, T., Kerr, J., Willingham, M., Ndousse-Fetter, S. B., White, G., & Altman, W. (2022). Exploring COVID-19 vaccine hesitancy in Black Americans: Contributing factors and motivators. *American Journal of Health Promotion, 36*(8), 1304–1315. doi: 10.1177/08901171221099270

Shmueli, L. (2021). Predicting intention to receive COVID-19 vaccine among the general population using the health belief model and the theory of planned behavior model. *BMC Public Health, 21*, 804.

Siegrist, M., & Bearth, A. (2021). Worldviews, trust, and risk perceptions shape public acceptance of COVID-19 public health measures. *Proceedings of the National Academy of Sciences, 118*(24), e2100411118.

Six, F., De Vadder, S., Glavina, M., Verhoest, K., & Pepermans, K. (2023). What drives compliance with COVID-19 measures over time? Explaining changing impacts with goal framing theory. *Regulation & Governance, 17*(1), 3–21.

Theocharis, Y., Cardenal, A., Jin, S., Aalberg, T., Hopmann, D. N., Strömbäck, J., … & Štětka, V. (2021). Does the platform matter? Social media and COVID-19 conspiracy theory beliefs in 17 countries. *New Media & Society 25*(12), 3412–3437.

Twardawski, M., Steindorf, L., & Thielmann, I. (2021). Three pillars of physical distancing: Anxiety, prosociality, and rule compliance during the COVID-19 pandemic. *Collabra: Psychology, 7*(1), 22511.

Uscinski, J. E., Enders, A. M., Klofstad, C., Seelig, M., Funchion, J., Everett, C., Wuchty, S., Premaratne, K., & Murthi, M. (2020). Why do people believe COVID-19 conspiracy theories? *The Harvard Kennedy School (HKS) Misinformation Review*, 1, Special Issue on COVID- 19 and Misinformation. doi: 10.37016/mr-2020-015. Website: misinforeview.hks.harvard.edu

Webb Hooper, M., Nápoles, A. M., & Pérez-Stable, E. J. (2021). No populations left behind: Vaccine hesitancy and equitable diffusion of effective COVID-19 vaccines. *Journal of General Internal Medicine, 36*(7), 2130–2133.

Woelfert, F. S., & Kunst, J. R. (2020). How political and social trust can impact social distancing practices during COVID-19 in unexpected ways. *Frontiers in Psychology, 11*, 572966.

Wong, C. M. L., & Jensen, O. (2022). The paradox of trust: perceived risk and public compliance during the COVID-19 pandemic in Singapore. In *COVID-19* (pp. 189–198). Routledge.

Wong, L. P., Alias, H., Wong, P. F., Lee, H. Y., & AbuBakar, S. (2020). The use of the health belief model to assess predictors of intent to receive the COVID-19 vaccine and willingness to pay. *Human Vaccines & Immunotherapeutics, 16*(9), 2204–2214.

World Health Organization. (2020). *Pandemic fatigue–reinvigorating the public to prevent COVID-19: Policy framework for supporting pandemic prevention and management* (No. WHO/EURO: 2020-1160-40906-55390). World Health Organization. Regional Office for Europe.

Zampetakis, L. A., & Melas, C. (2021). The health belief model predicts vaccination intentions against COVID-19: A survey experiment approach. *Applied Psychology: Health and Well-Being, 13*, 469–484.

Zhou, S., Villalobos, J. P., Munoz, A., & Bull, S. (2022). Ethnic minorities' perceptions of COVID-19 vaccines and challenges in the pandemic: A qualitative study to inform COVID-19 prevention interventions. *Health Communication, 37*(12), 1476–1487.

## Glossary of Key Terms and Concepts

**Compliance Response Framework** deals with differences between the strength of an individual's motivation to comply with policy measures and their beliefs about the advantages and disadvantages of policy outcomes and measures (Kaine et al., 2022).

**Conspiracy Theories** comprise the perception that a number of people are banded together join in order to achieve a hidden goal which is perceived to be unlawful or malevolent and do so in secret agreement (Proojien, 2018).

**Health Belief Model** a model developed in the 1950s which is one of the most widely used and recognized conceptual models for predicting health behavior (Mahindarathne, 2021). The HBM postulates several motivators for why people will take action to prevent, to screen for, or to control illness conditions. These motivators include susceptibility, seriousness, benefits and barriers to a behavior, cues to action, as well as self-efficacy (Champion & Skinner, 2008).

**Lindenberg's Goal Framing Theory,** comprises three overarching goals: the normative goal, (including variables pro-social behavior, trust in government, observed respect for rules and rule legitimacy), the hedonic goal, (including variables fear and opportunities for fun and happiness) and the gain goal, (including variable worsened income position) (Six et al., 2023).

**Motivational Interviewing** a framework that helps motivate behavior change from a patient-centered perspective, as a method for healthcare providers to reduce vaccine hesitancy (Boness et al., 2022).

**NPI** refer to non-pharmaceutical intervention.

**Pandemic Fatigue** is understood to be an expected and natural reaction to the prolonged nature of the COVID-19 pandemic and the associated inconvenience and hardship which poses a serious threat to efforts to control the spread of the virus (WHO, 2020).

**Risk Perception** how a person perceives the phenomenon of the probability of an adverse event multiplied by its magnitude (Oltedal et al., 2004).

**Vaccine Hesitancy** reluctance or refusal to get oneself or one under one's care vaccinated.

## Discussion Questions

1 What is the appeal of conspiracy theories and why are they so easily believed by some people?
2 Imagine you are asked to culturally tailor vaccine campaigns for African Americans and Hispanic populations in the U.S. Explain, using material from this chapter how you would go about doing this.

3 If you belonged to an ethnic minority group, why might it be more important for you to see others using the vaccine before using it yourself? Why would you be more likely to dislike complex messages about the vaccine?
4 Imagine you were visiting your grandmother during the beginning of the COVID-19 pandemic. Your grandmother, has few friends, has an underlying heart condition and does not have a computer and/or access to one. How would you persuade her that getting vaccinated is the best option for her? (Hint: please consider her likelihood of trusting the government, ways her age group could best be persuaded and other information from this chapter that will strengthen your argument).
5 Imagine you are writing an advertisement promoting getting COVID-19 vaccinations. What would you consider when creating your ad, to maximize persuasive appeal (what kinds of photos/videos would you include, how much information about safety of the vaccine and safety, how would you ensure your ad is trusted?)
6 Please watch the YouTube video: 'How Coronavirus Has Changed Lives Around the World' at: https://www.youtube.com/watch?v=MZrkwaYNioo

   How were your experiences of complying with social distancing orders similar and different to those you just watched? How would limited access to technology change this?

# 5

# CROSS-CULTURAL AND GENDER DIFFERENCES IN CRISIS MANAGEMENT STYLES

## Lessons from the COVID-19 Pandemic

### Chapter Learning Objectives

- Describe the characteristics of countries which managed the COVID-19 pandemic well
- Describe the characteristics of countries which mismanaged the COVID-19 pandemic
- Discuss what makes a good leader during times of crisis
- Define rhetorical analysis
- Describe some gender differences in leadership styles from heads of states during the pandemic
- Discuss what are some of the elements of communication styles employed by female leaders during the management of the COVID-19 pandemic

### Introduction

There has been unprecedented global government action to contain the rapid spread of COVID-19 (Hale et al., 2021). If we explore the management styles of countries that successfully managed the COVID-19 virus during the early stages, such as South Korea, Taiwan, Hong Kong and Singapore, we find some common themes in terms of decisive measures to implement mass testing and lockdowns, such as banning mass gatherings and religious services, imposing travel restrictions, quarantines, social distancing, and testing new comers to the country at the port. In South Korea the government mandated mass testing; not only people who exhibited physical symptoms of contacting the virus,

DOI: 10.4324/9781003394983-5

as was done in some countries. In Taiwan, rigorous screening procedures and home quarantines were strictly enforced for new arrivals to the country; fines ensured quarantines were followed. Hong Kong's focus was on containing the local transmission of the virus within the country, to this effect, existing facilities and local clinics were staffed with personnel who were legally required to report all persons exhibiting any symptoms who had traveled to Wuhan, China. In Hong Kong, individuals crossing the border from China were placed under a mandatory two week quarantine. At this time, social distancing was extensively implemented, and mass gatherings of all kinds were banned, including religious services. While schools and offices remained open in Singapore, health officials traced all contacts of people infected by the virus. Singapore and Hong Kong were two countries which placed citizens who were identified to be at-risk in state-controlled quarantine facilities (Rohrich et al., 2020).

While a common theme across these and other countries which successfully managed the spread of the COVID-19 virus within their countries, has been the implementation of social restrictions at the very early stages of the pandemic, South Korea seemed to be the only country to significantly slow the infection spread in the country without reliance on national lockdowns or other severe measures restricting public mobility. This raises an important question: are restrictive measures the only and best way to effectively manage the COVID-19 pandemic and similar global outbreaks?

One critique of the crisis management literature has been too much focus on improving the technological effectiveness of communication systems during a crisis without sufficient attention to various aspects of the crisis including human, communitarian and social aspects (Dückers et al., 2017; cited in McGuire et al). Given that good vs. poor leadership can have life altering consequences for the people of a nation (Wilson, 2020), this chapter seeks to amalgamate key lessons learned from the effective and not so effective government communication responses to the COVID-19 pandemic from countries around the world.

Countries have managed the COVID-19 pandemic in their own ways: what can we learn from good versus poor management styles? The chapter will begin with reviewing the management style of the pandemic in two countries that faced serious challenges but in the end of the first and second wave did not perform too badly. First, we review a unique framing strategy[1] adopted by the government of Singapore where a 'defensive pessimism' approach, a term first introduced by Elliot and Church (2003), was taken during the early stages of the coronavirus. In this strategy, the government framed communications to its nation to stress the seriousness of the virus and advocated the necessity to prepare for negative scenarios. Second, the case of Japan, a country faced with technological as well as leadership challenges will be explored; a country which illustrated how the impact of cultural values on behavior in the context of a large-scale disaster may be considered an asset for persuading citizens to comply with restrictive health measures. This review will be followed by the case of India a country which has the second largest population in the world, but with limited technological resources for mass testing of the virus and the needed resources for a national lockdown. We will analyze some of the key breakdowns in communication in India that are believed to have contributed to its disastrous rise in the spread of the virus and alarming rise in death toll once restrictions were eased. We conclude our review of India with a brief exploration of what can happen when cultural factors impede some of the citizens of a nation from not conforming to protective measures protocols further endangering the safety and lives of the nation.

The chapter will then delve into a comparison of two countries on polar opposites of 'miss-management' and 'exemplary management' of the COVID-19 pandemic: The US and New Zealand, respectively. In this comparison we will focus our attention on the importance of communication styles, hence, our discussion will include an exploration rhetorical tools employed to analyze speech content. Through exploration of timely policy adoption and policy easing, as well as key factors of leadership in both countries that promoted or hindered building trust with their citizens, the overview will highlight a few lessons learned on what 'worked and what did not work as well' when dealing with this global health crisis.

Given the central role of communication styles during crisis management, the chapter will conclude with further detailed exploration of speech analyses of three prominent heads of state during the COVID-19 pandemic. This analysis will comprise the focus topic for the current chapter: an in-depth investigation of key elements of female leaders' speeches during the pandemic. Employing the lens of Positive Psychology, we conclude this chapter with a discussion the results of Meyer et al.'s (2021) research which help to identify some of the unique elements of female heads of state in bringing unity to the nation during disastrous events such as the pandemic.

## Countries That Handled the COVID-19 Pandemic Well

### *Singapore's 'Defensive Pessimism Approach'*

On January 30, 2020, WHO declared coronavirus disease 2019 (COVID-19) as an international public health emergency. Singapore, which comprised nearly 6 million people, was among the first countries affected (Department of Statistics, Singapore, 2020). Until early April 2020, the COVID-19 pandemic was initially well contained in Singapore at which point there was a rise in cases.

These surges were for the most part attributed to a rise in local transmission as well as from the return of Singapore residents from hot spots overseas (Chou 2020). While Singapore initially received recognition from the WHO for its approach in COVID-19 containment (Teo, 2020) over time as more people continued to become infected the resilience of the country's health system began to be tested.

Scholars have noted a number of positive aspects of Singapore's response to the management of the COVID-19 pandemic including effective communication between government agencies (Chua et al., 2020), in addition to early response and disease surveillance, adequate preparation of public health clinics and extensive testing (Kuguyo et al. 2020; Lee & Ong, 2020). The government of Singapore had adopted a flexible approach in its management of the COVID-19 pandemic, what some scholars have termed the three-phase approach to "learning": which comprises in-between learning, trial-and-error learning, and contingency learning (Abdullah & Kim, 2020). With 24% of citizens in Singapore reporting a good amount of confidence in their government, Singapore has been considered to have a high level of trust in their government when compared to many other high-income countries (Wong et al., 2020).

What is of interest to us is how the government of Singapore chose to frame health risk communications about the seriousness of the COVID-19 virus. Given that high levels of trust in one's government may in certain situations result in less compliance with safety guidelines due to underestimation of risks during a public health crisis, (Wong & Jensen, 2022) it is interesting to note Singapore's adoption of what the Director General of the WHO described as "defensive pessimism" (Lanard, 2004; cited in Wong et al., 2020). The approach adopts the position that risks are very serious, should not be under-estimated and preparation for negative scenarios are anticipated (Wong et al., 2020). During the early stages of the Covid-19 outbreak in Singapore, two communication channels were employed. According to Feitelson et al. (2022) the narrative of *defensive pessimism* was a theme found in press conferences featuring key government officials. The first component of this defensive pessimism comprised the multi-lingual and multi-cultural contexts of the country of Singapore as this approach was deemed to build trust given it would be perceived to be a more direct form of address with the people. The second component of the defensive pessimism approach, according to Feitelson et al. (2022) was to openly discuss the scientific uncertainties that still existed at the time including the effectiveness of safety measures and the mode in which virus transmission was believed to have occurred.

The intention of such strategic framing of risk in public health messages is to warn the public about the urgency of safeguarding against such risks. For example, in order to test the effectiveness of the Singapore government's pandemic communication that the world order was threatened on citizens' disease preventative behaviors, Yeo et al. (2022) performed a content analysis of 7,128 news headlines on COVID-19. The results of their study found that 90% of news reports were framed to suggest a dangerous world. After surveying over 450 respondents in the main study, the researchers found that people's beliefs in a dangerous world were linked to their disease preventive behaviors.

### *A Country with Limited Technological Resources: The Case of India*

Let us take the case of India: by end of the first week of July 2020 the country had the third- highest number of confirmed COVID-19cases in the world (John Hopkins University, 2020).

India ranked 57th among 100 countries, according to the Global Health Security Index 2019 on a scale designed to assess the level of preparedness for the outbreak of serious infectious diseases (Tabish, 2020). This assessment is not difficult to understand if one considers that India at the time, faced two major challenges: a very large population and limited resources. Adding further complexity to India's limited infrastructure which included a shortage of healthcare facilities and equipment, was the countries' unhygienic conditions. With an average 10,000 tests conducted daily for a population of 1.38 billion, India was far behind in testing compared to many other countries in the world. Contact tracing was also weak with insufficient PPE and ventilators throughout the country (Tabish, 2020).

On March 24, 2020 until June 1, 2020, the government of India imposed a complete lockdown for the country, limiting the mobility of nearly 1.4 billion people. This action leads to highly unfortunate consequences for the economy resulting in an output loss of 8%. From a crisis communications perspective, the case of India illustrates an important lesson: during an emergency, unpredictable event, as important as it is to implement lockdown, an immediate lockdown without proper planning can lead to disastrous consequences. On March 24, 2020 the government of India ordered a sudden and severe nationwide lockdown which ended on June 1, 2020, and did not allow for sufficient time for proper planning. Consequently hundreds of thousands of migrant workers, manual laborers, and other sectors of informal workers were forced to walk very long distances to reach their homes located in rural areas as they had no other alternative during lockdown. It was speculated in hindsight that the government should have arranged for resources to pay for shelter, food and other basic needs (Tabish, 2020).

Given its innumerable challenges, the government of India implemented a Cluster Containment Strategy (CC strategy) in early April of 2020 in an attempt to contain the virus during the early stages of pandemic (Chetterje, 2020; Lancet, 2020; Tabish, 2020). The CC strategy entails containment of the pandemic within a defined region with high rate of infection, and in this way slowing the spread of the virus to new areas. This was followed up by citywide curfews, as well as extensive follow-up and testing of its residents, in addition to the implementation of travel bans. This model of virus containment is typically considered more efficient and flexible than a complete lockdown (Tabish, 2020).

Notwithstanding that the containment strategy initially appeared to be successful, India's overall performance in the handling of the pandemic remained doubtful. In other words, despite India's lockdown being considered one of the harshest in the world, the curve symbolizing the spread of the disease did not noticeably flatten or decline even after restrictions were first eased (Chaturvedi et al., 2020).

Indeed, Chaturvedi et al.'s (2020) analysis of India's disaster management framework identifies a number of key weaknesses with the system including un-clarity in the dissemination of information during the early stages when the order for lockdown was first issued, One issue of particular concern from their analysis was regarding the importance of government transparency by means of proactively releasing information about decision-making behind response strategies, so that its decisions are open to the public for scrutiny.

Another serious error from a communications perspective was confusion of the delegation of responsibilities. In their analysis Chaturvedi et al. (2020) provide ample evidence of how legislation such as the National Executive Committee (NEC) did not clarify which governing agencies had power over the administrative control over disaster management. For example, according to the Government of India's Allocation of Business Rules (ABR) the Ministry of Home Affairs (MHA) is enabled to take care of loss of human life as a result of man-made or natural disasters, while the DM act enabled power to the Ministry or Department of the central government over administrative rein over disaster management (Chaturvedi et al., 2020).

Further, another breakdown in communication identified in their analysis, is that guidelines were not followed (Chaturvedi et al., 2020). For example, according to the BDM which advises that surveillance be used to strategically identify as many cases as possible, especially during the early stages of a disaster event, the Indian Council of Medical Research limited testing to only those who had come abroad or had been in contact with such persons.

Of deep concern are reported cases of people escaping hospitals and quarantine which is a major factor in jeopardizing the success of any cluster containment strategies (Chetterjie, 2020; Kadram & Aatre, 2020). To better understand the driving force for so many to escape quarantine in India, it may be helpful to explore the stigma of COVID-19 in India. According to a study conducted by Joshi and Swarnakar (2021) there were clearly stigma-related beliefs among the individuals diagnosed or assumed susceptible to COVID-19, the researchers state: "[s]tigma is a risk in itself for society because it increases the burden of a disaster for already [marginalized] populations" (p. 501). Joshi and Swrnakar's

(2021) study found a relationship between risk perception and stigma generation for the COVID-19 spread in India. Specifically, the study found that social media contributed to a number of negative stereotyping, including, but not limited to perceived-shaming and circulating the contact information of suspected or quarantined people and further vilifying them as a 'super-spreader' in video streams and false messages during the lock-down in India. Such stigmatizing behavior was also observed in the current study, at a local level, in state authorities' use of 'stickers' on gates to mark confirmed COVID-19 cases. Previous scholars have pointed out the profound social implications of stigma in alienating at-risk individuals in India when we recall the social ostracization of leprosy (Barrett, 2005; cited in Joshi & Swarnakar, 2021) and HIV/AIDS patients (Bharat, 2011; cited in Joshi & Swarnakar, 2021) in India. From this it becomes -easy to understand the ramifications of stigma associated with having the COVID-19 virus for those attempting to escape quarantine in India.

### *India – Concluding Thoughts*

India's poor management of the COVID-19 pandemic during the second wave, may have been a result of multiple factors including very low technical resources to enable mass testing in a country with the world's second largest population (Choudhary et al., 2021; Radhakrishnan & Gupta, 2021; Samarasekera, 2021; Visaria & Dharamdasani, 2021). Some of these factors driving the second wave of COVID-19 in India may include, but are not limited to, the complex interplay of mutant strains, non-compliance of COVID appropriate behavior, as well as lack of sufficient government and public initiation of the vaccination drive (Choudhary et al., 2021). When full lockdowns were finally implemented, it was not to the country's advantage that the government did not prepare ahead for the working poor who were not equipped to deal with poverty that worsened as the pandemic progressed.

In sum, scholars have pointed out the need to exercise prudence when critiquing India's management of the second wave of the pandemic. For example, given harsh criticism the country has endured for allowing mass gatherings during the second wave, it has been pointed out that such situations bear some resemblance to similar cases in the US and other developed countries where groups of individuals had also refused to wear masks and gathered in large groups despite government guidelines and interventions (Ran et al., 2021 cited in Visaria & Dharamdasani, 2021).

## *The Role of Culture and Social Governance during the Pandemic: A Case Study of Japan*

The case study of Japan during the early phase of the pandemic teaches the world an important lesson: a country that lacked strong leadership as well as an efficient bureaucracy, and did not have advanced technology to tackle the global pandemic was ultimately successful in their management of the COVID-19 pandemic. This section will explore how the country emerged victorious with relatively low number of infection and death rates from the virus despite the multiple challenges the country faced compared to countries with more advanced technologies and other resources.

Especially noteworthy, is that early in the pandemic, the country lacked strong policy responses: there were no quick and widespread imposition of lockdown measures nor was there an employment of surveillance techniques such as those used in countries like Singapore and Israel to track those infected and subsequently monitor their interaction with others (Aldrich & Yoshida, 2020). Arguments have been put forth that on a social level, however, Japan's management of the COVID-19 pandemic is composed of what were essentially social or culturally based solutions referred to as the country's "secret sauces" (Aldrich & Yoshida, 2020). Aldrich and Yoshida (2020) describe the first part of this secret sauce to comprise Japan's hygiene practices requiring people to wear face masks which took place long before the COVID-19 pandemic took place. Social norms comprise the second part of the secret sauce such as the customary greeting which involves a blow that eliminates acts such as kissing, shaking hands or kissing that all require a shared social space. The final component of this secret sauce compress the Japanese language in spoken form which requires fewer sharper exhalations than other languages and therefore produces less infectious droplets when spoken.

In his analysis of the presence of 'cultural exceptionalism' in Japan's response to containing the COVID-19 virus, Matthews (2020) articulates the concept nicely when he explained how culture may influence compliance with public health interventions. He elaborated on how early on in the pandemic, there were many social media posts claiming the impact of culture on Japan's low infection numbers through the use of tweets on the importance of hygiene, hand-washing and the importance of cleanliness in people's homes.

Figures 5.1 and 5.2 depict data on stay-at-home measures for two different cities in Japan. Watanabe (2021) interpret the findings depicted in Figure 5.2 as follows: "[Figure 5.2] shows the impacts of the government's request to not leave home was effective in areas with low infection rates.

To summarize, a key characteristic of the Japanese response to the COVID-19 crisis has been that the central government did not have the legal authority to impose its pandemic policies across its various municipalities, even during a state of emergency (Chi & Pabyantara, 2022). Further complicating matters, in Japan, it is up to the governors to decide whether to follow the central government's instructions, and it is the governors who have the discretionary authority to impose restrictive measures within their jurisdictions. In sum, indeed, Japan was fortunate to benefit from relatively high compliance of social measures

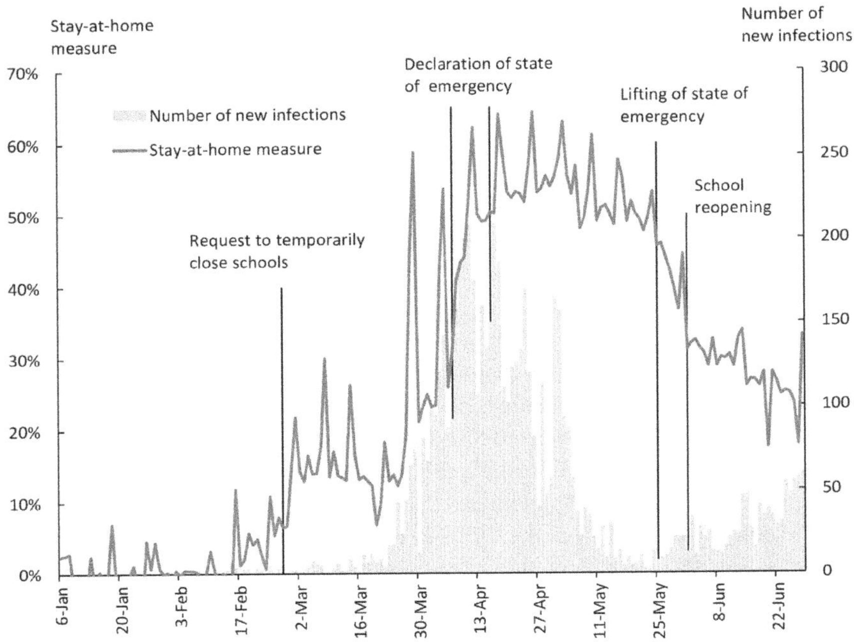


**FIGURE 5.1** Stay-at-home measure and number of new infections, Tokyo.
https://doi.org/10.1371/journal.pone.0252468.g001
(*Source:* Watanabe, 2021).

restrictions from its citizens given that no full lockdown policy was ever implemented by the government (Ripley, 2020). Specifically, while the Japanese Prime Minister announced a state of emergency on February 7, 2020, it was never sanctioned by police, and breach of the lockdown restrictions were never penalized through fines or arrests as they were in other countries. The large rates of social compliance behavior of the Japanese people, then, in a country where restrictions on social distancing and other health promoting behavior were not legally binding, suggests that fear of legal recourses were not the only reason the people of Japan changed their behavior (Watanabe, 2021). This is arguably a very powerful lesson for the world.

### *A Country Rich in Resources – What Went Wrong: Lessons Learned from the USA*

With the highest number of COVID-19 related cases and deaths than other countries in the world, COVID-19 has been a disaster for the US. Sadly for

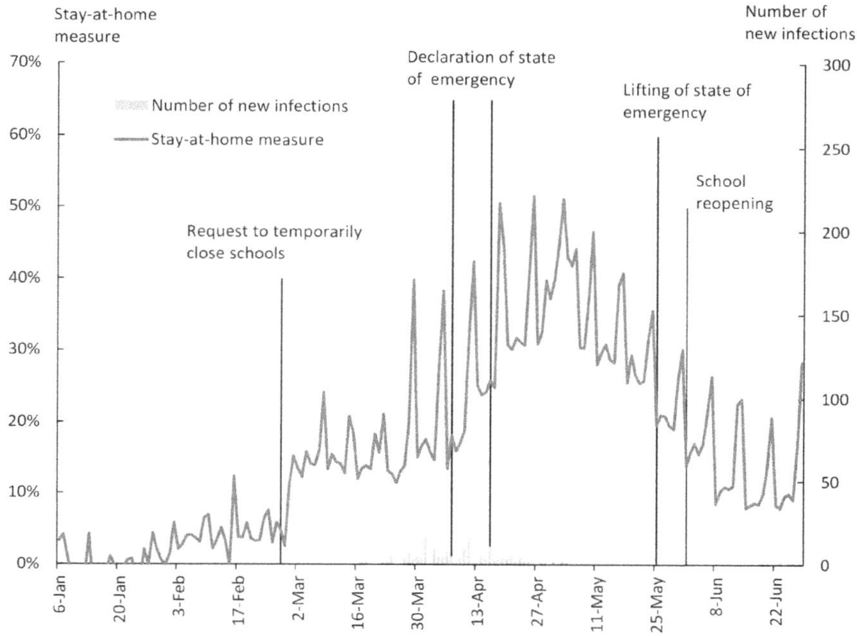


**FIGURE 5.2** Stay-at-home measure and number of new infections, Ibaraki.

https://doi.org/10.1371/journal.pone.0252468.g002

*Source:* Watanabe, 2021.

Americans, and the rest of the world, the US government's lack of action early on during the pandemic, allowed the virus to spread inside its borders, actively increasing the risk of the virus spreading to other countries.

Indeed, with almost one third of the world's total cases at the beginning of the pandemic, the US management of the COVID-19 pandemic has been heavily criticized especially during the early stages of the crisis. The bulk of the criticism lies in its decentralized political system where states were allowed to make decisions about containment, testing and treatment responses with little or no guidance from the federal government (Bergquist et al., 2020) as well as leadership styles described as confusing (Dyer, 2020) and misleading (Rufai & Bunce, 2020).

### *Denial/Slow Action*

Early on in the pandemic, from January to March 2020; President Trump assured American citizens that things were under control comparing the pandemic to seasonal influenza (Yarney & Gibsalves, 2020). He went on to assure the American public that the US is the most prepared and resilient country in the world for meeting pandemic threats (Yarney & Gibsalves, 2020).

Further, it took President Trump more than six weeks after the first documented case of coronavirus to take aggressive action to stop the spread of the virus. Indeed, despite being repeatedly warned about the seriousness of taking swift action by intelligence services, the former US president chose to focus on controlling the message and assuring the public the virus was not as serious as it was reported to be and had stated in April of 2020. Furthermore, he had stated "We're prepared, and we're doing a great job with it. And it will go away. Just stay calm. It will go away" (March 10) (Stevens & Tan 2020).

### *Decisions That Weakened the American Healthcare System*

It has been noted that in May 2018, before the pandemic was known to the world, the Trump administration eliminated the White House global health security office earlier established by former President Obama during the 2014–2016 Ebola epidemic (Yarney & Gonsalves, 2020). President Trump's decision to remind the American citizens of their right to bear arms in accordance with the second amendment has also been lauded by critics as a dangerous act in his handling of the pandemic (Yarney & Gonsalves, 2020).

### *Faulty Resources/Testing and Faulty Advice Not Based on Scientific Expertise*

One of the key problems identified with diagnostic kits in the US, during the early phases of the COVID-19 pandemic, appeared to be technical issues with the assay yielding in numerous false results. Many US labs did not operate at full capacity well into the end of 2020 (Maxmen, 2020). There have also been issues with the testing procedures themselves. For example, in their investigation of COVID-19 testing plans in over 500 American colleges and universities Booeshaghi et al. (2020) described many testing plans to be in a highly variable and muddled state with discrepancies to various scientific studies and federal guidelines. It was also reported that the CDC advised healthcare workers to use a bandana if they could not find a mask (Landsverk, 2020). On March 21, 2020 President Trump publicly promoted the anti-malaria medication hydroxychloroquine for immediate use despite no scientific basis for this decision.

### *Communication Breakdown: Delayed Transmission of Virus-Related Data*

In their exploration of the success of certain countries to contain the spreading of the COVID-19 virus more effectively than other countries, Xu and Basu

(2020) attributed a key factor in success to the timely and uniform communication between key stakeholders. For example Xu and Basu (2020) praised countries such as China, South Korea, Taiwan, and Singapore for their centralized public health, emergency management, and disease control system. Xu and Basu (2020) note that a difficulty in the US is that their federalist system is contingent upon the states to collect and report their disease-related data to the federal level, namely the National Center for Health Statistics (NCHS) and the US Centers for Disease Control and Prevention (CDC), which is perceived by the American public as the primary source for dissemination of disease-related information. Consequently, delays in data sharing and data transmission are likely to occur, even for highly infectious diseases like COVID-19, since it is protocol for each state to "conduct their own testing and then report the statistics to their own health departments and local communities before sharing the results with the CDC" (Xu and Basu, p. 569). While at first glance the drawbacks of such a -centralized government in impeding the quick and accurate sharing of critical health information during times of crisis may seem senseless, scholars have pointed out that one advantage of such a heterogeneous policy response is that it enables individual states to tailor their responses that are appropriate for local contextual factors (Bergquist et al., 2020).

### *The Country Which Fared Best during the Pandemic: Lessons Learned from New Zealand*

With no widespread, undetected community transmission of the virus during the early stages of the pandemic, New Zealand has led the world as an example of positive crisis management. The country took many measures to contain the virus early including decisive action, implemented rigorously during the early stages which arguably helped to slow down if not eliminate entirely, the spread of the deadly virus. There was also wide, mass testing, conducted as efficiently as possible. Non-pharmaceutical measures included social distancing during the early stages again with the intention to contain the spread of the virus (Tabish, 2020).

In her case study comparing the handling of the COVID-19 pandemic by the US government and the government of New Zealand, Wilson (2020) noted that a number of aspects of the New Zealand approach were align with the approach taken with the pre-existing Influenza Pandemic Plan comprising various phases including: planning for it, keeping it out, stamping it out, managing it, managing it post peak and recovering from it (Ministry of Health, 2017; cited in Wilson, 2020). A consistent theme noted by Wilson (2020) in New Zealand's management of the public health concerns of managing the COVID-19 virus has been reliance on the best available science and health advice (Clark, 2020; cited in Wilson, 2020). New Zealand also took very quick action to implement safety measures, after only 6 cases were identified in the country, the government announced restrictions on border crossing, self-isolation for those entering the country as well as other restrictions concerning mass gatherings. By March 21, 2020, Prime Minister Arden had announced the Four Level alert system comprising prepare, reduce, restrict, and lockdown.

## What Makes a Good Leader during Times of Crisis?

Before embarking on a comparison of how different world leaders managed the COVID-19 pandemic, let us first examine the characteristics of an effective leader. Berstein et al. defined the characteristics of a good leader during times of crisis as follows:

- Ability to communicate effectively
- Ability to make timely decisions
- Persuasive abilities
- Setting goals and following through

As we proceed to review the literature on what makes a good leader during times of crisis, namely the COVID-19 pandemic, let us note that in the sections to follow we will review a number of studies that employ rhetorical analysis which increases our awareness of the sometimes covert communicative strategies behind language that is integral to the study of the speeches of political figures. Of further note, the bulk of the studies discussed will be founded on data from speech analysis. There are ample studies employing speech analyses of political leaders during crisis events (Ahmad & Shamshul, 2021; Alyeksyeyeva et al., 2021; Berrocal et al., 2021; Dada et al., 2021; Hafner & Sun, 2021; Krishnatray & Shrivastrava, 2021; McGuire et al., 2020; Power & Crosswaithe, 2022; Yusanti et al., 2022). Political speeches may be understood to "be a broad, overarching, and heterogeneous genre of political discourse, inclusive of text types such as a press conference speech, or an address to the nation" (Berrocal et al., 2021, p. 2). This chapter draws upon 'discursive leadership studies' which characterize leadership as a process that involves influencing or otherwise managing others in order to reach a common goal (Hafner & Sun, 2021). When speeches are analyzed through Speech Act Theory, speech is categorized into the following five classes declaratives, representatives, expressive, directives, and commissives (see Searle, 1969 for a review). There are also a host of methodologies employed in speech analysis, including but not limited to discursive thematic analysis, corpus-based discourse analysis and other linguistic-based analyses.

Let us first turn our attention to the head of state of the country who managed the COVID-19 pandemic the best, Prime Minister Jacinda Arden of New Zealand. What were the unique features of Prime Minister Arden's leadership style?

Kearn's (2021) case study of daily press conferences from the Prime Minister and Director General of Health of New Zealand from March and April 2020 explored the presence of three key metaphors: bubbles, levels, and the team, and the perceptual and behavioral implications of the strategic use of these metaphors.

The first spatial metaphor discussed was the concept of level as used by the Prime Minister to describe what was meant by level 3, as a waiting room of sorts where one waited it out to see if they got it correct; levels are spaces that imply an upward ascent (Kearns, 2021). The second spatial metaphor was the concept of bubbles a concept first developed by Dr Tristram Ingham with the intention of making public health messages more clear and empowering enabling the public to more easily take action (Kearns, 2021). The third spatial metaphor identified was the concept of team, which can symbolized concepts such as employing an assertive style of play, everyone being delegated a role/responsibility and an emphasize on winning as evinced by Arden's referring to her team of 5 million having a part to play during her press briefings (Kearns, 2021).

Wilson's case study also highlights a number of key elements of Prime Minister Arden's leadership such as her willingness to be guided by the expertise of others, her empathetic attitudes toward citizens of her country creating and help her nation cope, all of which helped to build trust in a type of leadership needed to effectively manage the COVID-19 pandemic "the government's willingness to themselves be led by expertise, its efforts to mobilize the population, and to enable coping, all of which serve to build the trust in leadership needed for transformative, collective action such as the pandemic demands" (Wilson, 2020, p. 579). Let us examine each of these strategies in more detail.

*Developing sense-making* Pandemics are stressful times for all. It is noted by Wilson (2020) how PM Arden incorporated a lot of easy to understand terms into a number of her policies such as the term 'bubble' in her alerts which soon became a part of the daily lexicon of New Zealanders.

*Enabling kindness* It is noted that Arden expressed a number of public messages where she articulates people should be kind to each other and when landlords raised the cost of rent during the pandemic she proclaimed this action as "utterly unfathomable."

*Developing creative responses* Considering that a pandemic is an unexpected, unnatural occurrence that may require out of the box solutions, Wilson (2020) cited a number of initiatives taken by Prime Minister Arden including an easy to access wage subsidy program, as well as home schooling packages where resources are provided to parents and children to lighten the load of educating children from home.

In sum, Wilson (2020) argued that measures such as the above do much to facilitate trust in a nation that government is doing its best to safeguard their interests during a time of crisis and extreme uncertainty. Sense-making is a strategy for example, aimed to clarify common goals and shared responsibilities during a crisis situation, that is believed to instill a feeling of a common purpose between the government and its people.

Taking a crisis leadership approach, McGuire et al. (2020) analyzed the communication and leadership style of Prime Minister Arden during the early phases of the COVID-19 pandemic. In their analysis, McGuire et al. (2020) explored various linguistic and discursive aspects of Prime Minister Arden's communications with her nation. Their analysis also documents how discursive devices, such as images of social solidarity are used to co-create the crisis experience and ultimately establish a sense of trust with the citizens of New Zealand.

McGuire et al. (2020) argued that during the early stages of the pandemic, Arden's communications with her nation attempted to reassure the public that the government was employing decisive and evidence-based approaches. In this way, trust is established during the early stages of Arden's crisis leadership. Arden's tone later shifted during phases 2 and 3 of the pandemic, McGuire et al. (2020) argued, to a more empathetic approach. At this stage, a common understanding of a shared purpose is established in which the country is encouraged to move forward together from a sense of solidarity among the community. Here Arden repeatedly positioned herself on a common level with her public as part of "a team of 5 million" (McGuire et al., 2020). During Arden's series of six live Facebook broadcasts, the researchers noted that a main component of these broadcasts was how information was shared in an informal and relaxed tone in a direct personal nature (Kulkarni & Anantharama, 2020; cited in McGuire et al., 2020).

## Contrasting Communication Strategies New Zealand and the US

In her insightful comparison of how the US and New Zealand fared on opposite extremes on the continuum of success during the pandemic, Parker (2020) concedes that while both President Trump and Prime Minister Arden are both brilliant communicators, their messages comprised vastly different content in terms of pandemic risk, and proper response to this risk.

Prime Minister Arden warned her nation early:

> Like the rest of the world, we are facing the potential for devastating impacts from this virus .... We currently have 102 cases. But so did Italy once .... The situation here is moving at pace, and so must we .... If community transmission takes off in New Zealand the number of cases will double every five days. If that happens unchecked, our health system will be inundated, and tens of thousands of New Zealanders will die . . . .

After which, the Prime Minister talked about a unified national response that would take place in a clearly defined, series of restrictions. The restrictions would be administered in a manner where they would culminate in a nationwide lockdown. For example, after announcing the lockdown she asked her nation to sacrifice in a manner that would require them to work toward a common goal in saving lives:

> Everything you will all give up for the next few weeks, all of the lost contact with others, all of the isolation, and difficult time entertaining children—it will literally save lives. Thousands of lives .... If we after those four weeks have been successful, we will be able to ease up on restrictions. If we haven't, we'll find ourselves living with them for longer.
>
> That's why sticking to the rules matters. If we don't—if you hang out with that friend at a park or see that family member for lunch, you risk spreading COVID-19 and extending everyone's time in Level 4 [lockdown].
>
> *(Jacinda Arden, 2020)*

In contrast, President Trump posted more than 200 tweets and other statements in which he downplayed the severity of the virus, and implied in his messages, that the risk was already under control, or denying the seriousness of the situation warranting an immediate response from the federal government during a time when many US citizens were infected with the virus and these rates were increasing (Blake & Riger, 2021). Also, in direct contrast to the sense of unity Prime Minister Arden's speeches were creating in New Zealand, President Trump was creating further confusion precisely during a time when coordination between states was needed. For example, at this time, President Trump announced that his intention to leave the governors of each state to be primarily responsible for decisions regarding restrictions and when they would take place (Liptak et al., 2020). As can be anticipated, this policy position had profound implications for creating further confusion and lack of certainty, given that no single state had the power to articulate clear end dates for restrictions since the management of the pandemic required on the overall actions of other states which could not be controlled or predicted "[It] affected the messaging options of governors in dealing with their state populations. It meant that no state could offer its residents a clear end date for restrictions since success in managing the pandemic overall depended on the actions of other states whose actions could not be controlled or even foreseen"(Parker, 2020, p. 93). With no clear end date and no clear purpose, Parker (2020) noted that it was not surprising to understand the sentiments of many Americans' about rebelling against restrictions that had no clear end. In contrast, New Zealanders were informed by their leader that they would be working and sacrificing together to save lives with a clear end date in sight. Arguably, then, President Trump's refusal to organize a national response and consistently framing mandatory social distancing measures as *alternatives* to the reopening of businesses as opposed to framing these as essential and necessary steps to early reopening (Blake et al., 2020) created further mistrust in the government and rebellion in following rules for the American people. It is interesting to note that Prime Minister Arden's communication strategy comprised addressing the pandemic risk, while President Trump's theme was to "make America great again" without stipulating any clear direction on what he expected from his nation to make this happen (Parker, 2020).

Having analyzed the speeches of a number of political leaders during the COVID-19 pandemic, in the section to follow we will turn our attention to a more in-depth discussion of potential gender differences in these speeches. Our impetus for doing so will be to further explore if female and male leaders differ in their speech styles during their management of the COVID-19 pandemic.

## Gender Differences in the Speech Styles of World Leaders during COVID-19

Using an inductive approach, speeches made by heads of government from 20 countries around the world were analyzed in a study by Dada et al. (2021). Official statements about the COVID-19 crisis analyzed in this study included national addresses, statements or speeches made to the public, as well as press briefings, statements made to governing bodies and other statements created for the general public such as podcasts and video announcements. Ultimately a pool of 122 speeches were analyzed from ten male and ten female leaders; care was taken to ensure that countries from both groups ranged in economic productivity, geographical location and political systems.

The analysis sought to explore potential differences between male and female leaders in discussing COVID-19; speeches were coded for issues related to language and content. Gender differences were identified as follows: female leaders spoke more often about the impact of the economic aspects of the pandemic on the individual scale. The researchers further found female leaders to be more likely to describe a greater variety of social welfare services for the public. While both male and female leaders discussed supporting small businesses, the researchers noted, that male leaders tended to emphasize overall national economic recovery over individual support while female leaders tended to highlight the importance of protecting workers and individual families from the economic impact of the pandemic. While both male and female heads of state discussed vulnerable populations (for example, children, the sick and the elderly) the vulnerability of specific groups such as migrants and refugees, individuals with mental health substance use issues as well as victims of domestic violence were more likely to be noted by female leaders. Analysis of the speech transcripts and those video recordings that were analyzed revealed that when female leaders spoke, they made reference to these populations and that they did so with strong, empathetic, and persuasive language.

Although leaders of both genders spoke about global cooperation, it is interesting to note that this was emphasized more in the speeches of female leaders.

For example, the study found that four of the male-led countries (heads of state for France, Niger, UK, and the USA) discussed global cooperation (its importance and value), whereas seven female leaders (heads of state for Bangladesh, Bolivia, Finland, Germany, Norway, Sint Maarten, Taiwan) did as well. The researchers noted that even for male leaders who discussed global cooperation, their mention was far less frequent, with just one mention each. The only exception found was for President Trump who described working with other countries, and explained how America was "helping other nations—many other nations; we're helping them a lot" (Dada et al., 2021, p. 6). This contrast illustrates gender differences in word choice for cooperative behaviors.

In their rhetorical analysis of the speeches, Dada et al. (2021) identified gender differences in the emotions conveyed, noting that many of the male leaders described the response measures to the pandemic in blasé manner which is in contrast to some of the female leaders' use of empathy and compassion in their speeches to the public. As Dada et al. (2020) note:

> One poignant example is Norway's press briefings held specifically for children. On multiple occasions, Solberg held these events to answer the questions and concerns of the nation's children, including on 16 March when she said: 'Many children find this scary. I understand that well. It's allowed to get a little scared when so many big things happen at once. It is allowed to be a little scared to get infected by the coronavirus.' Women leaders such as Áñez and Ardern also empathized with parents and families by stressing their experiences as mothers. While the men leaders included in this analysis also have children, none of them mentioned their roles as fathers or experiences with family.
>
> *(p. 9)*

Employing a corpus-linguistic methodology, Power and Croswaithe (2022) analyzed written texts appearing on the websites of Prime Minister Scott Morrison of Australia and Prime Minister Jacinda Ardern's of New Zealand's website from the period December to January 2020. Using Scattertext software that enables visualization of lexical differences between each leader's corpus, followed by qualitative analysis of this data, the researchers identified gender differences in Arden's use of a more personalized communication style compared to her male counterpart's greater focus on government structures and overall less personal engagement with his nation.

The overview of gender differences in leadership style during the COVID-19 pandemic has shown us that female leadership styles hold certain merits that are of particular value during crisis management. Yet, statistics suggest that despite comprising over 70% of the global health workforce, only 25% of leadership roles in this area are held by women (Boniol, 2019). Clearly more needs to be done to include a greater number of women in the roles of agenda setting and decision-making during global crises management.

**TABLE 5.1** Examples of Gender Differences in Leadership Styles

| *Political Leadership* | *Chancellor Merkel (Germany)* | *PM Arden (New Zealand)* | *PM Ing-Wen (Thailand)* |
|---|---|---|---|
| Citizen Responsibility | • country that depends so much on our joint solidarity. what you do is tremendous<br>• learn from the international community | • through decisive action, and through working together Act now, or risk the virus taking hold<br>• we are all now preparing to go into self-isolation as a nation | • Assistance to the international community 'Taiwan is helping.'<br>• As we face the threat of COVID-19, our entire country has worked together |
| Own humanity | • I firmly believe that we will succeed in this task for [me] whom freedom of travel and movement was a hard-won<br>• and I thank you for it with all my heart | • I understand that self-isolation is a daunting prospect I do not underestimate what I am asking<br>• Be strong and be kind | • I want to emphasize that this kind of cooperation is possible [I] have seen countless acts of bravery and sacrifice from medical workers |
| Shared humanity | • we will succeed in this task if all citizens see it as their task. And we are a community in which every life and every person counts<br>• everything that could harm not only the individual, but also the community, we must reduce that now | • Everything you will all give up for the next few weeks [your sacrifice] will literally save lives. Thousands of lives<br>• What we need from you, is support one another | • Over the past months, we established a "national team." We will share our domestic electronic quarantine system<br>• we have kept the domestic outbreak well under control |

*Source*: Mayer et al. (2021).

## FOCUS TOPIC: Identifying Unifying Qualities of Female Leadership during the COVID-19 Pandemic

Mayer et al. (2021) analyzed the speeches of three female heads of state: New Zealand PM Jacinda Ardern, Taiwainese PM Tsai Ingwen and German Chancellor Angela Merkel using the framework of the Positive Psychology 2 (PP2.0) Framework. This model encourages the development of character strengths and

**TABLE 5.2** Examples of Gender Differences in Leadership Styles

| *Leaders and PP2.0* | *Chancellor Merkel (Germany)* | *PM Arden (New Zealand)* | *PM Ing-Wen (Thailand)* |
|---|---|---|---|
| Virtue | • Protection through common action Democratic values: transparency, open communication and decision-making, relatability<br>• Trust governmental decisions<br>• Act responsibly as individual and societal member<br>• Care for self and others | • Fighting the virus through decisive action and working together Government will do all to protect citizen and asks citizen to do all they can to protect "us all"<br>• Everybody to play their part to contain the virus to stop the spread<br>• Unite against Covid-19 in a kind and strong way<br>• Everybody to play their part to contain the virus to stop the spread Unite against Covid-19 in a kind and strong way | • Taiwanese people come together to protect Taiwan from the virus Fighting the virus<br>• Restrain from hostility and blame |
| Meaning | • Questioned normality and meaning in life New focus of meaning is on survival and defeating the virus | • Focus is to save lives and contain the virus Uniting against the virus | • Protecting the health of individuals, their families and thereby the nation |
| Resilience | • Manage loneliness and trust in finding new forms of connection, particularly in family relationships Care for self and others through new creative forms of connection | • Act now or risk the virus taking hold Empathy that restrictions will be daunting for all people<br>• Be kind and strong and let the government enforce the restrictions | • Resilience is shown in the national team's activities to manufacture items needed to contain the spread of the virus Resilience and strengths are strong in Taiwanese people |
| Well-being | • Empathy regarding missing social connection and contact Well-being through social support and action | • Move quickly and put action plans into action Awareness of socio-economic disruption and anxiety<br>• Well-being through planning keeping in touch, kindness and strongness | • Well-being is increased through helping to share accurate information and refrain from panicking, blaming and hostility |

*Source*: Mayer et al. (2021).

**TABLE 5.3** Examples of Gender Differences in Leadership Styles Using Positive Psychology

| *Leaders and PURE* | *Chancellor Merkel (Germany)* | *PM Arden (New Zealand)* | *PM Ing-Wen (Thailand)* |
|---|---|---|---|
| Purpose | • Defeat virus and survive Care for one another | • Slow down virus and save lives Work together to support each other | • Fighting the virus by working together Stand together and strengthen international cooperation |
| Understanding | • Deep understanding of the impact of this virus and the possibility of own approach and action | • Understanding how to stop the virus is easy, decisions to do so are not taken lightly | • Understanding the situation, working together, refraining from negative feelings and behaviors share accurate knowledge to understand the situation |
| Responsibility | • Responsibility of each and every single individual: self-care and care for others | • Responsible action needs to be taken – Ardern does not differentiate between government and people<br>• Stay home and stop interaction<br>• Self-isolate if necessary, even when daunting | • Responsibility through governmental proactive measure on all levels Awareness about the concern regarding the legal basis for the restrictions put in place and the need for international cooperation |
| Enjoyment and Evaluation | • Discipline to manage missing enjoyment through social connection and find new creative forms of entertainment | • Be practical and only leave home for walks, exercise and fresh air on your own and take children out | • Be confident and refrain from negative feelings and behavior |

*Source*: Mayer et al. (2021).

positive emotions which can help to offset the onset of negative emotions such as suffering whether it is directly or indirectly (Mayer et al. 2021). The impetus for this study was to better understand what components of PP2.0 may impact female political leadership in managing the COVID-19 pandemic. The researchers noted that they were further guided by how female leaders were able to transform negative emotions such as pain, fear, suffering and feelings of hopelessness or despair into more positive or meaningful actions during the COVID-19 pandemic. Summaries of their analysis are depicted in Tables 5.1–5.3.

As the researchers note, irrespective of individual differences in leadership style between the three leaders, caring natures, empathy and compassion are themes common to all three female leaders. In sum, solidarity is a theme common in the speeches of all three female leaders. As Berrocal et al. (2021) note: "One of the salient values addressed and highlighted in the COVID-19 crisis discourse is solidarity. Generally, solidarity is conceived as an element that is essential for social structuring, both on the interpersonal and intergroup levels" (Berrocal et al., 2021, p. 2).

## Key Lessons

Through its review of various international policies regarding the COVID-19 pandemic, this chapter highlights that there is no 'one size fits all' strategy when it comes to handling global disasters of such magnitude. For the most part, we find implementation of certain restrictive measures during the early stages of the pandemic to be a common theme in countries with high success rates (lower mortality rates and lower spread of the virus). We also found that certain cultural norms and values regarding hygiene customs can result in a higher percentage of the populace complying with social measures, even when a country's crisis-leadership style is poor.

When contrasting the management styles of the US (a country with consistently one of the highest mortality rates from the virus) with that of New Zealand (a country with consistently one of the lowest mortality rates from the virus) we again find early intervention of restrictive measures to be a key difference between the two countries. Despite its status as one of the wealthiest countries in the world, the US did not begin mass testing until well after the early stages when the virus was first discovered and there was a noted lack of seriousness or timeliness in doing so. We may compare this with the speed at which measures to contain the virus were taken in New Zealand.

When turning our attention to the communication styles of heads of states when dealing with the pandemic, we noted that compared to the speech of President Trump, Prime Minister Arden displayed a speech pattern that had ample evidence of trust-building elements. We also observed, that compared to President Trump, Prime Minister Arden's plans for action were clearer and more decisive resulting in her nation being better informed on what to expect at each stage, another element believed to promote trust between a head of state and her nation. Through the framework of Positive Psychology, our in-depth investigation of the gender styles of female world leaders, when dealing with COVID-19 pandemic identified a host of patterns including compassion, empathy as well as promoting a sense of working together as a team and shared responsibility to bring the pandemic to a successful end.

## Note

1 By elaborating upon the defensive pessimism strategy we are not suggesting that this was the only or main strategy adopted by Singapore in the management of the COVID-19 pandemic, rather it is one strategy of many that is the focus of this chapter.

## Bibliography

Abdullah, W. J., & Kim, S. (2020). Singapore's responses to the COVID-19 outbreak: A critical assessment. *The American Review of Public Administration, 50*(6–7), 770–776.

Ahmad Kamil, M., &ShamshulBahrn, F. F. (2020). A speech act analysis of the prime minister's speech pertaining to the movement control order (MCO) to address the covid-19 pandemic in Malaysia. *International Journal of Modern Languages and Applied Linguistics (IJMAL), 4*(4), 1–13.

Aldrich, D. P., & Yoshida, T. (2020). How Japan stumbled into a pandemic miracle. *Current History, 119*(818), 217–221.

Alyeksyeyeva, I., Kaptiurova, O., & Orlova, V. (2021). World war flu: War rhetoric of the Australian Prime Minister on coronavirus. *3L, Language, Linguistics, Literature, 27*(1), 90–101. doi10.17576/3L-2021-2701-07

Barrett, R. (2005). Self-mortification and the stigma of leprosy in Northern India. *Medical Anthropology Quarterly, 19*(2), 216–230.

Bharat, S. (2011). A systematic review of HIV/AIDS-related stigma and discrimination in India: Current understanding and future needs. *Sahara-J, 8*(3), 138–149.

Bergquist, S., Otten, T., & Sarich, N. (2020). COVID-19 pandemic in the United States. *Health Policy and Technology, 9*(4), 623–638.

Berrocal, M., Kranert, M., Attolino, P., Santos, J. A. B., Santamaria, S. G., Henaku, N., … & Salamurović, A. (2021). Constructing collective identities and solidarity in premiers' early speeches on COVID-19: A global perspective. *Humanities and Social Sciences Communications, 8*(1), 1–12.

Blake, H., Bermingham, F., Johnson, G., & Tabner, A. (2020). Mitigating the psychological impact of COVID-19 on healthcare workers: A digital learning package. *International Journal of Environmental Research and Public Health, 17*(9), 2997.

Blake, A., & Rieger, J. M. (2021). *Timeline: The 201 times trump has downplayed the coronavirus threat*, WASH. POST (Nov. 3, 2020, 1:07 AM), Retrieved from https://www.washingtonpost.com/politics/2020/03/12/trump-coronavirus-timeline/ ("It's going to disappear. One day, it's like a miracle, it will disappear."); *Totals for the* US, COVID Tracking Project, https://covidtracking.com/data/national (Feb. 3, 2021) (citing all of the case and death count data in the United States).

Booeshaghi, A. S., Tan, F., Renton, B., Berger, Z., & Pachter, L. (2020). Markedly heterogeneous COVID-19 testing plans among US colleges and universities. *MedRxiv*. doi: 10.1101/2020.08.09.20171223

Boniol, M., McIsaac, M., Xu, L., Wuliji, T., Diallo, K., & Campbell, J. (2019). *Gender equity in the health workforce: Analysis of 104 countries* (No. WHO/HIS/HWF/Gender/WP1/2019.1). World Health Organization.

Chaturvedi, S. (2020). Pandemic exposes weaknesses in India's disaster management response. *THE HINDU Centre for Politics and Public Policy.*

Chetterje, P. (2020). Gaps in India's preparedness for COVID-19 control. *The Lancet Infectious Diseases*, *20*(5), 544.

Chi, N., & Pabyantara, D. (2022). Living under Covid-19 in Asia: Tackling the challenges of the 'shadow pandemic' in Japan and Indonesia. *Annals, Public Policy Studies, 16*, 115–142.

Choudhary, O. P., Singh, I., & Rodriguez-Morales, A. J. (2021). Second wave of COVID-19 in India: Dissection of the causes and lessons learnt. *Travel Medicine and Infectious Disease*, *43*, 102126.

Chou, M. H. (2021). Sticky and slippery destinations for academic mobility: The case of Singapore. *Higher Education*, *82*(4), 749–764.

Chua, A. Q., Tan, M. M. J.,Verma, M, *et al.* (2020). Healthsystem resilience inmanaging the COVID-19pandemic: Lessons fromSingapore. *BMJ Global Health,* **5**:e003317. doi: 10.1136/bmjgh-2020-003317

Clark, D. (2020). Travel restrictions to remain in place as coronavirus precaution [Press release]. Retrieved on October 30, 2023 from www.beehive.govt.nz/release/travel-restrictions-remain-place-coronavirus-precaution.

Dada, S., Ashworth, H. C., Bewa, M. J., et al. (2021). Words matter: Political and gender analysis of speeches made by heads of government during the COVID-19 pandemic. *BMJ Global Health*, 6, e003910. doi: 10.1136/ bmjgh-2020-003910

Department of Statistics Singapore. (2020). Singapore population. Retrieved from: https://www.singstat.gov.sg/modules/infographics/population.

Dückers, M. L. A., Yzermans, C. J., Jong, W., & Boin, A. (2017). Psychosocial crisis management: The unexplored intersection of crisis leadership and psychosocial support. *Risks, Hazards & Crisis in Public Policy*, *8*(2), 94–112. doi: 10.1002/rhc3.12113.

Elliot, A. J., & Church, M. A. (2003). A motivational analysis of defensive pessimism and self- handicapping, *Journal of Personality, 71*(3), 369–396.

Eriksson, M., & Olsson, E.-K. (2016). Facebook and Twitter in crisis communication: A comparative study of crisis communication professionals and citizens. *Journal of Contingencies and Crisis Management, 24*(4), 198–208. doi: 10.1111/1468-5973.12116.

Feitelson, E., Plaut, P., Salzberger, E., Shmueli, D., Altshuler, A., Amir, S., & Ben-Gal, M. (2022). Learning from others' disasters? A comparative study of SARS/MERS and COVID-19 responses in five polities. *International Journal of Disaster Risk Reduction*, *74*, 102913.

Fouda, A., Mahmoudi, N., Moy, N., & Paolucci, F. (2020). The COVID-19 pandemic in Greece, Iceland, New Zealand, and Singapore: Health policies and lessons learned. *Health Policy and Technology, 9*(4), 510–524.

Hafner, C. A., & Sun, T. (2021). The 'team of 5 million': The joint construction of leadership discourse during the Covid-19 pandemic in New Zealand. *Discourse, Context & Media*, *43*, 100523.

Hale, T., Angrist, N., Goldszmidt, R., Kira, B., Petherick, A., Phillips, T. & Tatlow, H. (2021). A global panel database of pandemic policies (Oxford COVID-19 Government Response Tracker). *Nature Human Behaviour*, *5*(4), 529–538.

Hatzisavvidou, S., & Martin, J. (2022). Introduction to the special issue: Rhetorical approaches to contemporary political studies. Politics, 42(2), 149–155. doi: 10.1177/02633957211050272

Johns Hopkins University. (2020). COVID-19 dashboard by the Center for Systems Science and Engineering (CSSE) at Johns Hopkins University (JHU). Available at: https://coronavirus.jhu.edu/map.html (accessed 9 July 2020).

Joshi, B., & Swarnakar, P. (2021). Staying away, staying alive: Exploring risk and stigma of COVID-19 in the context of beliefs, actors and hierarchies in India. *Current Sociology, 69*(4), 492–511.

Kadam, A. B., & Atre, S. R. (2020). Negative impact of social media panic during the COVID-19 outbreak in India. *Journal of Travel Medicine, 27*(3), taaa057.

Kalokairinou, L., Zettler, P. J., Nagappan, A., Kyweluk, M. A., & Wexler, A. (2020). The promise of direct-to-consumer COVID-19 testing: Ethical and regulatory issues. *Journal of Law and the Biosciences, 7*(1), lsaa069.

Kearns, R. (2021). Narrative and metaphors in New Zealand's efforts to eliminate COVID-19. *Geographical Research, 59*(3), 324–330.

Kevin, L. et al. (n.d.). *Trump completes reversal, telling govs 'you (2020) are going to call your ownshots' and distributes new guidelines.* CNN, Retrieved from https://www.cnn.com/2020/04/16/politics/donaldtrump-reopening-guidelinescoronavirus/index.html.

Klopp, R. (2020). Does Japan's culture explain its low COVID-19 numbers? The Japan Times, Retrieved from https://www.japantimes.co.jp/community/2020/04/01/voices/japan-culture-low-covid-19-numbers

Krishnatray, P., & Shrivastava, S. (2021). Coronavirus pandemic: How national leaders framed their speeches to fellow citizens. *Asia Pacific Media Educator, 31*(2), 195–211.

Kulkarni, B. N., & Anantharama, V. (2020). Repercussions of COVID-19 pandemic on municipal solid waste management: Challenges and opportunities. *Science of the Total Environment, 743*, 140693.

Kuyuyo, O., Kengne, A. P., & Dandara, C. (2020). Singapore COVID-19 pandemic response as a successful model framework for low-resource health-care settings in Africa? *OMIC: A Journal of Integretative Biology, 24*(8), 470–478.

Lafortune, G. (2020). How much do we know about countries preparedness to respond to pandemics? Insights from two country-level indices. *Sustainable Development Solutions Network (SDSN), 20.*

Lanard. (2004). "WHO expert consultation on outbreak communications – Singapore's SARS Outbreak Communications." Keynote presentation, World Health Organization conference "Outbreak Communications," Singapore, September 21, 2004. Retrieved from https://www.psandman.com/articles/sarscomm.htm

Landsverk, G. (2020). The CDC says healthcare workers who can't get a mask should use a bandana or scarf as a 'last resort' as supplies run short. Business Insider (March 19, 2020). Retrieved from https//www.businessinsider.com/cdc-recommends-health-workers-use-bandanas-face-masks-crisis-2020-3

Lee, W. C., & Ong, C. Y. (2020). Overview of rapid mitigating strategies in Singapore during the COVID-19 pandemic, *Public Health, 185*, 15–17.

Liptak, K., Holmes, K., & Noblies, R. (2020). Trump completes reversal, telling govs 'You Are Going to Call Your Own Shots' and distributes new guidelines. *CNN News.* https://edition.cnn.com/2020/04/16/politics/donald-trump-reopening-guidelines-coronavirus/index.html

Matthews, J. (2020). "Cultural exceptionalism" in the global exchange of (mis) information around Japan's responses to COVID-19. *Media and Communication, 8*(2), 448–451.

Maxmen, A. (2020). Thousands of coronavirus tests are going unused in U.S. labs. *Nature, 580*(7803), 312+.

Mayer, C.-H., & May, M. S. (2021). Women leaders transcending the demands of Covid-19: A positive psychology 2.0 perspective. *Frontiers in Psychology,* 12, 647658. doi: 10.3389/fpsyg.2021.647658

McGuire, D., Cunningham, J. E., Reynolds, K., & Matthews-Smith, G. (2020). Beating the virus: An examination of the crisis communication approach taken by New Zealand Prime Minister Jacinda Ardern during the Covid-19 pandemic. *Human Resource Development International*, *23*(4), 361–379.

Ministry of Health (New Zealand). (2017). *New Zealand influenza pandemic plan: A framework for action* (2nd ed.). Available at www.health.govt.nz/publication/new-zealand-influenza-pandemic-plan-framework-action (accessed October 30, 2023).

Ministry of Health. (n.d.). 20 August 2020 daily report on COVID-19, 2020. Retrieved from https://www.moh.gov.sg/docs/librariesprovider5/2019-ncov/20200820_daily_report_on_covid-19_cabinet.pdf

Number One News. (2020). Full speech: Prime Minster Ardern's address to the nation. Retrieved on September 17, 2023 at: https://www.1news.co.nz/2020/03/23/full-speech-prime-minister-jacinda-arderns-address-to-the-nation/

Parker, R. W. (2020). Why America's response to the COVID-19 pandemic failed: Lessons from New Zealand's Success. https://papers.ssrn.com/sol3/papers.cfm?abstract_id=3794725

Patrick, P. (2020). Has Japan cracked the coronavirus? *The Spectator*. Retrieved from https://www.spectator.co.uk/article/has-japan-cracked-coronavirus-

Power, K., & Crosthwaite, P. (2022). Constructing COVID-19: A corpus-informed analysis of prime ministerial crisis response communication by gender. *Discourse & Society*, *33*(3), 411–437. doi: 10.1177/09579265221076612

Radhakrishnan, N., & Gupta, D. K. (2021). India's COVID-19 response: Science first. *The Lancet*, *397*(10293), 2464–2465.

Ran, J., Zhao, S., Han, L., et al. (2021). The changing patterns of COVID-19 transmissibility during the social unrest in the United States: A nation wide ecological study with a before- and-after comparison. *One Health*, *12*, 100201.

Ripley, W. (2020). There are fears a coronavirus looms in Tokyo. Is it too late to change course? CNN. Retrieved from https://edition.cnn.com/2020/04/03/asia/tokyo-coronavirus-japan-hnk-intl/index.html

Rohrich, R. J., Hamilton, K. L., Avashia, Y., &Savetsky, I. (2020). The COVID-19 pandemic: Changing lives and lessons learned. *Plastic and Reconstructive Surgery Global Open*, *8*(4), e2854. doi:10.1097/GOX.0000000000002854.

Samarasekera, U. (2021). India grapples with second wave of COVID-19. *The Lancet Microbe*, *2*(6), e238. sctm27. (2020). Japan's corona mystery [Tweet]. Retrieved from https://twitter.com/sctim_27/status/1242653182053892097

Searle, J. R. (1969). Expression and meaning: Studies in the theory of speech acts. New York: Cambridge University Press.

Searle, J. R., Kiefer, F., & Bierwisch, M. (Eds.). (1980). *Speech act theory and pragmatics* (Vol. 10). Dordrecht: D. Reidel.

Stevens, H., & Tan, S. (2020). "From 'It's going to disappear' to WE WILL WIN THIS WAR.'" *Washington Post*, March 31.

Tabish, S. A. (2020). Covid-19 pandemic: Emerging perspectives and future trends. *Journal of Public Health Research, 9*(1), 1786. doi: 10.4081/jphr.2020.1786

Tan, Y. T., & Kesselheim, A. S. (2020). Implementing US Covid-19 testing: Regulatory and infrastructural challenges. *The Journal of Law, Medicine & Ethics, 48*(3), 606–612.

Teo, J. (2020). Coronavirus: WHO praises Singapore's containment ofCOVID-19 outbreak. *The Straits Times*. Retrieved from: https://www.straitstimes.com/singapore/health/coronavirus-who-praisessingapores-containment-of-covid-19-outbreak

Todd, B. (2020). The US COVID-19 testing failure. *AJN The American Journal of Nursing, 120*(10), 19–20.

Visaria, A., & Dharamdasani, T. (2021). The complex causes of India's 2021 COVID-19 surge. *The Lancet, 397*(10293), 2464.

Watanabe, T., & Yabu, T. (2021). Japan's voluntary lockdown. *PLoS One, 16*(6), e0252468. doi: 10.1371/journal.pone.0252468

Wilson, S. (2020). Pandemic leadership: Lessons from New Zealand's approach to COVID-19. *Leadership, 16*(3), 279-293. https://doi.org/10.1177/1742715020929151

Wilson, S. (2020). Pandemic leadership: Lessons from New Zealand's approach to COVID-19, *Leadership, 16*(3), 279–293. doi: 10.1177/1742715020929151

Wong, C. M. L., & Jensen, O. (2020). The paradox of trust: Perceived risk and public compliance during the COVID-19 pandemic in Singapore. *Journal of Risk Research, 23(*7–8), 1021–1030.

Xu, H. D., & Basu, R. (2020). How the United States Flunked the COVID-19 test: some observations and several lessons. *The American Review of Public Administration,* 50(6–7), 568–576.

Yarney, G., & Gonsalves, G. (2020). Donald Trump: A political determinant of covid-19. *British Medical Journal*, Volume 396.

Yeo, S. L., Phua, D. Y., & Hong, Y. Y. (2022). The effects of dangerous world beliefs on COVID-19 preventive behaviors in Singapore: The moderating role of public health communication. *International Journal of Strategic Communication, 16*(3), 485–498. doi: 10.1080/1553118X.2022.2036742

Yusanti, G., Ningrum, A. S., Aini, N., & Al Aziz, E. N. (2022). Speech act analysis on Joe Biden's speech about Covid-19. *JurnalArbitrer, 9*(1), 57.

## Glossary of Key Terms and Concepts

**Corpus linguistic analysis** comprises the collections of electronically searchable texts that represent a given genre or register that is under investigation (this refers to corpora) which are analyzed through corpus linguistic procedures that show patterns of language use which may be difficult to decipher with manual discourse analysis (Power & Crosthwaite, 2022).

**Discursive leadership studies** draw upon empirical observational techniques to explore how leadership is performed through discourse (Hafner & Sun, 2021).

**Health system resilience** refers to a population's ability to effectively prepare for and respond to crises while maintaining core functions (Chua et al., 2020, p. 1).

**Political speeches** are a category of political discourse that has the purpose of informing the audience and are also a communicative channel to convey the speaker's beliefs, ideas and the speaker's cognitive representation of these beliefs within a certain political, social and ideological context" (Alyeksy-eyeva et al., 2020).

**Rhetorical analysis** cautions us to the distinctive techniques of speech and performance that give meaning and force to ideas and is attuned to the concrete rather than the universal forms of language and meaning (Hatzisav-vidou & Martin, 2022).

**Speech Act Theory.** In linguistics, a speech act is an utterance defined in terms of a speaker's intention and the effect it has on a listener. Speech acts are verbal actions. Speech-act theory considers the levels of action at which utterances are said to perform these are locutionary, illocutionary and perlocutionary (Searle et al., 1980).

## Discussion Questions

### *Cultural Issues*

1 In this chapter we noted a number of cultural differences that impacted the public's compliance with government implementations of safety measures. In the case of India, what are steps that could have been taken to overcome the issue of stigmatization of quarantine when people were trying to escape restrictions?
2 What lessons can some Western countries learn from some of the hygienic practices of Japan during the earlier stages of the pandemic, that helped safeguard the country from the spread of the coronavirus?

### *Gender Issues*

1 In general, what are some characteristics of female leadership compared to male leadership, in the handling of the COVID-19 pandemic?
2 Explain how the principles of Positive Psychology was applied in this chapter to better understand key elements of female leadership styles in the handling of the COVID-19 pandemic.

# 6

# 'FRAMING-RISK'

## An In-Depth Exploration of the Role of Semiotic Analysis in Message Persuasion

### Chapter Learning Objectives

- Differentiate between loss and gain framed messages
- Define semiotic analysis in the context of crisis communication
- Describe what is meant by color analysis
- Explain what studies suggest about how social media have changed the media sphere in portraying the coronavirus compared to previous media portrayals of the H1N1 flu
- Differentiate between verbal and non-verbal signs
- Explain the advantages of multi-modal framing in portraying messages about the coronavirus
- Discuss some of the framing techniques used to persuade people to practice self-protective measures during the COVID19 pandemic used in advertisements

### Introduction

When a strange and new experience occurs, it is human nature to attempt to make the foreign familiar. In this way, cultural narratives have been created during the COVID-19 pandemic. Cultural narratives have broken our old reality, to the new 'normal' brought about by the COVID pandemic that attempted to 'make sense' of the phenomena and regulate affect in doing so. Indeed, studies have found that changes in the everyday lives of persons in the pandemic might have influenced peoples' temporalities (the subjective experience of time)

DOI: 10.4324/9781003394983-6

which have, in turn, altered their shared meaning of time (Kahawage et al., 2022; Kosak et al., 2022). Other studies have found that our shared understanding of hybrid and domestic spaces have been altered even a year after the implementation of Covid-19 related restrictions. For example, in their community-based participatory study of 20 UK households, Tulfi (2022) identified alterations in semiotic markings[1] of domestic space as a result of the reorganization of domestic space and time routines.

During a global health disaster, information is only empowering if it is understood properly and ultimately used to prevent further infections and deaths. This requires a common understanding of the world around us.

There is therefore a growing need for public health communication research to be employed in the identification of the information needs of the populace at large, who can then use this information to take better control of their health and self-care through health literacy information (Kreps & Maibach, 2008). An important question that needs to be considered is what are the variables that prevent certain people from refusing (or even incite rebellion against) measures to mitigate the spread of the virus? Some studies suggest that defiance of COVID-19 mitigation guidelines may be a combination of emotions and rational choice considerations (Burruss et al., 2021).

If a message is not persuasive it will not lead to desired action. The safety of millions of people during the COVID-19 pandemic depended on effective vaccine implementation strategies as well as other preventative healthcare measures such as social distancing. Prior to the development and dispersion of the COVID-19 vaccine and even now, as of this writing, with new mutations evolving, behavioral change such as hand washing, social distancing and staying home were the principal ways to manage the pandemic (World Health Organization (WHO), 2020).

We will begin the chapter with an overview of what is meant by message framing. Here it should be noted that **multi-modal framing** refers to how framing is contingent upon a multi-modal approach which refers to assuming how language (speech or written form) is one of many forms of representation for meaning-making (Kress, 2012). We will then examine the literature on the impact of two types of framing strategies: loss vs. gain framed messages as it relates to the desire to comply.

In this chapter we chose to review studies that analyze COVID-19 messages via semiotic analyses as it will enable us to better understand how narratives created by the interplay of textual and pictorial information impact the persuasive ability of COVID-19 messages that promote self-preventative measures. This will lead to an overview of semiotic studies that have explored the visual (verbal and non-verbal) aspects of COVID-19 message content. The chapter will conclude with a discussion of some of the main themes that emerge from these studies as a guide to lessons learned of the persuasive techniques used in COVID-19 message framing.

## Framing of COVID-19 Preventative Healthcare Messages

### *Loss/Gain Frames of COVID-19 Messages and Intention to Comply*

**Prospect theories** explore how people evaluate risk in uncertain situations (Barberis, 2013). This typically involves decision-making regarding potential gains and losses; there is ample evidence to suggest the power of gain- and loss-framed messages in behavior change (Gantiva et al., 2021; Jiménez-Leal et al., 2020; Prakesh et al., 2022; Steffen & Cheng, 2021). According to a study conducted by Gantiva et al. (2021, gain-framed health messages were more effective in increasing intentions to comply with self-care measures, as well as increasing message strength and motivating more self-care behavior. In their study, 319 participants were presented with an unforced choice task where they selected the message they believed to be more effective in promoting health preventative behaviors from COVID-19 messages that were either gain or loss-framed. The results of this study suggest that while loss-framed health messages were perceived to be higher risk messages, gain-frame health messages resulted in higher intention to adopt self-care behaviors and were judged to be stronger by participants in the study. Other studies have found the opposite results where loss-framed messages were more effective in promoting compliant behavior during the COVID-19 pandemic (Steffen & Cheng, 2021).

Reflection: *Look through cigarette ads from twenty or so years back, can you think of some examples of loss and gain-framed messages? Which were more effective and why? How do you think this would apply to messages regarding COVID-19?*

In the section to follow, we will delve into how narratives can be employed to deliver gain-framed messages in the health communication literature.

## The Power of Narratives in Health Communications

Narratives are a powerful tool of persuasion in the realm of health communication (Bosticco & Thompson, 2009; Dunlop et al., 2008; Jennings et al., 2018; Kim et al., 2012; Langer & Ribarich, 2008; Ooms et al., 2017; Petraglia, 2009; Shen & Sheer, 2015). A plethora of studies have been conducted which have explored the impacts of narratives on message persuasiveness in a variety of contexts, including anti-smoking campaigns (Ma & Nan, 2019), eating intention (Wirtz & Kulpavaropas, 2014), willingness to engage in exercise (Gray & Harrington, 2011) and engagement in climate-change philosophies and activities (Connor et al., 2020; Liu & Yang, 2020). As Kim et al. (2012) note in the case of anti-smoking messages, smokers reading an article with an exemplar exhibited a higher intention to quit smoking than when they read an article without an exemplar. Indeed arguably, a great power of the image is in its speed of reach (Gibbs, 2011). This may be because of the ability of narratives to evoke emotion of fear, especially where a health-related risk is present.

Recently some studies have investigated the impact of narratives in the context of COVID-19 messages (Ye et al., 2021). Perhaps lessons about the power of narratives can be learned from countries such as Sweden where there was less overall regulation, including less lockdowns and more voluntary action expected of citizens and organizations compared to many other countries in the world during the COVID-19 pandemic. Nygren and Olofosson (2021)'s critical discourse analysis of editorials and opinion articles in Sweden's largest morning newspaper, Dagens Nyheter, during the spring of 2020 identified three crisis narratives which dominated the debates: health, the economy, and democracy. Their analysis revealed several conflicting perspectives or paradoxes within and between these narratives, including Swedish exceptionalism versus the world, centralization versus decentralization, and herd immunity versus herd humanism.

Semiotic analysis is a powerful technique for investigating how we process non-verbal information. The reason we chose to explore COVID-19 messages through the lens of semiotic analysis in this chapter is twofold. First, we are following the concept of metaphorical networks (Danesi, 2003) which postulates that the structure of human cognition is highly associative and that verbal discourse is structured by metaphorical reasoning. Second, we also believe that semiotic analysis provides a powerful tool through which we can explore the interconnectedness of language, culture, and cognition (Danesi, 2003).

Let us now turn our attention to defining what is meant by semiotic analysis.

## *Semiotic Analyses of COVID-19 Self-Preventative Healthcare Messages*

The semiotic approach is primarily based on the work of Roland Barthes, Fernindand de Sassure and Charles Pierce. "[as stated earlier] the visual has massive impact on our society as we enter the field of images, perceptions, constructs and culture brought together" (Tukus & Lubar, 2021). Signs and symbols provide much insight, indeed:

> [t]hrough signs and symbols, we recognize how the realistic style of representation actually reflects a culturally shaped code. The concept of image

> persuasiveness draws from Barthes's paradigmatic study in 1964 and largely relies on the two main hypotheses: first, that there is no neutral documentation and second, that denotation is only the first level of meaning (of a photograph, for example). Accordingly, we need to first know something about what we are looking at in order to be able to understand the image. As for the social functioning, the signification, communication and culture were brought together by Eco's "doctrine of the sign and communication" (1976). The sign production tends to communicate something"
>
> *(Tukus & Lubar, 2021, p. 14).*

Given the literature reviewed in Chapter 4 where we discussed how religious attitudes may influence the reluctance to receive vaccination, it follows that moral perspective in how COVID-19 messages are framed. Indeed, some scholars assert that emotions (Venkateswaran, 2021) and moral values can be used to explain human behaviors related to vaccination (Zhang et al., 2023) and that individual may apply an ethical lens when making decisions about vaccinating when processing message about vaccination. In this way, the moral values attached to a message resonate with individuals, individuals are more likely to show approval of the message (Wang & Liu, 2021) and ultimately align their behavior (to vaccinate or not) with it.

Scholars have argued that advertisement may be considered to be one of the most effective ways to provide education and understanding about COVID-19 (Trisnavanti et al., 2021). In a study conducted by Trisnavanti et al. (2021) hidden messages in COVID-19 advertisements were investigated through analysis of the verbal and non-verbal signs used in the advertisement entitled "Stay Home Save Live." The data were analyzed by semiotic theory (Saussure, 1983) as well as the theory of meanings proposed by Barthes (1977). Results of the study suggested that both verbal and visual signs in the advertisement "Stay Home Save Lives" have hidden message. The aim of semiotic analysis is better understanding of how humans interpret their surroundings. In Trisnavanti et al.'s (2021) study, both verbal and non-verbal signs were analyzed, where:

> A verbal sign is communication that may be in form of spoken or written text. Meanwhile, According to (Chandler, 2007), the non-verbal sign is known as visual communication to deliver an idea, through image or illustration that combines with a symbol, art, color, gesture, facial expression, graphics, and posture
>
> *(Trisnavanti, p. 25)*

A number of interesting findings were discovered in this study. For example, in their analysis of verbal signs, the researchers explain how the first sign in scene 1 of the video conveys staying home with 'pleasantness' or at least, not a bad thing. Their analysis of the second scene involves the symbolism of feelings and experiences associated with nature, more specifically trees with associations such as spiritual nourishment, fertility and liberty. Other verbal signs are also associated with positive connotations such as freshness, growth, and a clean, quiet environment as more people stay home. Analyses of verbal signs included associations of fun activities and past times with staying at home such as time with puppies, books and other adventures; these messages were further analyzed to include fun bonding activities with family. Again these are pleasant connotations associated with the concept (self-protective measure) as well as the potential for new experiences possible when staying home, in addition to becoming more creative and productive.

The analysis of non-verbal signs is equally informative as Trisnavanti et al. (2021) note:

> The non-verbal sign is the picture of three boys who pouring food for birds. They help each other to hang it on the tree branch. It implied two messages. First, it represents teamwork which is needed during the global pandemic of COVID-19. Second, it implicitly shows that although we just stay at home there are always ways to share with others. This signifier portrays hidden meaning since the advertiser provides a message which aims to convince people that teamwork is very important to prevent the spread of COVID-19.

Semiotic analysis of COVID19 messages can also be helpful in understanding the psychological roots of framing techniques. For example, Gulzer et al. (2021) conducted a multimodal analysis of visuals that comprised public service messages for society to better understand how to better cope in a world with the fast-spreading virusCOVID-19. The study comprised a comparative analysis of semiotic aspects of COVID-19 visuals of two public message ads from two Asian countries (Pakistan and India). The findings of the study suggested that India employed visuals which conveyed fear among people whereas Pakistan has used motivational messages through visuals to combat the disease. A similar theme of fear in the strategic framing of COVID-19 preventative public health messages were also found in a UK study. Gill and Lennon's (2022) analysis of 17 COVID-19 adverts identified four sequential phases to the Government's pandemic response: responsibility, management, mitigation, and reflection. An in-depth Multimodal Critical Discourse Analysis of four selected adverts (one screenshot per advert, per phase), found that fear was constructed using implicit multimodal semiotic interactions. By "portraying a 'good' pandemic subject as one who makes 'moral' and 'rational' decisions to comply with COVID-19 policy, pre-existing societal inequalities which might hinder compliance, particularly for the socioeconomically disadvantaged groups of society, were reduced and problematised" (Gill & Lennon, 2022, p. 22).

Al-Ghamdi et al. (2020) explored the discourse of COVID-19 social media posts using an approach that integrated the social semiotics and multimodal approaches to better understand the dynamic Saudi discourse on COVID-19 posts. The results of the investigation identified a dynamic multi-layered nature of governmental, individual, and public voices pertaining to COVID-19 multi-discoursal themes. A specific semiotics, tailored to the cultural semiotics of Saudi Arabia was also identified. For example, certain signs signified an integrated national identity where symbols of government authority were strategically used to give additional credence and authority to certain messages where a sense of community was strengthened (national symbols as well as the use of the color green). As well, the use of certain clothes, as symbols, was argued by the researchers to further create socio and cultural contextual meanings tailored for the Arab people.

### *Coronavirus Prevention Campaign by the Police*

Venkateswaran (2022) conducted a frame analysis as well as structural narrative analysis on two videos on coronavirus prevention measures that were created by the Kerala and Tamil Nadu police. Their study revealed that emotion was employed to elicit compliance through the use of emotional language that highlighted the facilitation of fear as well as through intimidating images. Characterization was also employed in a way that instead of inducing an empathetic bonding with the audience, it focused instead on evoking a sense of terror and repulsion with the pandemic; overall messages were framed to promote a self-interest angle toward persuading people to adopt preventative measures for their own well-being and survival.

### *Semiotic Analysis of COVID19 Messages through Cartoons*

Humor is created from identifying congruity when two or more opposing ideas are brought together (Sen, 1996) and arguably the pandemic has provided a breeding ground of absurdities into the world around us (Barkadis, 2021). There is a lot of literature demonstrating the power of humor as a cathartic release during difficult times (Dziegielewski, 2003; Leak, 1974; Sen, 1996). Through an analysis of memes, Barkadis (2021) investigated quarantine lifestyle issues in Greek social media groups during Covid-19 and how quarantine impacted everyday lives for the Greek people during this time. The author notes, "the primary role of meme humor in social media is to create a vernacular metalanguage, giving people the opportunity to reconsider their attitudes, beliefs, and actions about significant aspects and issues in their lives through an exaggerated perspective" (p. 42). Barkadis' study employed a mixed methodology, emphasizing a multi-semiotic approach. As Barkadis (2021) notes

> This coexistence of two different semiotic systems seems to conduct a semiotic synergy since meaning is created and complemented by different semiotic codes and expressed in a compact semiotic text. [T]he main focus [of the section of this paper which deals with the interpretation of the memes examined is] on text-image relationships and how reframing some aspects of

social reality into syncretic semiotic texts, such as memes, can lead to humor construction

*(Barkadis, 2021, p. 32).*

Barkadis found some interesting reflections from both the first and second lockdown. During the first lockdown memes the emerging theme was expression of the importance of taking preventative measures for the greater safety of the public good, while the theme from the second lockdown expressed weariness and other signs of psychological fatigue from enduring the government's strict measures. Some of the memes analyzed, taken from Facebook and Instagram, featured open dialogs between the government and the feelings of the public with sarcasm conveyed in discrepancies between image and textual discourse.

In 'Visualizing the Pandemic: A Semiotic Study of Contemporary Arab Media Cartoons on COVID-19,' Hameed and Afzal (2021) conducted a semiotic analysis of 12 cartoons from the Arab and Gulf area. As the authors note the purpose of their study was to conduct a semiotic analysis of COVID-19 cartoons from selected Arab newspapers to better understand how the COVID-19 pandemic was visually conveyed through these images. The major themes included the regular interruption of normal human life activities, the nippy collapse of the world economies, the glum miseries of the working class, the duple downfall of the terror-struck countries, the unfair hold of the COVID-19 vaccine, the capitalistic issues with vaccine supply, and the deplorable botch of the world advancement.

Kadim and Abbas (2022) conducted a semiotic analysis on cartoons and posters of the coronavirus that espouse health and other quarantine instructions against the COVID19 virus to explore how different human, political, and cultural messages are depicted to viewers. The literal and non-literal analyses of the cartoons revealed how certain actions and values that would help facilitate quarantine measures are highlighted in various ways. For example, in certain posters the words 'we're apart' took precedence over 'love' and 'heart' and this message was reinforced by visual depictions of a male and female standing apart (visual illustration of social distancing). In this vein, visually, pointing gestures are often used to attract attention to a certain message, and on a verbal level, words such as "find" "treat" and "early" are grouped together and/or otherwise given prominence by strategic positioning and/or boldface or capitalization of the words themselves. In this way, gestures are also used to grab attention and draw attention to important words that signify important actions relating to social distancing and other quarantine-associated measures. The researchers note in their visual analysis of prominent colors employed in the posters and cartoons that the use of light and dark blue, white, red, brown and pink each signify different emotions associated with compliance to self-protective health measures during the pandemic. For example, brown was associated with a sense of responsibility, faithfulness and devotedness, white was associated with purity, red was associated with forward movement and the courage to fight dangerous enemies, calmness, blue was associated with peace and security (blue) and pink was associated with faith in a better future.

### *Semiotic Representation of COVID19 in Children's Literature*

In their analysis of the book covers and selected contents of a number of children's books that discuss narratives about the coronavirus, Tufail et al. (2021) note that a sense of action and motivation to fight the dangers of the pandemics typically created between superheroes trying to kill the virus. Attractive and adventurous visual images are believed to promote a sense of interest and grabbing children' attention to the topic of the pandemic, and the perception that it is something that needs to be fought, which, in turn, may promote a sense of empowerment during these times.

### *Public Service Advertisements*

Putrasusila (2021) conducted semiotic analysis of two public service advertisement videos entitled Anak Kost and Restu Ibu published by the Ministry of Education and Culture, in Indonesia. Through exploration of the storyline, shooting techniques and the visual cues present in this video, the researchers discussed the good characters that were featured in the videos (a daughter informing her mother of her decision to stay home during the pandemic) portrayed feelings and values of empathy, helping each other and a sense of responsibility for the health and safety of oneself and others during this public message.

Zhao's (2021) study of COVID-19 public service announcements in China investigated questions related to (1) the attitudes that were constructed in the Covid-PSAs in China (2) how these attitudes were constructed (text, visual images or both), (3) the communicative purposes/functions of these attitudes, and the identification of (4) what any identifiable patterns may reveal about the speaker/society/culture in China. The results of the study revealed that the PSAs were created to build the public's confidence in battling the virus, to persuade people to be grateful and united and finally to brand a good image of China on an international level.

As Zhao (2021) note, many psychological theories were employed to guide this research. For example, affect theory (a psychological theory that categorizes subjectively experienced feelings into discrete categories and in so doing, typifies their physiological, social, interpersonal, and internalized manifestations) was used to manipulate the public's emotion. Face theory was used to maintain the image of China and report more positively to the public (by reporting few patients). And additionally, cooperation theory was used to address and better understand what the audience needed to hear (for example, the need for more emotional support and confidence, which resulted in broadcasters reporting more content related to social values).

### *National Health Sites*

In a similar vein, Andriani's (2022) investigation of the signifier and signified of verbal and non-verbal signs of COVID-19 advertisements in Indonesia identified verbal signs that the COVID-19 virus is dangerous as well as verbal signs with clear denotative and connotative meanings. In the case of the latter, the importance of removing waste that could spread infection rates, and the denotative meaning of making this message more appealing to viewers. In their application of color analysis, the researchers further note that color was identified in this study, particularly the background color of blue, to signify the seriousness of adhering to safety precautions, explaining how the colors blue and white have traditionally been used to denote seriousness, health, and healing (Andriani, 2022).

### *Fast Food Businesses on Social Media*

As a unique medium of communication in the public health crisis context, the COVID-19 poster is arguably an interesting genre to explore. Given the unexpected nature of a crisis, when stocks of signs were not readily available, this created an immediate need for the creation of new signs to communicate specific messages (Chen, 2020). Employing semiotic analysis, Kudus et al.'s (2022) explored how products and services are branded in a manner during the COVID-19 pandemic to most effectively resonate with consumers. When analyzing the content of KFC, Pizza Hut, and McDonald's Instagram posts during the March 18 to May 3, 2020, the first Movement Control Order was being carried on in Malaysia.

Given the plethora of visual content on a platform such as Instagram, marketers need to create advertisements that are engaging enough to draw the viewer's attention sufficiently long enough to process the information before moving onto to other images (Kusumasondjaja & Tjiptono, 2019). Kudus et al. (2022) found that the images employed were used to develop a dynamic engagement with consumers that stressed the first-person point of view in a number of captions. Humor and empathy were also highlighted in posts that portrayed certain humorous ideas and empathizing with the need for delivery services during the lockdown. The researchers also discussed the use of hashtags by all three companies to create a spirit of unity and togetherness in the fight against COVID-19.

### *Semiotic Analysis of the WHO YouTube Video: Stay at Home*

Arguably the representation of COVID-19 on the official homepage of the WHO homepage demonstrates the complexity of communicating health-specific messages about the nature and consequences of COVID-19 semiotically. Octarensa and Aras (2020) conducted a semiotic analysis of a 60 second 'Stay at Home' video created by the WHO. Their study analyzed the signifier and signified as well as the overall message or lesson for various scenes in all 20 videos. For example, in the first scene, the non-cheerful atmosphere of a housing complex served as the signified for the signifier which comprised a residential roof that was located in a quiet atmosphere; for this it was determined that the overall message comprised the feelings of isolation that is commonly reported during a pandemic. The overall message for scene seven was enjoyment of time alone where the signifier comprised a lady in a chair at home and the signified a woman relaxing at home alone. This analysis was conducted as previously mentioned, for all 20 scene numbers in this study.

In sum, the various scenes taken together illustrate the WHO's social campaign messages which is for people of all ages, socio-economic statuses, ethnicities etc. to Stay at Home: whether or not it is pleasant or not, it is simply what must be done (Octarensa & Aras, 2020).

### *Lessons from Semiotic Analyses of COVID-19 Messages*

#### *How Fear Impacts Language/Communication and Behavior during the Pandemic*

According to Terror Management Theory (Greenberg & Arndt, 2012) it is normal to react to anxiety, associated with our fear of death, by increasing our adherence to affect-laden and identity grounded generalized beliefs. It is believed that this typically manifests in our language as ingroup-outgroup polarization. For example, this polarization may express itself in the militarization of language as well as in idealized and counter-idealized representation of otherness (Venuleo, 2020). We may recall seeing evidence of this in Chapter 5 in the discourse analysis of female heads of state, where analysis of speech transcripts identified an 'us vs. them' discourse. This was also evinced in the speech patterns of certain male heads of state as well as in the case for the heads of state for the US and France.

## Key Lessons

By means of reviewing several studies which employed a semiotic analysis of COVID-19 messages promoting adherence to self-protective measures, we learned the value of framing techniques in enhancing message appeal. Specifically we found many of these messages were framed in such a manner that appeals were made to viewers' emotions. In certain cases, messages were also framed to appeal to viewers' morals and ethics as well. Finally, framing techniques were also found to employ a dichotomy of good and bad in a battle where viewers' perceived messages promoting health preventative measures in the context of winning a battle against the virus.

Our review of semiotic studies that analyzed COVID-19 advertisements advocating preventative social distancing and other self-care measures were instructive in several respects. Indeed, one of the principal lessons learned in this chapter was the power of emotion in evoking behavior change, a finding consistent with much of the advertising literature (Edell & Burke, 1987; Vakratsas & Ambler, 1999). Adhering to social restrictions during a pandemic is clearly not a pleasant prospect for most people, as it entails loss of freedom in one's personal and work life on a number of levels. Through the power of evoking emotion, via carefully selected images, much of the semiotic analyses reviewed suggested two persuasive techniques in convincing readers and audiences to adopt positive behavior change for people who may have been reluctant to do so.

First, the argument was presented that adhering to social distancing and other restrictive measures is the 'moral' thing to do. This was illustrated in the analyses of public service advertisements in India, Pakistan, China and Saudi Arabia where national symbols and signs were strategically employed to denote a sense of responsibility to one's country (sometimes through the use of fear). This message was also found in a number of studies in children's literature where a 'you vs. them' mentality was advocated, and battles fought between the virus and society. In these studies, vilification was often used to construe the virus as a bad force that needs to be fought. Arguably, children growing up with exposure to such narratives will learn that the COVID-19 virus is a bad entity that needs to be destroyed.

Second, other studies suggested that even restrictive measures are not always necessarily unpleasant. Examples of this found in the YouTube video, 'Stay Home Save Lives' included associating social distancing measures such as 'stay at home' with positive connotations such as more family bonding time where indoors activities at home were associated with fun and other pleasant experiences.

In sum, through strategic highlighting of certain key words in the COVID-19 messages we found that certain self-protective health measures were being advocated. Along similar lines, a number of visual expressions were used to grab attention and convey certain feelings to the viewer as to why adhering to self-protective health measures should be appealing from an emotional and/or ethical perspective. Irrespective of whether messages analyzed in the studies reviewed were cartoons, messages in print form, online or specific to social media, this theme of associating an emotive aspect with the message to comply with health protective measures appeared to be a common theme.

## Note

1 The researchers state that due to space limitations they do not define what constitutes public vs. private space. In the study the participants provided their own reflections and comments via words and images on how they felt their space had changed.

## Bibliography

Al-Ghamdi, N. A., & Albawardi, A. H. (2020). Multivocality of Saudi COVID-19 Discourse in Social Media Posts: A Socio-Semiotic Multimodal Perspective. *GEMA Online Journal of Language Studies*, *20*(4), 228–250.

Andriani, N. K. A. (2022). Semiotic Analysis Found in COVID-19 Advertisements by National Institutes of Health Websites (Doctoral dissertation, Universitas Mahasaraswati Denpasar).

Andriani, N. K. A., Pratiwi, D. P. E., & Juniartha, I. W. (2022, November). Semiotic analysis found in COVID-19 advertisements by National Institutes of Health Websites. In *The First International Conference on Language, Culture, and Communication (ICLCC) 2022* (pp. 100–106).

Axelrod, R. (2000). On six advances in cooperation theory. *Analyse & Kritik*, *22*(1), 130–151.

Barberis, N. C. (2013). Thirty years of prospect theory in economics: A review and assessment. *Journal of Economic Perspectives*, *27*(1), 173–196.

Bardakis, T. (2021). A semiotic approach to Greek internet memes during the covid-19 pandemic. *Punctum International Journal of Semiotics, 7*(1), 31–43.

Barrett, L. F. (2006). Solving the emotion paradox: Categorization and the experience of emotion. Personality and Social Psychology Review, 10(1), 20–46. doi: 10.1207/s15327957pspr1001_2

Barthes, R. (1968). *Elements of semiology* (1st ed.). New York: Hill and Wang.

Bosticco, C., & Thompson, T. L. (2009). Let me tell you a story: Narratives and narration in health communication research. In *Emerging perspectives in health communication* (pp. 49–72). Routledge.

Burruss, G. W., Jaynes, C. M., Moule, J. & Fairchild, R. (2021). Modeling individual defiance of COVID-19 pandemic mitigation strategies: Insights from the expanded model of deterrence and protection motivation theory. *Criminal Justice and Behavior*, *48*(9), 1317–1338. doi: 10.1177/00938548211010315

Chandler, D. (2007). *The Basic Semiotic* (second). Canada: Routledge.

Chen, N. (2020). Semiotic resourcefulness in crisis risk communication: The case of COVID-19 posters. *Language and Semiotic Studies*, *6*(3), 1–27.

Connor, J., Madhavan, S., Mokashi, M., Amanuel, H., Johnson, N. R., Pace, L. E., & Bartz, D. (2020). Health risks and outcomes that disproportionately affect women during the Covid-19 pandemic: A review. *Social Science & Medicine, 266*, 113364.

Danesi, M. (2003). Metaphorical "networks" and verbal communication: A semiotic perspective of human discourse. *Σημειωτκή-Sign Systems Studies*, *31*(2), 341–364.

Dewi, O. C. (2022). Face masks, between social and political messages in Covid-19 pandemic: A semiotic analysis. *Metahumaniora, 12*(2), 196–203.

Dunlop, S., Wakefield, M., & Kashima, Y. (2008). Can you feel it? Negative emotion, risk, and narrative in health communication. *Media Psychology*, *11*(1), 52–75.

Dziegielewski, S. F. (2003). Humor: An essential communication tool in therapy. *International Journal of Mental Health*, *32*(3), 74–90.

Edell, J. A., & Burke, M. C. (1987). The power of feelings in understanding advertising effects. *Journal of Consumer Research, 14*(3), 421–433.

Gandiva, C., Jimenez-Leal, W., Urriago-Rayo, J. (n.d.). Framing messages to deal with the COVID-19 crisis: The role of loss-gain frames and content. *Frontiers in Psychology*.

Gibbs, A. (2011). Affect theory and audience. In Virginia Nightingale (Ed.), *The handbook of media audiences* (pp. 251–266). Blackwell Publishing Ltd.

Gill, K. A., & Lennon, H. (2022). Conformity through fear: A multimodal critical discourse analysis of COVID-19 information adverts. *Critical Approaches to Discourse Analysis Across Disciplines*, *14*(1), Art 2.

Gray, J. B., & Harrington, N. G. (2011). Narrative and framing: A test of an integrated message strategy in the exercise context. *Journal of Health Communication*, *16*(3), 264–281.

Greenberg, J., & Arndt, J. (2012). Terror management theory. In P. A. M. Van Lange, A. W. Kruglanski & E. T. Higgins (Eds.), *Handbook of theories of social psychology* (pp. 398–415). Thousand Oaks, CA: Sage Publications.

Greenberg, J., Pyszczynski, T., & Solomon, S. (1986). The causes and consequences of a need for self-esteem: A terror management theory. In *Public self and private self* (pp. 189–212). New York: Springer New York.

Hameed, A., & Afzal, N. (2021). Visualizing pandemic issues: A semiotic study of contemporary Arab media cartoons on COVID-19. *Eurasian Journal of Applied Linguistics*, *7*(2), 84–102.

Hansen, F., & Christensen, S. R. (2007). *Emotions, advertising and consumer choice*. Copenhagen Business School Press DK.

Jiménez-Leal, W., Gantiva, C., & Urriago, J. (2020). Framing effects on intentions and effectiveness related to Covid-19 messages contrasting economic and health concerns. https://osf.io/6rfeu/download

Jennings, W., Bond, C., & Hill, P. S. (2018). The power of talk and power in talk: A systematic review of Indigenous narratives of culturally safe healthcare communication. *Australian Journal of Primary Health*, *24*(2), 109–115.

Kadim, E. N., & Abbas, A. H. (2022). Signs are sometimes more humane than some people: A semiotic-discourse analysis of selected COVID-19 cartoons and posters. *Journal of Global Scientific Research*, *7*(9), 2633–2645.

Kahawage, P., Crowe, M., Gottlieb, J., Swartz, H. A., Yatham, L. N., Bullock, B., ... & Murray, G. (2022). Adrift in time: The subjective experience of circadian challenge during COVID-19 amongst people with mood disorders. *Chronobiology International*, *39*(1), 57–67.

Kim, H. S., Bigman, C. A., Leader, A. E., Lerman, C., & Cappella, J. N. (2012). Narrative health communication and behavior change: The influence of exemplars in the news on intention to quit smoking. *Journal of Communication*, *62*(3), 473–492.

Kooistra, E. B., & Rooij, B. V. (2020). Pandemic compliance: A systematic review of influences on social distancing behavior during the first wave of the COVID-19 outbreak. *Working Paper*.

Kosak, F., Schelhorn, I., & Wittmann, M. (2022). The subjective experience of time during the pandemic in Germany: The big slowdown. *PLos One*, *17*(5), e0267709.

Kudus, N. V., Zulkifli, C. N., & Amin, N. M. (2022). Semiotic analysis of three QSR Instagram posts during COVID-19 Outbreak. *Pertanika Journal of Social Sciences & Humanities*, *30*(3), 1383–1404.

Kusumasondjaja, S., & Tjiptono, F. (2019). Endorsement and visual complexity in food advertising on Instagram. *Internet Research*, *29*(4), 659–687. doi: 10.1108/IntR-11-2017-0459

Kreps, G. L., & Maibach, E. W. (2008). Transdisciplinary science: The nexus between communication and public health. *Journal of Communication*, *58*(4), 732–748.

Kress, G. (2012). Multimodal discourse analysis. *The Routledge handbook of discourse analysis* (pp. 35–50). https://www.taylorfrancis.com/chapters/edit/10.4324/97810030 35244-12/multimodal-discourse-analysis-gunther-kress-jeff- bezemer

Langer, N., & Ribarich, M. (2008). Using narratives in healthcare communication. *Educational Gerontology*, *35*(1), 55–62.

Leak, G. K. (1974). Effects of hostility arousal and aggressive humor on catharsis and humor preference. *Journal of Personality and Social Psychology*, *30*(6), 736.

Liu, S., & Yang, J. Z. (2020). Incorporating message framing into narrative persuasion to curb e-cigarette use among college students. *Risk Analysis*, *40*(8), 1677–1690.

Ma, Z., & Nan, X. (2019). Positive facts, negative stories: Message framing as a moderator of narrative persuasion in antismoking communication. *Health Communication, 34*(12), 1454–1460.

Nygren, G. K., & Olofsson, A. (2021). Swedish exceptionalism, herd immunity and the welfare state: A media analysis of struggles over the nature and legitimacy of the COVID-19 pandemic strategy in Sweden. *Current Sociology, 69*(4), 529–546.

Octarensa, V., & Aras, M. (2020). Semiotic analysis of video COVID-19 by World Health Organization. *International Journal of Innovative Science and Research Technology, 5*(7), 145–151.

Ooms, J. A., Jansen, C. J., Hommes, S., & Hoeks, J. C. (2017). Health communication|"Don't make my mistake": On the processing of narrative fear appeals. *International Journal of Communication, 11*, 22.

Peirce, C. P. (1965). Basic concepts of Peircean sign theory. In M. Gottdiener, K. Boklund-Lagopoulou & A. P. Lagopoulos (Eds.), *Semiotics*. London: Sage Publications.

Petraglia, J. (2009). The importance of being authentic: Persuasion, narration, and dialogue in health communication and education. *Health communication, 24*(2), 176–185.

Prakash, A., Jeyakumar Nathan, R., Kini, S., & Victor, V. (2022). Message framing and COVID-19 vaccine acceptance among millennials in South India. *PloS One, 17*(7), e0269487.

Psychology Today. (2023). Terror management theory. Retrieved on November 21, 2023 from https://www.psychologytoday.com/ca/basics/terror-management-theory#

Putrasusila, H. (2021). *Semiotic analysis on COVID-19 public service advertisements of the Ministry of Education and culture of Republic Indonesia* (Doctoral dissertation, Universitas GadjahMada).

Rutherford, D. (2016). Affect theory and the empirical. *Annual Review of Anthropology, 45*, 285–300.

Sa, A. S. P., & Putrib, I. P. (2021). The semiotics analysis in delivering message how to prevent Covid-19 on grab advertisement. *Jurnal Ilmiah LISKI (Lingkar Studi Komunikasi), 7*(2).

de Saussure, F. (1983). Course in general linguistics. C. Bally, & A. Sechehaye (Eds.), with collaboration of A. Riedlinger, R. Harris (Trans.). London: Duckworth.

Schmidt, U., Starmer, C., & Sugden, R. (2008). Third-generation prospect theory. *Journal of Risk and Uncertainty, 36*, 203–223.

Sen, D. (1996). What is Humour? Unpublished Independent Study Paper. Carleton University.

Shen, F., Sheer, V. C., & Li, R. (2015). Impact of narratives on persuasion in health communication: A meta-analysis. *Journal of Advertising, 44*(2), 105–113.

Snoussi, T., & Korbi, W. (2021). Cyber anti-hate speech during the Covid-19 pandemic: Semiotic analysis. *The Asian ESP Journal, 17*(4.2), 169–189.

Starr, R. L., Go, C., & Pak, V. (2022). 'Keep calm, stay safe, and drink bubble tea': Commodifying the crisis of Covid-19 in Singapore advertising. *Language in Society, 51*(2), 333–359.

Steffen, J., & Cheng, J. (2021). The influence of gain-loss framing and its interaction with political ideology on social distancing and mask wearing compliance during the COVID-19 pandemic. *Current Psychology*, 1–11.

Toro-Ascuy, D., Munoz, N. C., Avaria, A., Pereira-Montecinos, C., Cruzat, G., Peralta-Arancibia, K., Zorondo-Rodriguez, F., & Fuenzalinda, L. F. (2022). Factors influencing the acceptance of COVID-19 vaccines in a country with a high vaccination rate, *Vaccines, 10*(5), 681.

Trisnavanti, N. M. D., Pratiwi, D. P. E., & Candra, K. D. P. (2021). Discovering hidden messages in Covid-19 advertisement "stay home save lives": A semiotic analysis. Retorika: *JurnalIlmu Bahasa, 7*(1), 25–31. doi: 10.22225/jr.7.1.3137.

Tufail, H., Khan, M. Y., & Qureshi, U. (2021). Visual representation of COVID-19 in children's literature: A semiotic analysis. *Sir Syed Journal of Education & Social Research, 4*(2), 423–430.

Tufi, S. (2022). Hybrid places: The reconfiguration of domestic space in the time of Covid-19. *Linguistic Landscape, 8*(2–3), 202–218.

Tuksar, S., & Labaš, D. (2021). Every cloud has a silver lining': humour and persuasiveness in social media images during lockdowns. *Medijska istraživanja: znanstveno-stručni časopis za novinarstvo i medije, 27*(2), 7–35.

Venkateswaran, T. V. (2022). Tale of two videos: Frame and narrative structure analysis of two COVID-19 communication social media messages. *Journal of Scientific Temper (JST), 8*(1–2), 18–37.

Venuleo, C., Gelo, O. C. G., & Salvatore, S. (2020). Fear, affective semiosis, and management of the pandemic crisis: Covid-19 as semiotic vaccine? *Clinical Neuropsychiatry, 17*(2), 117–130. doi: 10.36131/CN20200218.

Wang, R., & Liu, W. (2021). Moral framing and information virality in social movements: A case study of #HongKongPoliceBrutality. *Communication Monographs,* 88(3): 350–370. doi: 10.1080/03637751.2021.1918735.

Wirtz, J. G., & Kulpavaropas, S. (2014). The effects of narrative and message framing on engagement and eating intention among a sample of adult Hispanics. *Journal of Nutrition Education and Behavior, 46*(5), 396–400.

World Health Organization (WHO). (2020). *Rolling updates on coronavirus disease (COVID-19)*. Geneva: WHO.

Ye, W., Li, Q., & Yu, S. (2021). Persuasive effects of message framing and narrative format on promoting COVID-19 vaccination: A study on Chinese college students. *International Journal of Environmental Research and Public Health, 18*(18), 9485.

Zhao, R. (2021, June). A social semiotic analysis of covid-19 public service advertisements in China. In *2nd International Conference on Language, Art and Cultural Exchange (ICLACE 2021)* (pp. 256–259). Atlantis Press. https://www.atlantis-press.com/proceedings/iclace-21/125957524

Zhang, W., Wang, R., & Liu, H. (2023). Moral expressions, sources, and frames: Examining COVID-19 vaccination posts by Facebook public pages. *Computers in Human Behavior, 138*, 107479.

## Glossary of Key Terms and Concepts

**Affect theory** is a psychological theory that explores how behavior can be driven by affect, understood to be subjectively experienced feelings and even unconscious responses to stimuli (Rutherford, 2016).

**Affective semiosis** shapes the global pairing between an organism and the environment without interruption, as a kind of neuro-physiological gauge. It is believed to be active even when outside the focus of consciousness (Barrett, 2006).

**Cooperation theory** addresses the common tension between what is good for the individual in the short-term, compared to what is good for a group inthe long-term (Axelrod, 2000).

**Framing draws** upon empirical observational techniques to investigate the performance of leadership through discourse.

**Multi-modal framing** refers to how language (speech or written form) is one of many forms of representation for meaning-making. In multi-modalframing this framing is contingent upon a multi-modal approach (Kress, 2012).

**Prospect theory** explores how people make decisions about risk in uncertain situations. In the many versions of this theory, we may consider that the subjective value of a given monetary lottery, viewed from a given certain reference point, comprises a weighted average of the subjective values of the monetary gains or losses associated with the lottery outcomes (Schmidt et al., 2008).

**Signs constitute** the core concept of semiotics and stand for a concept or object (Octarensa & Aras, 2020).

**Signified refers** to the meaning expressed by the sign.

**Signifier refers** to the sign in physical form.

**Terror Management Theory** posits that fear (especially of death) can influence behavior and that cognition is often biased to protect our self-esteem and the belief that we play a meaningful part in the world (Greenberg et al., 1986; Psychology Today, 2023).

## Discussion Questions

1 How does semiotic analysis contribute a different way of understanding messages than more quantitative methods? What different kinds of questions are asked?
2 Explain how time has been reconfigured during the pandemic and the psychological reason for this
3 Explain how Trisnavanti's (2021) study persuades viewers about three positive connotations of staying home during the pandemic.
4 Please answer the following questions after clicking the link at: 'Stay at Home' from Belfast Health and Social Care Trust at https://www.youtube.com/watch?v=R6JLomdYups

   a How do the speakers' levels of expertise influence your decision to stay at home?
   b What is your emotional reaction to the various tones of voice from these experts? Which are more convincing and why?
   c Analyze the overview shot (where we are looking down onto the various speakers who are about to talk). What impression does this angle give to the video? For example, doesit make us feel closer or more distant to the speakers?
   d How do the colors used in this video impact how much you are persuaded by this message?
   e What, if anything, would you do to improve this video and make it more persuasive?

# 7

# POSITIVE PSYCHOLOGY

## Enhancing Well-Being During COVID-19

### Chapter Learning Objectives

- Define Positive Psychology
- Discuss some of the negative impacts of the COVID-19 pandemic on well-being
- Discuss how some vulnerable populations such as the elderly and people with disability are impacted differently by the pandemic in terms of social isolation.
- Discuss some lessons from the COVID-19 pandemic that could actually promote well-being.

### Introduction

The negative impacts of the COVID-19 pandemic on mental health have been well documented (O'Connor et al., 2021; Qiu et al., 2020; Torales et al., 2020). Faulker et al.'s (2021) on-line cross-sectional survey administered to 8,425 adults living in the UK, Ireland, Australia, and New Zealand ten days to six weeks after government mandated lockdown procedures found that those who reported exercising less after restrictions were administered had poorer mental health and well-being. Dwidienawati et al.'s (2021) survey conducted in Indonesia implemented between February and March 2021 found that even one year after government mobility restrictions were enforced, people reported being less happy and satisfied with life. O'Connor et al.'s (2021) longitudinal analysis of over 3,000 adults in the UK found significant rates of suicidal thoughts, especially for young people, across the first three waves of the pandemic.

DOI: 10.4324/9781003394983-7

The pandemic, however, has also resulted in a number of positive effects on social and environmental welfare. For example, with more people staying closer to home due to stay-at-home orders being implemented across the world, there has been a dramatic reduction in certain crimes such as assault and robbery (Dazio & Tarm, 2020). There have also been significant reductions in air pollution, as has been documented by NASA satellites as much as 20–30% in several major cities around the world (NASA, 2020).

In this chapter we will review literature that shows some of the positive impacts of the COVID-19 pandemic on the populace at large. We begin with a review of studies that explore the impacts of the pandemic on vulnerable populations. This leads to a discussion of the role of emotional regulation strategies during the pandemic and its ramifications on our mental well-being. We cannot escape the restrictions that this global event has made on our world, but how do we deal with it: do we allow isolation to cause us to be depressed, or do we perceive new opportunities within these restrictions? From this, we turn our attention to discussing Positive Psychology and use it as a framework for better understanding potential positive impacts of the pandemic on our well-being.

## The Well-Being of Vulnerable Populations

Research suggests that socially vulnerable populations such as healthcare workers, front-line workers, people with disability, as well as the elderly, are also more likely to perceive greater stress as a result of greater distress from fear of contracting the virus and spreading it to family and friends (Ferreira, 2020; Waters et al., 2022). For example, in their on-line survey of 825 American adults aged 60 and older, Whitehead et al. (2021) found that feelings of loneliness, concern for others and restrictions/confinement were common stressor reported during the pandemic. The study found that the most popular sources of joy and comfort included relationships with family and friends, digital social contact, and hobbies.

Yet other studies suggest the opposite may be true and that some of these vulnerable groups may be faring better, despite the extreme distress they are facing at work during the pandemic, than we might expect. For example, in the case of healthcare workers, there is some evidence that the COVID-19 pandemic might have encouraged a type of post-traumatic growth manifested in higher appreciation for and intrinsic satisfaction in their work. Fiengold et al.'s (2022) study of healthcare workers in New York city found 76.8% of FHCWs endorsed moderate or greater post-traumatic growth; the areas in which there were the highest rates of increase included having an appreciation of life (67.0%), improved relationships (48.7%), and greater personal strength (44.1%).

Indeed, there is some evidence to suggest that the negative impacts of lockdowns on mental health are less significant than is currently believed for vulnerable groups, as well as the populace at large. For example, employing a random effects model, Prati et al.'s (2021) meta-analyses and reviews of 25 cross-sectional studies comprising over 72,000 participants with 58 effect sizes found that lockdowns had only a small impact on mental health of participants including feelings of anxiety and depression. The study also found that the negative psychological impact of COVID-19 lockdowns do not impact the mental health of all individuals in the same way and that many people are psychologically resilient to their effects (Prati et al., 2020). Using a repeated measures design with data gathered during the peak phase of the COVID-19 pandemic and compared with data taken when the lockdown was lifted, Kimhi et al. (2020) found that certain psychological attributes may help lower the negative impacts of the COVID-19 pandemic. The study conducted in Israel using a sample size of 300 found that the higher an individual's resilience and well-being, the lower their sense of danger and distress during the pandemic.

What is especially interesting about the results of this study is that the researchers note that this finding was robust *irrespective* of economic support. That is, individual resilience is present even without government support, which contradicts the finding that people cannot remain resilient after a natural disaster such as a pandemic after financial loss.

Kimhi et al. (2020) point out, that one limitation of Prati et al.'s study is that the second repeated measure results were gathered shortly after the lockdown release. For this reason, more research is needed to assess the presence of well-being and resiliency after some time has passed after lockdown measures have ceased to be implemented and people have had a chance to fully comprehend and process the ramifications of economic loss in their lives. Such a study was conducted involving surveys from three nationally representative cross-sectional studies in the Czech Republic. Winkler et al. (2021) assessed the prevalence of mental disorders (mood and anxiety disorder, alcohol related disorders and suicide risk) during the second wave of COVID-19 pandemic. This data was compared with the baseline data as well as data from the first wave of the pandemic. Their study found that the proportion of individuals experiencing at least one mental disorder was highest during the second wave of the pandemic, when compared to the baseline and the first wave of the pandemic. The study also found that younger adults, including students, who had only elementary education or had experienced financial hardship such as loss of their job, displayed disproportionally high prevalence of mental disorders suggesting that financial loss had taken a toll on people's mental health.

Clearly the literature is mixed in regard to vulnerable populations as well as the population at large with respect to well-being during the pandemic. Financial loss, no doubt has had some detrimental impacts, but why might some individuals do better? Are there coping skills or various mindsets that can be helpful when dealing with a global event such as the COVID-19 pandemic?

## The Role of Psychologically Coping Mechanisms During Covid-19

In their investigation of the potential relationship between coping strategies and psychological well-being during the pandemic, Guszkowska and Dabrowska-Zimakowska (2022) administered a general well-being index to 1,330 university students in Poland. The study found that the most commonly used strategies for coping with stress during the second wave of the pandemic included acceptance, engaging in alternative activities, active coping, as well as physical activity. Similar results were obtained by Khan et al.'s (2021) study which explored the impact of COVID-19 on psychological well-being and associated factors among the Pakistani general population. They assessed well-being using an online survey of 1,756 people. A number of coping strategies during lockdown were found to be significantly associated with mental well-being. These included spending time with loved ones, self-care activities that promoted physical health such as eating healthy food, exercising and getting sufficient sleep, spending time on hobbies and contributing in social welfare work.

## Role of Emotional Regulation Strategies During the Pandemic

In their longitudinal study, Gutiérrez-Cobo et al. (2021) explored how cognitive reappraisal and expressive suppression, which are two strategies for the regulation of our emotions, mediated the impact of engagement in pleasant activities during the COVID-19 lockdown. In their study comprising 88 participants, evaluations on emotional regulation and cognitive/affective happiness were performed. In this study frequency in engagement with pleasant activities were noted during two time points: before the COVID-19 pandemic and during the COVID-19 lockdown. According to the results of this study, cognitive reappraisal was significantly related to participating in more pleasant activities during the lockdown and these pleasant activities were also found to be related to more affective happiness during the lockdown when compared to levels of affective happiness before the pandemic had taken place. The researchers also noted an association between affective happiness and cognitive happiness. In this research the researchers found the cognitive reappraisal to be a protective factor for affective and cognitive happiness, which occurred through the mediating role of participating in enjoyable activities during lockdown.

It has been argued that the root of the mental health crisis during the pandemic is that social isolation has inhibited much of the basis of positive emotions such as joy, comfort, gratitude, love, and happiness, which are typically developed during social interaction (Yamaguchi et al., 2020). For this reason, Yamaguchi et al. (2020) have posited that we have essentially two choices: learn to endure our negative emotions or learn new ways of maintaining joy, happiness and other positive emotions during the pandemic. This has led to initiatives such Japanese musician Gen Hoshino's proposal to embellish his song, "Dancing on the Inside," through multi-modal components which involved layering sounds and images in different ways, leading to world-wide attention where people responded similarly resulting in joyful connections being established at the global level. Another example is the Nintendo Co., Ltd.'s online videogame called Animal Crossing: New Horizons in which the players go freely back and forth between each other's houses to engage in social interaction in virtual space (Strampe, 2020, as cited in Yamaguchi, 2020).

## Leisure and Well-Being: The Impacts of the COVID-19 Pandemic on Mental Health

While numerous studies have found that stay-at-home order status from the COVID-19 pandemic has had adverse and other negative impacts on daily life (Benke et al., 2020; Gratz et al., 2020; Marroquín et al., 2020) such as greater health anxiety, financial worry, and loneliness (Tull et al., 2020), other studies have found that more time at home has resulted in greater time for leisure activities which have had positive impacts on well-being. By means of a structured on-line survey conducted in Güler and Haseki (2021) found that increased culinary experiences during the COVID-19 lockdown was associated with higher levels of hedonic well-being which, in turn, may have impacted increased feelings of self-actualization and self-enrichment. Using a sample of 3,438 participants during the Spring 2020 lockdown in Czechia, Cosma et al. (2021) investigated if there was any association between leisure domains and mental well-being. The results of their study found that leisure time, whether socially active leisure or physical activity such as sports, formed the strongest positive predictors of mental well-being. More passive activities such as time spend online and time spent on electronic media was found to be negative predictors on mental well-being., Morse et al. (2021) administered an online leisure activities questionnaire and the World Health Organization Five Well-Being Index on a sample of 3,827 participants from 74 countries. Logistic regression analysis from their study found that gender, age, social distancing adherence, and employment status significantly predicted leisure engagement during the COVID-19 pandemic. The researchers noted that participation in creative activities was generally more likely to increase during this period, while the opposite was true for participation in non-creative activities. Study results also indicated that spending the same amount of time or spending more time on leisure activities significantly predicted well-being during COVID-19. More specifically, higher well-being was associated with a wide variety of leisure activities including home crafts, music, language activities as well as sports and other outdoor physical activities. The researchers concluded from their study results that participation in both physical and creative leisure activities may offer protective benefits for well-being during COVID-19.

## Positive Psychology

Positive Psychology, first introduced in 1998 by psychologist Martin Seligman, is the scientific study of what makes people happy in life, with a focus on individual as well as societal well-being (Seligman & Csikszentmihalyi, 2020). This area of psychology focuses on happiness, well-being, building on the humanistic movement pioneered by Abraham Maslow during the 1960s. One of the tenets of Positive Psychology is that times of uncertainty and transition may provide opportunities for personal growth and potentially even enhance well-being (Waters et al., 2022). Gratitude comprises a large part of this philosophy, and there is evidence to suggest that the more appreciation we have for things and people in our lives the happier we become (Seligman & Csikszentmihalyi, 2014). Given the unique ways the COVID-19 pandemic has altered our lifestyles, particularly in regards to unpredictable and prolonged social isolation from intermittent lockdowns, it easy to understand how this may impact feelings of well-being and happiness. When assessing the impact of the current pandemic on our happiness and well-being, it is important to understand our conceptualizations of these concepts. For example, according to PERMA Seligman's conceptualization of happiness, our sense of well-being is contingent on the following factors: Positive emotions, Engagement, Relationships, Meaning in life, and Achievement (under the acronym "PERMA," Seligman, 2011). Because many of the components of PERMA are context-dependent or relational, as noted by Carreno et al. (2021), people who score high on well-being according to the PERMA model may be particularly impacted by the current pandemic:

> Many people who are used to experiencing high levels of well-being (according to PERMA) can be simultaneously suffering to a great extent from the present collective crisis. For example, let us think of a person who presents high levels of PERMA components, that is, they often experience positive emotions, are highly engaged in what they do, have positive relationships, have found meaning in their life, and have achieved worthy life goals. Although these can be important factors that contribute to their well-being, it is not difficult to imagine that this person can still suffer from serious inner conflicts and distress because of confinement, trauma, worry about the future, and fear of contagion. We believe that this may be just one potential example out of millions worldwide.
>
> *(p. 2)*

In contrast to the PERMA, the concept of mature happiness is contingent upon living in harmony with the good and bad in one's life. For the reasons noted above, Carreno et al. (2021) conducted an on-line survey of 12,203 participants from 30 countries which assessed two models of happiness, namely the PERMA, and the concept of Mature Happiness as predictors of well-being during the

COVID-19 pandemic. The study found that inner happiness was a better predictor of well-being during adverse events such as the COVID-19 pandemic.

### *Could Covid-19 Promote Better Well-Being?*

As stated earlier, one of the tenets of Positive Psychology is that times of uncertainty and transition may provide opportunities for personal growth; and potentially even enhance well-being. Studies have identified positive effects of the COVID-19 pandemic in a number of areas, including, but not limited to, increased quality of leisure activities (Güler et al., 2021), positive environmental effects (El Zowalaty et al., 2020), higher quality of job satisfaction (Fiengold et al., 2021; Jain, 2020), as well as an opportunity to re-discover physical, psychological, and social resources around us and in doing so, build resilience (Yamaguchi et al., 2020). In the case of Jain's (2020) study, journalists were found to navigate their roles as educators and to provide hope without arousing undue alarm; this could certainly be interpreted as making a positive difference to their viewers. Other studies have suggested that psychological capital can have a buffering influence on the negative effects of the COVID-19 pandemic on mental health (Kim, 2020).

When the principles of Positive Psychology have been applied via intervention strategies during the COVID-19 pandemic, there is some evidence to suggest that these principles can be effectively used to improve or enhance performance during this time (Brouzos et al., 2023; van Nieuwerburgh et al., 2021). For example, Positive Psychology Coaching (PPC) is a new intervention strategy that aims to enhance well-being a central aspect of the intervention. For example, van Nieuwerburgh et al. (2023) conducted an Interpretative Phenomenological Analysis (IPA) in the UK, to examine the daily life experiences of six employees of a financial services company who received PPC during the COVID-19 pandemic while working from home. The study found that PPC can increase well-being for employees by promoting: valuing opportunity for safe reflection; increasing awareness; alleviation of negative emotions; re-energization by identifying a way forward; and renewed self-confidence.

Similar results were found in Brouzos et al.'s (2023) study in which 82 Greek adults were administered a multi-component Online Positive Psychology Intervention (OPPI) where an effort was made to improve participants' resilience and personal strengths to better cope with the negative impacts of social distancing. The results of the study showed that the intervention group exhibited greater resilience than the control group after the intervention, and also that participants in the intervention group exhibited more empathetic behaviors such as greater effort to understand others' point of view in the role of perspective taking. The researchers noted that the intervention group were better at imagining themselves in fictional situations and also felt less anxious when seeing others' hardship and personal distress, after the intervention, compared to the control group. It may be speculated that this greater ability to see and empathize with others' distress during a crisis situation may have contributed toward the intervention group's higher resilience and lower levels of anxiety and other negative mood during the pandemic.

### *The Application of PERMA to the COVID-19 Pandemic*

Waters et al. (2022) shows how the PERMA model may be applied to COVID-19 to show potential positive effects on well-being that result from uncertain times that require an even greater focus on self-care and resilience. For example, for family relationships Waters et al. (2022) noted that more time at home during the COVID-19 pandemic may strengthened family bonds with more time working from home. The increased solitary time during the pandemic may also have resulted in more time to reflect meaning more self-awareness and feelings of gratitude and appreciation for life.

## Key Lessons

This chapter discussed some of the positive impacts of the COVID-19 pandemic on society at large including impacts on our environment and our mental and emotional well-being. After exploring the impacts of the pandemic on vulnerable populations, we discussed the role of emotional regulation strategies during the pandemic and its ramifications on our mental well-being. This led to more discussion of positive and negative impacts of the COVID-19 pandemic on our mental health. The chapter concluded with a review of Positive Psychology and the application of the PERMA framework for better understanding potential positive impacts of the pandemic on our well-being.

## Bibliography

Benke, C., Autenrieth, L. K., Asselmann, E., & Pané-Farré, C. A. (2020). Lockdown, quarantine measures, and social distancing: Associations with depression, anxiety and distress at the beginning of the COVID-19 pandemic among adults from Germany. *Psychiatry Research, 293*, 113462.

Brouzos, A., Vassilopoulos, S. P., Baourda, V. C., Tassi, C., Stavrou, V., Moschou, K., & Brouzou, K. O. (2023). "Staying Home–Feeling Positive": Effectiveness of an online positive psychology group intervention during the COVID-19 pandemic. *Current Psychology, 42*(4), 2749–2761.

Burke, M. (2020). Covid-19 reduces economic activity, which reduces pollution, which saves lives. G-FEED.org. 8 March 2020. www.g-feed.com/2020/03/covid-19-reduces-economic-activity.html.

Carreno, D. F., Eisenbach, N., Perez-Escobar, J. A., & Garcia-Montes, J. M. (2021). Inner Harmony as an esssential facet of well-being: A multi-national study during the COVID-19 pandemic. *Frontiers in Psychology, 12*, 648280. doi: 10.3389/fpsyg.2021.648280

Cohen-Louck, K., & Levy, I. (2022, July 11). Happiness during a mass trauma: Predicting happiness during the COVID-19 pandemic through function, stress, anxiety, and coping. *Psychological Trauma: Theory, Research, Practice, and Policy*. Advance online publication. doi: 10.1037/tra0001314

Cosma, A., Pavelka, J., & Badura, P. (2021). Leisure time use and adolescent mental well-being: Insights from the COVID-19 Czech spring lockdown. *International Journal of Environmental Research and Public Health, 18*(23), 12812.

Dazio, S., Briceno, F., & Tarm, M. (2020). Crime drops around the world as COVID-19 keeps people inside. Associated Press. 11 April 2020. https://apnews.com/bbb7adc88d3fa067c5c1b5c72a1a8aa6.

Dwidienawati, D., Tjahjana, D., Gandasari, D., & Faisal, M. (2021). Happiness and satisfaction, one year after the COVID-19 pandemic. *Journal of Southwest Jiaotong University, 56*(2). doi: 10.35741/issn.0258–2724.56.2.10

El Zowalaty, M. E., Young, S. G., & Järhult, J. D. (2020). Environmental impact of the COVID-19 pandemic–a lesson for the future. *Infection Ecology & Epidemiology, 10*(1), 1768023.

Faulker, J., O'Brien, W. J., McGrane, B., Wadsworth, D., Batten, J., Askew, C. D., Badenhorst, C., Byrd, E., Coulter, M., Draper, N., Elliot, C., Fryer, S., Hamlin, M. J., Jakeman, J., MacKintosh, M. A., McNarry, M. A., Mitchelmore, A., Murphy, J., Ryan-Stewart, H., Saynor, Z., Schaumberg, M., Stone, K., Stoner, L., Stuart, B., & Lambrick, D. (2021). Physical activity, mental health and well-being of adults during initial COVID-19 containment strategies: A multi-country, cross-sectional analysis, *Journal of Science and Medicine in Sport, 24*, 320–326.

Ferreira, R. J., Buttell, F., & Cannon, C. (2020). COVID-19: Immediate predictors of individual resilience. *Sustainability, 12*(16), 6495. doi: 10.3390/su12166495

Fiengold, J. H., Hurtado, A., Feder, A., Peccoralo, L., Southwick, S. M., Ripp, J., & Pietzrak, R. H. (2022). Posttraumatic growth among health care workers on the frontlines of the COVID-19 pandemic. *Journal of Affective Disorders, 296*, 35–40. doi: 10.1016/j.jad.2021.09.032

Gratz, K. L., Tull, M. T., Richmond, J. R., Edmonds, K. A., Scamaldo, K. M., & Rose, J. P. (2020). Thwarted belongingness and perceived burdensomeness explain the associations of COVID-19 social and economic consequences to suicide risk. *Suicide and Life-Threatening Behavior, 50*(6), 1140–1148.

Güler, O., & Haseki, M. I. (2021). Positive psychological impacts of cooking during the COVID-19 lockdown period: A qualitative study. *Frontiers in Psychology, 12*, 635957.

Guszkowska, M., &Dąbrowska-Zimakowska, A. (2022). Coping with stress during the second wave of the COVID-19 pandemic by Polish university students: Strategies, structure, and relation to psychological well-being. *Psychology Research and Behavior Management*, 15, 339–352.

Gutiérrez-Cobo, M. J., Megías-Robles, A., Gómez-Leal, R., Cabello, R., & Fernández-Berrocal, P. (2021). Is it possible to be happy during the COVID-19 lockdown? A longitudinal study of the role of emotional regulation strategies and pleasant activities in happiness. *International Journal of Environmental Research and Public Health, 18*, 3211. doi: 10.3390/ijerph18063211

Jain, P. (2021). The COVID-19 pandemic and positive psychology: The role of news and trust in news on mental health and well-being. *Journal of Health Communication, 26*(5), 317–327.

Khan, A. A., Lodhi, F. S., Rabbani, U., Ahmed, Z., Abrar, S., Arshad, S., … & Khan, M. I. (2021). Impact of coronavirus disease (COVID-19) pandemic on psychological well-being of the Pakistani general population. *Frontiers in Psychiatry, 11*, 564364.

Kim, S. Y. (2020). A convergence study of stress caused by the epidemic of COVID-19, quality of life and positive psychological capital. *Journal of the Korea Convergence Society, 11*(6), 423–431.

Kimhi, S., Marciano, H., Eshel, Y., & Adini, B. (2020). Recovery from the COVID-19 pandemic: Distress and resilience. *International Journal of Disaster Management.* doi: 10.1016/ijdrr.2020.101843

Marroquín, B., Vine, V., & Morgan, R. (2020). Mental health during the COVID-19 pandemic: Effects of stay-at-home policies, social distancing behavior, and social resources. *Psychiatry Research, 293*, 113419.

Morse, K. F., Fine, P. A., & Friedlander, K. J. (2021). Creativity and leisure during COVID-19: Examining the relationship between leisure activities, motivations, and psychological well-being. *Frontiers in Psychology, 12*, 609967.

NASA. (2020). Airborne nitrogen dioxide plummets over China. 2 March 2020. www.earthobservatory.nasa.gov/images/146362/airborne-nitrogen-dioxide- plummets-over-china.

van Nieuwerburgh, C., Barr, M., Fouracres, A. J., Moin, T., Brown, C., Holden, C., … & Thomas, P. (2021). Experience of positive psychology coaching while working from home during the COVID-19 pandemic: An Interpretative Phenomenological Analysis. *Coaching: An International Journal of Theory, Research and Practice*, 1–18. doi: 10.1080/17521882.2021.1897637

O'Connor, R. C., Wetherall, K., Seonaid Cleare, McClelland, H., Melson, A. J.,Niedzwiedz, C. L., O'Carroll, R. E., O'Connor, D. B., Platt, S. Scowcroft, E., Watson, B., Zortea, T. Ferguson, E., & Robb, K. A. (2021). Mental health and well-being during the COVID-19 pandemic: Longitudinal analyses of adults in the UK COVID-19 Mental Health & Wellbeing study. *The British Journal of Psychiatry, 218*, 326–333. doi: 10.1192/bjp.2020.212

Palmer, S., Panchal, S., & O'Riordan, S. (2020). Could the experience of the COVID-19 pandemic have any positive impact on wellbeing? *European Journal of Applied Positive Psychology, 4*(10), 1–13. http://www.nationalwellbeingservice.org/volumes/volume-4-2020/volume-4-article-10/

Prati, G., & Mancini, A. D. (2021). The psychological impact of COVID-19 pandemic lockdowns: A review and meta-analysis of longitudinal studies and natural experiments. *Psychological Medicine, 51*, 201–211. doi: 10.1017/S003329172100001

Qiu, J., Shen, B., Zhao, M., Wang, Z., Xie, B., & Xu, Y. (2020). A nationwide survey of psychological distress among Chinese people in the COVID-19 epidemic: Implications and policy recommendations. *General Psychiatry, 33*, e100213. doi: 10.1136/gpsych-2020–100213

Seligman, M. (2011). *Flourish: A Visionary New Understanding of Happiness and Well-being*. New York: Free Press.

Seligman, M. E. P., & Csikszentmihalyi, M. (2000). Positive psychology: An introduction. *American Psychologist, 55*(1). doi: 10.1037/0003 066x.55.1.5. PMID 11392865

Seligman, M. E., & Csikszentmihalyi, M. (2014). Positive psychology: An introduction. In *Flow and the foundations of positive psychology* (pp. 279–298). Dordrecht: Springer. doi: 10.1007/978-94-017-9088-8_18

Strampe, L. (2020). Animal crossing: New horizons is the game we all need right now. Wired. Retrieved from https://www.wired.com/story/rave-animal-crossing-new-horizons/

Takiguchi, Y., Matsui, M., Kikutani, M., & Ebina, K. (2023). The relationship between leisure activities and mental health: The impact of resilience and COVID-19. *Applied Psychology: Health and Well-Being, 15*(1), 133–151.

Torales, J., O'Higgins, M., Castaldelli-Maia, J. M., & Ventriglio, A. (2020). The outbreak of COVID-19 coronavirus and its impact on global mental health. *International Journal of Social Psychiatry, 66*, 317–320.

Tull, M. T., Edmonds, K. A., Scamaldo, K. M., Richmond, J. R., Rose, J. P., & Gratz, K. L. (2020). Psychological outcomes associated with stay-at-home orders and the perceived impact of COVID-19 on daily life. *Psychiatry Research, 289*, 113098.

Waters, L., Algoe, S. B., Dutton, J., Emmons, R., Fredrickson, B. L., Heaphy, E., Moskowitz, J. T., Neff, K., Nilemiec, R., Pury, C., & Steger, M. (2020). Positive psychology in a Pandemic: Buffering, bolstering, and building mental health, *The Journal of Positive Psychology, 17*(3), 303–323.

Whitehead, B. R., & Torossian, E. (2021). Older adults' experience of the COVID-19 pandemic: A mixed-methods analysis of stresses and joys. *The Gerontologist, 61*(1), 36–47. https://doi.org/10.1093/geront/gnaa126

Winkler, P., Mohrova, Z., Mlada, K., Kuklova, M., Kagstrom, A., Mohr, P., & Formanek, T. (2021). Prevalence of current mental disorders before and during the second wave of COVID-19 pandemic: An analysis of repeated nationwide cross-sectional surveys. *Journal of Psychiatric Research, 139*, 167–171.

Yamaguchi, K., Takebayashi, Y., Miyamae, M., Komazawa, A., Yokoyama, C., & Ito, M. (2020). Role of focusing on the positive side during COVID-19 outbreak: Mental health perspective from positive psychology. *Psychological Trauma: Theory, Research, Practice, and Policy, 12*(S1), S49–S50. doi: 10.1037/tra0000807

## Glossary of Key Terms and Concepts

**Mature happiness** refers to living in harmony between with both positive and negative aspects of one's life (Seligman, 2011).

**PERMA Model** is a multidimensional questionnaire that assesses well-being through assessments of the PERMA model (**P**ositive emotion, **E**ngagement, positive Relationships, **M**eaning, and **A**ccomplishment) (Seligman, 2011).

**Positive Psychology** investigates the emotions, strengths, processes, conditions, and relationships that contribute toward the optimal functioning in people, groups, and institutions (Waters et al., 2022).

**Positive Psychology Coaching (PPC)** is a new intervention strategy that aims to enhance well-being which is a central aspect of the intervention (van Nieuwerburgh et al., 2021).

## Discussion Questions

1 How have you dealt with the COVID-19 pandemic? Are there any ways you can think of that you have experienced improvement in your life (e.g., being closer to loved ones, or other experiences?). Did you expect this when the pandemic first began? Why or why not?
2 Are you a front-line worker or know anyone who is? If so, discuss some of the unique stresses you or they have faced during the pandemic. Have you or they used any special coping strategies? Do you think those strategies have or would help?

# 8

# MOVING FORWARD

## Re-thinking Communication During and Post COVID-19 with Special Consideration to Marginalized and Vulnerable Populations

### Key Lessons

- How COVID-19 has altered communication issues for vulnerable and marginalized groups
- How the pandemic has impacted frontline healthcare workers
- How are older adults sufficiently understanding digital communications about COVID-19 to maintain social ties
- How can communicating digitally or via video (vs. face to face) impact the mental health of older adults
- How the pandemic has increased health disparities between ethnic minority groups and the population at large
- What are some ways Disability Inclusiveness Post COVID-19 can be implemented in research?
- What are some barriers faced by the transgender and non-binary communities during the COVID-19 pandemic?
- How has ableist rhetoric changed perceptions of how people with disability and/or people with underlying health conditions are more at risk of acquiring the COVID-19 virus during the beginning of the pandemic

### Introduction

There is ample evidence that minority groups already living with health inequities are unduly impacted by COVID-19 (Layton et al., 2021) and that pre-existing health disparities are worsened by COVID-19. **Marginalized Populations** are groups as well as communities of people who may experience social, political, and/or economical discrimination as a result of unequal power relationships.

DOI: 10.4324/9781003394983-8

According to the **Knowledge Gap Hypothesis** pre-existing health disparities will worsen when information flows to those in high socioeconomic status before reaching those in the lower socioeconomic status. This chapter will explore the special challenges faced by the following vulnerable and marginalized populations: frontline healthcare providers, substance abusers, incarcerated individuals, migrant workers, older adults, and people with disability and transgender/non T binary populations. Specifically, we will take an in-depth look at the concept of access: is information available and is it being understood? Are physical issues limiting the ability to find information and are cognitive issues also acting as barriers to proper information-processing (for example language barriers for migrants)? In the cases of physical and potentially psychological barriers to finding information, this chapter will explore how healthcare providers have been urged to find innovative and patient-centered ways to provide care to marginalized groups.

## Groups That Have Been Further Alienated and Marginalized

### *COVID-19 Impact on Access to Treatment Facilities for Substance Abusers*

It has been stated by scholars that the COVID-19 pandemic has urged healthcare providers to find innovative and patient-centered ways to provide care to marginalized groups such as people with addictions and other substance abuse disorders (Krawczyk et al., 2021; Narayan & Balkrishnan, 2021; Samuels et al., 2020). Over 138 million or 50.0% of people aged 12 and over have used drugs illicitly in their lifetime(NCDAS, 2023). Given the limited number of specialized COVID-19 resources in hospitals and clinics, people with addiction, who are already stigmatized and underserved by the healthcare system, have faced additional barriers to treatment since the pandemic. If we consider the reduction in hours of services in many addiction centers and rehabilitation facilities, this has resulted in additional obstacles to already limited access for people with addiction. For individuals with opioid use disorder, physical distancing and the associated social isolation can lead to fatal consequences because isolation can lead to an increased risk of death by overdose which is related to limiting access to a safe supply, as well as fewer supervised injecting sites and outpatient treatments (Vigo et al., 2020).

Given their exploration of the needs of substance abusers across the world and how different countries have found innovative ways to ensure treatment for chronic substance abusers, Dunlop et al. (2020) discuss alternative methods of ensuring access to treatment during the COVID-19 pandemic. They argue how social distancing may not be practical due to the number of patients and size of waiting areas which poses a major challenge to treatment.

Considering these issues and the availability of new long depot formulations, number of plans that will more efficiently maximize the utilization of these resources during the COVID-19 pandemic are being developed (please refer to Dunlop et al. (2020) for a detailed review of some of these considerations). Given that substance abusers face increased risk of death with reduced hours at many addiction centers Samuels et al. (2020) discuss the development of a new model use of audio-only telehealth encounters for buprenorphine induction without requiring an in-person evaluation or video interface.

In their scoping review of new services and harm reduction programs for people who use opioid (PWUOs) Krawczyk et al. (2021) employed a narrative synthesis approach to identify major themes around key service modifications and innovations implemented across programs serving PWUO. Their review found that innovative service modifications to adapt to COVID-19 circumstances typically comprised further employment of tele-health services, virtual individual or group therapy sessions, greater availability of donated or publicly available phones. The study also found beneficial effects of home delivery of services as they increased outreach and temporary services for delivering MOUD and naloxone, and the provision of a safe supply of opioid.

### *COVID-19 Impact on Reduced Communication with Family for Incarcerated Individuals*

The COVID-19 pandemic has undoubtedly wreaked havoc on structurally vulnerable populations (James et al., 2022) and there is ample evidence of the detrimental impacts of lockdown related restrictions on the mental and physical health of incarcerated individuals (Garrihy et al., 2023; James et al., 2022; Johnson et al., 2021; Kim et al., 2022; Song et al., 2023).

Ample studies suggest a strong association between social support and reduced recidivism for incarcerated individuals (Bales & Mears, 2008; Breese et al., 2000; Cochran, 2014; Dallaire et al., 2021). This leads to the question of what happens when COVID-19 measures restrict family visits, and the potential impacts on future violent behaviors.

By promoting stronger social bonds between incarcerated individuals and their family members, video visitations show promise, for building and maintaining relationships during incarceration (Skora Horgan & Poehlmann-Tynan, 2020). For incarcerated parents, it is believed that frequent, high-quality parent–child interactions are critical in preventing recidivism in addition to being beneficial for the healthy development of children with parents in prison (Muñiz et al., 2024). Some studies have found that enabling video visitations for families of incarcerated individuals allowed families to stay connected. For example, Muñiz et al. (2024) gathered publicly available information related to each of the US's 50 states regarding COVID-19 safety protocols and prison visitation policies and found 39 states offered video visits as an alternatives in this way, providing the need for safe, accessible, and family-friendly alternatives to in-person visits.

In their mixed-design study, Charles et al. (2022) collected qualitative and quantitative data for 33 adults, the majority Black Americans, in mid-sized county jails. The study found that a number of pandemic-related changes including the use of segregation, delayed court proceedings, inadequate health responses, and suspended programming and visits with limited contact alternatives. The researchers noted that this may have resulted in the depleted mental health of incarcerated individuals further contributing to strained family relations as well as feelings of isolation and concerns for the well-being of family members.

### *The Impact of COVID-19 on Front-Line Workers*

The detrimental impacts of the COVID-19 pandemic on frontline workers have been well documented and includes but is not limited to a rise in feelings of depression (Gilleen et al., 2021), loneliness (Kotera et al., 2022), anxiety and distress (Vindrola-Padros et al., 2020) and insomnia (Hassinger et al., 2022). Frontline workers (FLW) have been at increased risk of mortality from contracting the virus (Jackson et al., 2020) as well as facing increased workloads and shortage of PPEs in addition to greater harassment during work (Green et al., 2020).

Resiliency has been argued to safeguard against negative psychological effects from the COVID-19 pandemic (Huffman et al., 2021). Despite their increased vulnerability, studies have identified ways FLWs have adopted coping skills and have built resiliency during the pandemic. For example, thematic analysis of Jordan et al.'s (2022) structural interviews of 18 front-line healthcare workers identified the need for more timely, accurate and transparent communication as healthcare professionals reported facing new patient safety and communication challenges during the pandemic. Munawar and Choudry's (2021) study of FLW's coping strategies in Pakistan identified media to be a source of stress, whereas religious coping and a desire to serve one's country were reported to be effective manners of coping with the stresses of the pandemic. Religious coping by FLW as well as coping through situation acceptance and peer support were also found in Taremwa et al.'s (2023) study conducted in Uganda.

### *Migrant and Ethnic Minority Populations*

The COVID-19 pandemic has increased health disparities between ethnic groups and the population at large. Ethnic minorities in most countries such as Black and Hispanic populations in the US are at a particular disadvantage as many already assume the status of a marginalized group (Garcia et al., 2021; Laurencin & McClinton, 2020). The underlying factors that contribute to health disparities are complex and include social and structural determinants of health, racism and discrimination, economic and educational disadvantages, biological and individual factors as well as access to quality healthcare (Hooper et al., 2020).

Studies have shown that poor communication is a barrier for many migrants and ethnic minorities that impacts vaccine uptake hesitancy (Abba et al., 2020). Language barriers have been found to be in particular problematic (Abba-Aji et al., 2022; Bhandari et al., 2021). Deal et al. (2021)'s UK study of 32 migrants comprising refugees, asylum seekers, undocumented migrants as well as migrants with limited leave to remain from 15 different countries found that participants communicated concerns reflecting lack of knowledge about vaccines. These concerns included information about vaccine content, side-effects, lack of accessible information in an appropriate language. The study also found some participants reported being concerned about getting vaccinated as they worried about the cost and also facing immigration checks. In other words, there was a worry about how to access vaccines and being assured this would not lead to immigration checks. The researchers noted that one way to address vaccine hesitancy issues such as insufficient awareness about relevant access points and information about entitlement would be to create more tailored information campaigns that are clear, accessible that are preferably delivered by trusted sources within marginalized, migrant communities

In the case of groups dealing with language barriers, another question of interest is where are these groups getting information about the COVID-19 vaccine? Roble et al.'s (2022) study of Swedish immigrants with limited proficiency in Swedish found that immigrants were primarily using school, social media, and the media (at large) for their primary sources of information and that there is a need to improve how health communications reach people in the entire nature.

Let us look at some of the challenges faced by Indigenous People during COVID-19 in the case study below.

## CASE STUDY: INDIGENOUS PEOPLE AND COVID-19

Historically, Indigenous Peoples have suffered higher infection rates, and more severe symptoms and death than the general population, across the world, due to a number of factors including the effects of colonization (Hillier et al., 2020), as well as the powerful forces of the social and cultural determinants of health and lack of political power (Power et al., 2020). Angela Nodin offers a first-hand account of some of the experiences of Indigenous

Peoples during the COVID-19 pandemic, which may help us to better understand some of the unique challenges faced by this population:

> In Whites and First Nation, health coordinator Angela Nodin is doing her best to support members of her community who are self-isolating, including those who live off-reserve.
>
> Nodin sent her children into the bush with her parents when she feared she had come into close contact with COVID-19 as a front-line worker. After that scare, the band council issued a notice to end social gatherings. Nodin took her van and blocked off the road to the community and recorded a message urging members to stay home.
>
> But Nodin felt she couldn't ask people to self-isolate, on or off the reserve, without also offering supports like food hampers and cleaning supplies. The band bought a cow and a pig to help see the community through. Nodin sent hunters to the land to catch moose, fishermen to Lake Nipigon, and medicine pickers to gather cedar, Labrador tea and other traditional medicines. "We've been able to send three shipments of fresh lake trout and whitefish to our members in Thunder Bay," Nodin says.
>
> The band has also offered incentives for children to stay home, including by distributing craft supplies and hosting an online puppet show competition. Nodin reminds people to use 24-hour helplines and online supports and has talked with people about their concerns, sometimes until the early hours of the morning"
>
> (Banning, 2020, pp. E787–E788).

Pickering et al. (2023) conducted a scoping review of the state of understanding of the experiences of Indigenous Peoples during the first 18 months of the COVID-19 pandemic. Their review explored how COVID-19 is impacting the health and livelihoods of Indigenous peoples, the kinds of system level challenges Indigenous peoples are and how Indigenous peoples are responding. The kinds of system level challenges found in this review included those which impacted exposure and livelihoods such as ecological, poverty, communication challenges, as well as challenges regarding education and healthcare services. A chronic challenge found in this study was inadequate access to healthcare as was poor communication strategies about COVID-19 prevention in Indigenous languages that were also culturally appropriate.

## People with Disabilities

'Disablism' may be defined as discourses and practices that exclude, discriminate against, and/or otherwise oppress people with disability (Rotarou et al., 2021). There are currently over one billion people with disabilities world-wide (Banks et al., 2021). Individuals with disabilities are defined as people with long-term physical, mental, intellectual, or sensory impairments, which may hinder these individuals' full and effective participation in society on an equal basis with others when interacting with various barriers (OHCHR, 2006). Scholars have cautioned to not ignore the needs of people with disability during the pandemic (Kuper et al., 2020). **Direct Disability Inclusive Measures** attempt to ensure the well-being of people with a disability from the impact of the pandemic (Rotarou et al., 2021). **Indirect Disability Inclusive Measures** the purpose of indirect measures is to protect the general population, and in this manner, people with disabilities are included as well, from the impact of the pandemic (Rotarou et al., 2021).

Three risks typically faced, to a higher degree, by people with disabilities during the COVID-19 pandemic include a greater risk of contracting the disease, of developing a severe form of the disease which may lead to death, and of new or worsening health conditions as a result of contracting the virus (Pearce et al., 2022).

In the sections to follow we will review a few of the issues faced by people with disabilities during the COVID-19 pandemic.

### *Older Adults*

Disability scholars have argued that some of the earliest reporting of the pandemic by mainstream media employed an ableist rhetoric where the disease primarily impacted people with preexisting medical conditions and older adults, and not much has changed since that time (Goggin, 2020). The impact of the COVID-19 pandemic has not been equally distributed across all populations, indeed, an important impact on vulnerable subpopulations, includes the older adults some of whom have previous health conditions (Liu et al., 2020). Skalaka and Pajestka (2021) conducted a study on the living situation of older adults (aged $\geq$ 60 years) during the later stages of the pandemic and found that in-person communication was more beneficial to the mental health in people aged more than digital communication. The study also found that the older the individual, the less beneficial digital communication was for their mental health, especially during interactions with their children.

Another study conducted by Banovic et al. (2022) found that while the older adults are using digital technologies, they are for the most part, dissatisfied with their skills in using digital technologies. The researchers found that most of the information during the COVID-19 pandemic was provided to older adults via television and telephone (video) conversations with family members and friends. Further, the study found that 57.7% of older adults stated that they very much missed direct communication; and as many as 4/5 of the respondents in this study reported feelings of anxiety, fear, loneliness, and depression. However, given this study was conducted in Bosnia, it would be interesting to explore if similar results are obtained in other countries across the world.

### *The Hearing Impaired*

People with hearing impairment have faced a host of communication-related challenges during the COVID-19 pandemic, including the use of masks and other protective equipment which reduce speech volume, and difficulty in seeing and reading nonverbal cues during communication (Cox et al., 2021). Jansen et al. (2022) evaluated the impact of COVID-19 preventative measures on hearing and communication among individuals with normal and impaired hearing. Their study found that participants with poor and insufficient hearing had more difficulty understanding other people sufficiently through masks, behind plastic screens, and from a one and a half meter distance, compared to those with good hearing.

Yap et al. (2020) explored, by means of a virtual audit, if pandemic related press briefings and press conferences issued by governments and international organizations to assess if information dispersion about the pandemic were inclusive to the hearing-impaired communities in low- and middle-income countries(LMICs). COVID-19 press conferences and press briefings issued during the second to fifth months of 2020, for over 123 LMICs and for international organizations were analyzed. The findings suggested that only 65% of countries had a sign language interpreter (SLI) who was present during COVID-19 press briefings and conferences, with smaller percentages found in low-income countries and Sub-Saharan African countries. Another study exploring the concept of inclusion in terms of the COVID-19 pandemic's impact on hearing impaired adults, children, and their families in Ghana was conducted by Swanwick et al. (2020) who found that the pandemic deepened societal inclusion for hearing impaired adults and their families. The study found that fear was overwhelmingly associated with lack of access and understanding information about the pandemic. Further, the study found sign language announcements were not sufficient for in-depth understanding of COVID-19 and how one protects themself from the virus.

In order to ascertain the experiences of people with **functional disabilities** defined as difficulties performing daily living tasks, during the first wave of the COVID-19 lockdown Hall et al. (2022) analyzed the first 100 comments regarding functional disability and COVID-19 published on VICE's YouTube channel. During the time the study was conducted, the video had over 600 comments and over 700K views. The study identified four themes including isolation and lifestyle changes, difficulty accessing healthcare and other services, mental health consequences and peer support.

Test yourself: *How do the results of Hall et al.'s (2022) study suggest that social support systems may need to be improved for people with disabilities even in developed countries? What are some considerations that need to be taken?*

### *The Visually Impaired*

Currently more than 260 million people with moderate to severe visual impairments of BVI throughout the world were at an increased risk during the COVID-19 pandemic (Orbis, 2021). Specifically, individuals with visual impairments (i.e., people who are blind or have low vision) have several additional complications: (1) greater vulnerability to being infected by the disease, (2) more difficulties implementing preventive strategies against COVID-19 and also need to implement additional strategies, and (3) may have more mental health problems due to COVID-19 and its consequences (Jondani, 2021). Indeed, there are ample studies suggesting the greater barriers visually impaired people face accessing important pandemic-related information, as well as accessing healthcare and other important services (Battistin et al., 2021; Senjam, 2020; Siu et al., 2021).

Let us explore some of the special everyday challenges faced by BVI people:

**CASES STUDY OF BVI PERSON DURING COVID-19 (SOURCE: ADAPTED FROM RIZZO ET AL., 2021)**

The Coronavirus environment had made many everyday behaviors for BVI individuals dangerous for themselves and others. For example, let us consider the case of physical contact and proximity as illustrated by a trip to the store.

In this case study 'Caitlin' who is BVI, visits a store where her primary manner of navigation is through touch and exploration through her hand. When opening a door, a sighted person might open the door with their elbow (or other body regions) and/or wear gloves thereby lowering risk for virus spread. However, given gloves lower tactile perception, this may not be a practical option for someone who is visually impaired. If the handle cannot be seen, it is even more difficult for a visually impaired person to open the door with their hands.

### *People with Disability and Accessible Healthcare*

Ned et al. (2020) argue that both inaccessible healthcare systems and the presence of underlying health conditions have put people with disabilities at additional risk and highlight a number of key considerations demonstrating the vulnerability of people with disability in the context of the COVID-19 pandemic. These risks include greater vulnerability to contracting COVID-19 especially in cases comprising under-resourced health systems, as well as more difficulty accessing health services. For example, people with disabilities often have difficulty accessing routine medical and rehabilitation services with critical care resources such as intensive care unit (ICU) beds and ventilators as they are limited resources during emergency events. During a disaster event, individuals with disabilities also typically have greater difficulty accessing health information and communication on prevention measures during when information is not in accessible format. There is also the issue of facing unequal access to water, sanitation and hygiene facilities, for this reason, for some individuals with disabilities, social distancing and isolation may be not be a realistic option. This may be even more true for people who live in residential institutions and/or are dependent on personal care-takers. As a result, for certain people with pre-existing mental health conditions, other health conditions may become prevalent among people with disabilities during the COVID-19 pandemic. Finally, for some people with disabilities who have become unemployed during the pandemic, pre-existing conditions may worsen the cycle of poverty and disability during the pandemic.

### *Government Measures to Promote Disability Inclusiveness*

As previously discussed, governments across the world have created measures to protect the rights and well-being of people with disability during the COVID-19 pandemic (Aboagye et al., 2022; Colon-Cabrera et al., 2021; Rotarou et al., 2021; Sakellariou et al., 2020). Here we explore a self-initiated case study of a disability support network in China to better understand the coordination process as well as impacts of having a family member with a disability during the pandemic and attending to special needs.

#### FIGURE CASE STUDY OF SELF-INITIATED DISABILITY SUPPORT NETWORK IN CHINA

This Case Study reports the key findings of a self-initiated Disability Support Network conducted in China by Dai and Hu (2022) which demonstrates the communication difficulties experienced by people with disabilities in emergency situations. The study employed a WeChat ethnography research method. Data were collected from both participant-observation in the online chat rooms and semi-structured interviews with Network participants. COVID-19 related information was provided in different accessible formats including sign language videos and screen-readable text. Twelve support plans were also compiled and provided for the larger disability community based on communal needs. Each support plan was a step-by-step guide to address a specific issue faced by people with disability based on their real-life experiences.

In this study, the Network connected approximately 190 volunteers domestically and internationally, among which half were persons with disabilities and family members of people with disability. The Network included the diverse needs of the community, including the issues faced by women with disabilities and local hearing impaired people and older adults. People with disabilities in the Network were in full action mode, from coordination and distribution of feminine hygiene products, to transportation and dissemination of protective supplies to serve other disability community members. (Dai & Hu, 2022).

### *Challenges of Disability Data and the Need for More Inclusive Research Methods*

**Direct Disability Inclusive Measures** attempt to ensure the well-being of people with disability from the impact of the pandemic (Rotarou et al., 2021). As it has been stated that the COVID-19 pandemic has impacted the inner equilibrium, outer relations as well as the overall societal systems of countries around the world, it seems appropriate to consider a **Systems Thinking (ST) approach** understood to comprise a set of synergistic analytic skills working together as a system that are employed to improve the capability of identifying and understanding systems, as well as predicting their behaviors, and devising modifications to them in order to produce desired effects (Arnold & Wade, 2017) which helps to provide insight into response patterns where a system is considered to compromise interrelated components, as opposed to responses impacting only isolated components (Jesus et al., 2020). Indeed, it is for this reason, among many, that the ST lens has been increasingly adopted to identify and solve complex challenges in global public health (Chughtai & Blanchet, 2017; Leischow et al., 2008), health policy and healthcare transitions for youth (Hamdani et al., 2021) and rehabilitation (Abboudi et al., 2022; Jesus et al., 2022).

## Impacts of COVID-19 on the Well-Being and Access to Healthcare for Transgender and Binary Populations

A number of studies have identified negative impacts of the COVID-19 pandemic on the mental health and access to healthcare for binary and transgender populations (Burgess et al., 2021; Radusky et al., 2021; Wang et al., 2020). By means of an online survey conducted on 182 participants, Radusky et al. (2021)

explored self-reported changes in mental health, substance use, experiences of violence, and access to healthcare and basic services among transgender and non-binary populations in Argentina. Transmasculine (TM) and Nonbinary (NB) participants reported higher frequencies of intense negative emotions and suicidal thoughts than the other groups. The study also found that Transfeminine (TF) participants reported a greater proportion of negative changes in the socioeconomic factors in their lives, including losses in income and barriers in accessing basic services including food, housing, hygiene products, and financial help.

## Applying Communication Principles to Creating More Inclusive Digital Technologies

Employing a sample comprising 35 men and boys, and 38 women and girls, from infants to people over 90 years of age, Layton et al. (2020) conducted a thematic analysis of the experiences of assistive technology (AT) users pre and post COVID-19. In addition to exploring the experiences of AT users during the COVID-19 pandemic in relation to AT access and service delivery, the study also investigated how the COVID-19 pandemic may have played a role in strengthening AT systems.

Analyses of narratives from this study suggested that the experiences of AT users during the COVID-19 pandemic could be categorized under the themes of feeling excluded from pandemic responses, feeling that governments did not perceive AT services to be essential and feeling an underlying weakness of the AT systems themselves. Respondents spoke about a number of ideas and solutions, which contributed to a set of recommendations for strengthening AT systems. From this a subtheme was found regarding enabling technologies to create inclusion. Communication technology, in essence, allowed AT users with physical restrictions to more effectively participate in community, social and civic life.

> All the services that were meaningful to me were all closed. However, my exercise physiologist and my drama group started to offer video link appointments or group activities. I did not have the technology or internet to access these, and I needed help to learn how to use this … I was still able to participate in my drama group sessions with my classmates, friends and trainers through a virtual environment. It is undoubtedly true that this iPad and internet connection, has become an important part of my daily activities since the beginning of the pandemic. I believe having a stable and economical internet plan is essential for me to fully participate in meaningful activities and essential services."
>
> *(SU66, Australia, p. 13)*

For some respondents, AT created new opportunities, such as learning new skills in the online environment,

> The self-isolation impacted me positively because I could explore calls via Zoom and Teams. Using Teams, Zoom, and headphones enables me to focus more on my speech, and understand people clearly. Online calls have actually proved to be an advantage because I must rely on just one sense-hearing. This has made me more sensitive and empathetic to others' voices, honing my abilities along the way.
>
> *(SU13, UK, p. 13)*

In other cases, some AT users had specific needs in relation to digital technologies, such as one person living with hearing loss who described exclusion they experienced with a shift to an online environment,

> During COVID I reduced my participation in [classroom competitions] as it becomes a bit difficult to communicate effectively over a call as compared to communication in person.... Access to good internet service helped, also, I am a persistent person, I don't give up easily
>
> *(SU10, India, p. 13)*

Another woman with hearing loss was able to coordinate Muslim women's group in the UK states,

> I have tried to keep my Muslim Group going as many really wanted support. Possibly no one really thought how much we rely on AT until we have these restrictions—it certainly made me think once my hearing started to deteriorate; I just need to be patient to get the new equipment. With hearing aids and the hearing clinic I can run my home, engage in discussions and online meetings with my hearing aids-otherwise I would not be able to be active.
>
> *(SU06, UK, p. 14)*

Overall, the researchers acknowledged the opportunity to rebuild and improve systems through co-creation between AT service users and service providers to be an empowering outcome

> Test yourself: *How has technology helped to empower some of the people you know who may have been more isolated during the pandemic due to physical limitations in accessing the outside world during the pandemic? In particular, older adults or people with disability you may know?*

## Future Directions for Disability Inclusive Research

People with disabilities have been underrepresented in research and this underrepresentation has magnified since the pandemic given additional concerns regarding the accessibility of technology and tools for remote data collection, as well as the challenge of recruiting difficult-to-reach populations (Banks et al., 2022). A study conducted in the UK by Kuper et al. (2020) stated that the right to healthcare for people with disability is a right that must be protected within the COVID-19 pandemic, and is a right that is non-negotiable. He recommended that greater effort be placed by scholars to disability-inclusive responses are included in the planning stage which will require consultation with people with disability and their supporters, leadership at policy and program level, and realistic levels of funding. They further recommend the tracking of differences between people with disability and able-bodied individuals, given the usefulness of this information in the identification of differences in contracting the virus, becoming critically ill or dying between the two populations for disability-inclusive planning and data collection. The authors also recommend the use of large-scale qualitative studies, in which individuals with various types of impairment can be included.

Using the experience of research teams working on disability-focused studies across ten different countries Banks et al. (2022) overview a number of key challenges, strategies and opportunities for academics interested in conducting disability-inclusive research during the pandemic, some of which are listed below:

- Adapting informed consent to potentially include oral consent in addition to written consent.
- Instruct data collectors to assess the capability of a person with disability to give consent rather than rely on the reports of others, including family members or friends of the disabled person.
- In the case of sensitive topics, carefully consider how much information about the topic will be given to caregivers.
- In the case of remote data collection, consider that certain manners of data gathering such as through phone calls may not be completely confidential. This will be even more challenging for sensitive topics (this may require asking for additional information only if the participant is in a private space at the time).
- Be aware of the limitations of remote data collection. For example, access to mobile phones may be limited for people with disability living in poverty or older individuals with disabilities who may not have access to smart phones. In certain cases, alternative technologies such as video calls through another platform may be needed.

## Key Lessons

The COVID-19 pandemic has further marginalized vulnerable populations in our society. In this chapter we explored some of the ways certain groups such as older adults, people with disability, incarcerated individuals and individuals with substance use disorder have been further disadvantaged by the pandemic and proactive steps that can be taken to empower these groups with improved access to facilities that will support their unique healthcare needs.

Our review of the special needs of substance abusers, suggested serious consideration for re-designing services that are more accessible during the pandemic. Given the dangers of withdrawal, as well as the risk of confusing symptoms of withdrawal with signs of acquiring the COVID-19 virus, more attention needs to be focused on the needs of this marginalized group in society.

When reviewed how the lives of people with long-term incarcerations have changed with the pandemic, we found literature that discusses the impact of maintaining visitations during time spent in prison with lowering recidivism rates. While the majority of the studies reviewed were conducted in the US, it can still be extrapolated that a number of pandemic-related changes including reduced number of visits and reduced contact alternatives had negative impacts on incarcerated individuals' mental health and may potentially impact future recidivism.

The older adults were found to have difficulty understanding some of the information presented to the public at large concerning the COVID-19 virus. This brings to question if the older adults are sufficiently empowered to act upon the knowledge they have acquired or need special coaching or other types of assistance to better access and understand available information. As social ties were heavily impacted by altered modes of communication during the pandemic, mostly virtually based, this was also found to negatively impact the mental health of many older adults.

Our review of people with disability identified a number of issues related to accessing current information about the pandemic made available to the public, For example, many telemedicine platforms, which during the pandemic, are in some cases the only means (vs. an alternative to accessing healthcare) may not have custom features to facilitate healthcare communications for individuals with hearing and vision impairments or for persons with cognitive disabilities (Annaswamy et al., 2020). The hearing-impaired were found to face a number of challenges when communicating during the pandemic, as many PPE such as masks impair the ability to lip read, which can be a primary manner of interacting with non-hearing impaired people.

As in the case with other marginalized groups, it was found that many transgender/non-binary populations faced increased stigmatization and discrimination during the COVID-19 pandemic. This was evinced in increased barriers to basic services, loss of income and negative impacts on mental health such as feelings of depression and anxiety.

The chapter concluded with a discussion of more inclusive steps that can be taken in disability research and how communication principles can be applied to public health messages about the pandemic that can more effectively reach these vulnerable groups.

## Bibliography

Abba-Aji, M., Stuckler, D., Galea, S., & McKee, M. (2022). Ethnic/racial minorities' and migrants' access to COVID-19 vaccines: A systematic review of barriers and facilitators. *Journal of Migration and Health*, *5*, 100086.

Abboudi, C., Maignant, G., & Choplin, A. (2022). Systems thinking epistemological underpinnings of practice among rehabilitation professionals: Case study of the major text of a French physiotherapy founder. *Systems Research and Behavioral Science*, *39*(4), 824–839.

Aboagye, E. M., Mensah, F., Owusu, N. O., Effah, K. O., & Erzuah, M. (2022). Disability inclusiveness in Covid-19 pandemic policies in West Africa: "Are we left behind?" *Cogent Social Sciences*, *8*(1), 2079803.

Annaswamy, T. M., Verduzco-Gutierrez, M., & Frieden, L. (2020). Telemedicine barriers and challenges for persons with disabilities: COVID-19 and beyond. *Disability and Health Journal*, *13*(4), 100973.

Arnold, R. D., & Wade, J. P. (2015). A definition of systems thinking: A systems approach. *Procedia Computer Science*, *44*, 669–678.

Bales, W. D., & Mears, D. P. (2008). Inmate social ties and the transition to society: Does visitation reduce recidivism? *Journal of Research in Crime and Delinquency*, *45*(3), 287–321.

Banks, L. M., Davey, C., Shakespeare, T., & Kuper, H. (2021). Disability-inclusive responses to COVID-19: Lessons learnt from research on social protection in low-and middle- income countries. *World Development*, *137*, 105178.

Banks, L. M., Willan, S., Inglis-Jassiem, G., Dunkle, K., Ganle, J., Shakespeare, T., … &Hanass-Hancock, J. (2022). Adapting disability research methods and practices during the covid-19 pandemic: Experiences from the field. *IDS Bulletin*, *53*(3), 129–152.

Banning, J. (2020). How Indigenous people are coping with COVID-19. https://www.cmaj.ca/content/192/27/E787

Battistin, T., Mercuriali, E., Zanardo, V., Gregori, D., Lorenzoni, G., Nasato, L., & Reffo, M. E. (2021). Distance support and online intervention to blind and visually impaired children during the pandemic COVID-19. *Research in Developmental Disabilities*, *108*, 103816.

Banovic, S., Sinanovic, O., Jankovic, S., Patkovic, N., & Smajlovic, S. (2022). Communication of the elderly during the COVID-19 pandemic. *Acta Informatica Medica*, *30*(4), 324.

Bhandari, D., Kotera, Y., Ozaki, A., Abeysinghe, S., Kosaka, M., & Tanimoto, T. (2021). COVID-19: Challenges faced by Nepalese migrants living in Japan. *BMC Public Health*, *21*(1), 1–14.

Breese, J. R., Ra'el, K., & Grant, G. K. (2000). No place like home: A qualitative investigation of social support and its effects on recidivism. *Sociological Practice*, *2*, 1–21.

Burgess, C. M., Batchelder, A. W., Sloan, C. A., Ieong, M., & Streed, C. G. (2021). Impact of the COVID-19 pandemic on transgender and gender diverse health care. *The Lancet Diabetes & Endocrinology*, *9*(11), 729–731.

Centre for Population Health. (2018). *NSW clinical guidelines: Treatment of opioid dependence GL2018_019*. North Sydney: NSW Ministry of Health.

Charles, P., Muentner, L., Jensen, S., Packard, C., Haimson, C., Eason, J., & Poehlmann-Tynan, J. (2022). Incarcerated during a pandemic: Implications of COVID-19 for jailed individuals and their families. *Corrections*, *7*(5), 357–368.

Chughtai, S., & Blanchet, K. (2017). Systems thinking in public health: A bibliographic contribution to a meta-narrative review. *Health Policy and Planning*, *32*(4), 585–594.

Cochran, J. C. (2014). Breaches in the wall: Imprisonment, social support, and recidivism. *Journal of Research in Crime and Delinquency*, *51*(2), 200–229.

Colon-Cabrera, D., Sharma, S., Warren, N., & Sakellariou, D. (2021). Examining the role of government in shaping disability inclusiveness around COVID-19: A framework analysis of Australian guidelines. *International Journal for Equity in Health*, *20*, 1–11.

Cox, A., Iedema, R., Li, S., Sabbe, M., Salaets, H., & Dauby, N. (2021). Adding barriers to barriers during the COVID-19 pandemic: A call for interdisciplinary research on communication with migrant patients in the emergency department. *European Journal of Emergency Medicine*, *28*(1), 5–6.

Dallaire, D. H., Shlafer, R. J., Goshin, L. S., Hollihan, A., Poehlmann-Tynan, J., Eddy, J. M., & Adalist-Estrin, A. (2021). COVID-19 and prison policies related to communication with family members. *Psychology, Public Policy, and Law*, *27*(2), 231.

Dai, R., & Hu, L. (2022). Inclusive communications in COVID-19: A virtual ethnographic study of disability support network in China. *Disability & Society*, *37*(1), 3–21.

Deal, A., Hayward, S. E., Huda, M., Knights, F., Crawshaw, A. F., Carter, J., … & Hargreaves, S. (2021). Strategies and action points to ensure equitable uptake of COVID-19 vaccinations: A national qualitative interview study to explore the views of undocumented migrants, asylum seekers, and refugees. *Journal of Migration and Health*, *4*, 100050.

Dunlop, A., Lokuge, B., Masters, D., Sequeira, M., Saul, P., Dunlop, G., & Maher, L. (2020). Challenges in maintaining treatment services for people who use drugs during the COVID-19 pandemic. *Harm Reduction Journal*, *17*(1), 1–7.

Duwe, G., & McNeeley, S. (2021). Just as good as the real thing? The effects of prison video visitation on recidivism. *Crime & Delinquency*, *67*(4), 475–497.

Etti, M., Fofie, H., Razai, M., Crawshaw, A. F., Hargreaves, S., & Goldsmith, L. P. (2021). Ethnic minority and migrant underrepresentation in Covid-19 research: Causes and solutions. *EClinicalMedicine*, *36*, 100903. doi: 10.1016/j.eclinm.2021.100903

Friedman, C., & Owen, A. L. (2017). Defining disability: Understandings of and attitudes towards ableism and disability. *Disability Studies Quarterly*, *37*(1). doi: 10.18061/dsq.v37i1.5061

Garcia, M. A., Homan, P. A., García, C., & Brown, T. H. (2021). The color of COVID-19: Structural racism and the disproportionate impact of the pandemic on older Black and Latinx adults. *The Journals of Gerontology: Series B*, *76*(3), e75–e80.

Garrihy, J., Marder, I., &Gilheaney, P. (2023). 'Cocooning' in prison during COVID-19: Findings from recent research in Ireland. *European Journal of Criminology*, *20*(3), 996–1015.

Gaziano, C. (2017). Knowledge gap: History and development. In: Roessler P. (Ed.), *The International Encyclopedia of Media Effects* (pp. 840–850). London: Wiley-Blackwell.

Gilleen, J., Santaolalla, A., Valdearenas, L., Salice, C., & Fusté, M. (2021). Impact of the COVID-19 pandemic on the mental health and well-being of UK healthcare workers. *BJPsych Open*, *7*, e88.

Goggin, G., & Ellis, K. (2020). Disability, communication, and life itself in the COVID-19 pandemic. *Health Sociology Review*, *29*(2), 168–176.

Gonzales, M. (2020). *Systems thinking for supporting students with special needs and disabilities*. New York: Springer Publishing. doi: 10.1007/978–981-33-4558-4_18.

Green, D., Fateen, D., Gupta, T., McHale, T., & Nelson, R. (2020). Mishori Providing women's health care during COVID-19: Personal and professional challenges faced by health workers. *International Journal of Gynecology & Obstetrics*, *151*(1), 3–6.

Hall, K. A., Deusdad, B., D'Hers Del Pozo, M., & Martínez-Hernáez, Á. (2022). How did people with functional disability experience the first COVID-19 lockdown? A thematic analysis of youtube comments. *International Journal of Environmental Research and Public Health*, *19*(17), 10550.

Hamdani, Y., Jetha, A., & Norman, C. (2011). Systems thinking perspectives applied to healthcare transition for youth with disabilities: A paradigm shift for practice, policy and research. *Child: Care, Health and Development*, *37*(6), 806–814.

Hassinger, A. B., Breuer, R. K., & Mishra, A. (2022). Sleep patterns of US healthcare workers during the first wave of the COVID-19 pandemic. *Sleep and Breathing= Schlaf & Atmung*, *26*(3), 1351–1361. doi: 10.1007/s11325-021-02515-9.

Hillier, S. A., Chaccour, E., Al-Shammaa, H., & Vorstermans, J. (2020). Canada's response to COVID-19 for indigenous peoples: A way forward? *Canadian Journal of Public Health*, *111*(6), 1000–1001.

Hooper, M. W., Nápoles, A. M., & Pérez-Stable, E. J. (2020). COVID-19 and racial/ethnic disparities. *Jama*, *323*(24), 2466–2467.

Huffman, E. M., Athanasiadis, D. I., Anton, N. E., Haskett, L. A., Doster, D. L., Stefanidis, D., & Lee, N. K. (2021). How resilient is your team? Exploring healthcare providers' well- being during the COVID-19 pandemic. *The American Journal of Surgery*, *221*(2), 277–284.

Jackson, D., Anders, R., Padula, W. V., Daly, J., & Davidson, P. M. (2020). Vulnerability of nurses and physicians with COVID-19: Monitoring and surveillance needed. *Journal of Clinical Nursing*, *29*(19–20), 3584–3587.

James, J. E., Riddle, L., & Perez-Aguilar, G. (2022). "Prison life is very hard and it's made harder if you're isolated": COVID-19 risk mitigation strategies and the mental health of incarcerated women in California. *International Journal of Prisoner Health*, *19*, (–1), 95–108. doi: 10.1108/IJPH-09-2021-0093

Jansen, L. A., van Wier, M. F., Lissenberg-Witte, B. I., & Kramer, S. E. (2022). A comparison of the impact of the COVID-19 pandemic on communication among individuals with and without hearing impairment. *International Journal of Audiology*, *63*(3), 182–189. doi: 10.1080/14992027.2022.2152742.

Jesus, T. S., Landry, M. D., & Jacobs, K. (2020). A 'new normal'following COVID-19 and the economic crisis: Using systems thinking to identify challenges and opportunities in disability, telework, and rehabilitation. *Work*, *67*(1), 37–46.

Johnson, L., Gutridge, K., Parkes, J., Roy, A., & Plugge, E. (2021). Scoping review of mental health in prisons through the COVID-19 pandemic. *BMJ Open*, *11*(5), e046547.

Jondani, J. A. (2021). Strategies for addressing the special needs of people with visual impairments during the COVID-19 pandemic. *Journal of Visual Impairment & Blindness*, *115*(3), 263–267.

Jordan, S. R., Connors, S. C., & Mastalerz, K. A. (2022). Frontline healthcare workers' perspectives on interprofessional teamwork during COVID-19. *Journal of Interprofessional Education & Practice, 29*, 100550.

Kim, H., Hughes, E., Cavanagh, A., Norris, E., Gao, A., Bondy, S. J., & Kouyoumdjian, F. G. (2022). The health impacts of the COVID-19 pandemic on adults who experience imprisonment globally: A mixed methods systematic review. *PLoS One, 17*(5), e0268866.

Kings College London: C-19 COVID Symptom tracker.2020; [cited 2020 30.3]

Krawczyk, N., Fawole, A., Yang, J., &Tofighi, B. (2021). Early innovations in opioid use disorder treatment and harm reduction during the COVID-19 pandemic: A scoping review. *Addiction Science & Clinical Practice, 16*, 1–15.

Kotera,Y.,Ozaki,A.,Miyatake,H.,Tsunetoshi,C.,Nishikawa,Y.,Kosaka,M.,&Tanimoto,T. (2022). Qualitative investigation into the mental health of healthcare workers in Japan during the COVID-19 pandemic. *International Journal of Environmental Research and Public Health, 19*(1), 568.

Kuper, H., Banks, L. M., Bright, T., Davey, C., & Shakespeare, T. (2020). Disability-inclusive COVID-19 response: What it is, why it is important and what we can learn from the United Kingdom's response. *Wellcome Open Research, 5*, 79. doi: 10.12688/wellcomeopenres.15833.1

Laurencin, C. T., & McClinton, A. (2020). The COVID-19 pandemic: A call to action to identify and address racial and ethnic disparities. *Journal of Racial and Ethnic Health Disparities, 7*, 398–402.

Layton, N., Mont, D., Puli, L., Calvo, I., Shae, K., Tebbutt, E., & Sidiqi, M. (2021). Access to assistive technology during the COVID-19 global pandemic: Voices of users and families. *International Journal of Environmental Research and Public Health, 18*(21), 11273.

Leischow, S. J., Best, A., Trochim, W. M., Clark, P. I., Gallagher, R. S., Marcus, S. E., & Matthews, E. (2008). Systems thinking to improve the public's health. *American Journal of Preventive Medicine, 35*(2), S196–S203.

Liu, K., Chen, Y., Lin, R., & Han, K. (2020). Clinical features of COVID-19 in elderly patients: A comparison with young and middle-ged patients. *The Journal of Infection, 80*(6), e14–e18. doi: 10.1016/j.jinf.2020.03.005

Loeb, M., Eide, A. H., Jelsma, J., Toni, M. K., & Maart, S. (2008). Poverty and disability in Eastern and Western Cape Provinces, South Africa. *Disability & Society, 23*(4), 311–321.

Loomis, J. M., & Lederman, S. J. (1986). Tactual perception: Chapter 31. In K. Boff, L. Kaufman, & J. Thomas (Eds.), *Handbook of Perception and Human Performance* (Vol. 2). New York, NY: Wiley.

McFarlane, S. J., Yook, B., & Wicke, R. (2023). Knowledge gaps, cognition and media learning: Designing tailored messages to address COVID-19 communication inequalities. *Journal of Health Communication, 28*(sup1), 97–106.

Munawar, K., & Choudhry, F. R. (2021). Exploring stress coping strategies of frontline emergency health workers dealing Covid-19 in Pakistan: A qualitative inquiry. *American Journal of Infection Control, 49*(3), 286–292.

Muñiz, J. O., Corcoran, F., Marzougui, J., Shlafer, R., Eddy, J. M., & Dallaire, D. (2024). Towards family preservation: A systematic jurisdiction analysis of prison visitation policies during the COVID-19 pandemic. *Psychology, Public Policy, and Law, 30*(1), 91–103.

Narayan, A., & Balkrishnan, R. (2021). A health crisis within a health crisis: Opioid access in the COVID-19 pandemic. *Substance Abuse, 42*(2), 148–152.

Ned, L., McKinney, E. L. M., McKinney, V., & Swartz, L. (2020). COVID-19 pandemic and disability: Essential considerations. *Social and Health Sciences, 18*(2), 136–148.

NCDAS. (2023). Retrieved on November, 18, 2023 from https://drugabusestatistics.org/#:~:text=Substance%20Abuse%20Statistics&text=138.543%20million%20or%2050.0%25%20of,over%20is%20down%200.4%25%20YoY.

OHCHR. (2006). United Nations convention on the rights of persons with disabilities, Office of the United Nations High Commissioner for Human Rights (accessed 5 January 2022).

Orbis. (2023). Retrieved on November 18, 2023 from https://www.orbis.org/en/news/2021/new- global-blindness-data?fbclid=IwAR1XVfXYPPMKHXswl8Jcdb9-fTKwyA7S8xrRqBXEjmfq3MMAggfVaf1tbP8#:~:text=2021%20has%20seen%20the% 20official,%2Dto%2Dsevere%20visual%20impairment

Parida, M., & Sinha, M. (2021). Pandemic and disability: Challenges faced and role of technology. *Technology and Disability, 33*(4), 245–252.

Pearce, E., Kamenov, K., Barrett, D., & Cieza, A. (2022). Promoting equity in health emergencies through health systems strengthening: Lessons learned from disability inclusion in the COVID-19 pandemic. *International Journal for Equity in Health, 21*(3), 1–7.

Pickering, K., Galappaththi, E. K., Ford, J. D., Singh, C., Zavaleta-Cortijo, C., Hyams, K., … & Anza-Ramirez, C. (2023). Indigenous peoples and the COVID-19 pandemic: A systematic scoping review. *Environmental Research Letters*. https://iopscience.iop.org/article/10.1088/1748-9326/acb804

Power, T., Wilson, D., Best, O., Brockie, T., Bearskin, L. B., Millender, E., & Lowe, J. (2020). COVID-19 and indigenous peoples: An imperative for action. *Journal of Clinical Nursing, 29*(15–16), 2737–2741. doi: 10.1111/jocn.15320

Radusky, P. D., Cardozo, N., Duarte, M., Fabian, S., Frontini, E., Sued, O., & Aristegui, I. (2021). Mental health, substance use, experiences of violence, and access to health care among transgender and non-binary people during the COVID-19 lockdown in Argentina. *International Journal of Transgender Health, 24*(3), 320–333. doi: 10.1080/26895269.2021.1943593.

Reddy, B. V., & Gupta, A. (2020). Importance of effective communication during COVID-19 infodemic. *Journal of Family Medicine and Primary Care, 9*(8), 3793.

Rizzo, J. R., Beheshti, M., Fang, Y., Flanagan, S., & Giudice, N. A. (2021). COVID-19 and visual disability: Can't look and now don't touch. *PM&R, 13*(4), 415–421.

Roble, S., Wångdahl, J., & Warner, G. (2022). COVID-19 information in Sweden: Opinions of immigrants with limited proficiency in Swedish. *Health Communication, 37*(12), 1510–1519.

Rotarou, E. S., Sakellariou, D., Kakoullis, E. J., & Warren, N. (2021). Disabled people in the time of COVID-19: Identifying needs, promoting inclusivity. *Journal of Global Health, 11*, 03007. doi: 10.7189/jogh.11.03007.

Rothan, H. A., & Byrareddy, S. N. (2020).The epidemiology and pathogenesis of coronavirus disease (COVID-19) outbreak. *Journal of Autoimmunity, 109*, 102433.

Sakellariou, D., Malfitano, A. P. S., & Rotarou, E. S. (2020). Disability inclusiveness of government responses to COVID-19 in South America: A framework analysis study. *International Journal for Equity in Health, 19*, 131. doi: 10.1186/s12939-020-01244-x

Samuels, E. A., Clark, S. A., Wunsch, C., Keeler, L. A. J., Reddy, N., Vanjani, R., & Wightman, R. S. (2020). Innovation during COVID-19: Improving addiction treatment access. *Journal of Addiction Medicine, 14*(4), e8–e9. doi: 10.1097/ADM.0000000000000685

Senjam, S. S. (2020). Impact of COVID-19 pandemic on people living with visual disability. *Indian Journal of Ophthalmology, 68*(7), 1367.

Siu, A. F., Fan, D., Kim, G. S., Rao, H. V., Vazquez, X., O'Modhrain, S., & Follmer, S. (2021). COVID-19 highlights the issues facing blind and visually impaired people

in accessing data on the web. In *Proceedings of the 18th International Web for All Conference* (pp. 1–15). https://hci.stanford.edu/publications/2021/w4aSiu/siu2021dataCovid-2.pdf
Song, M., Kramer, C. T., Sufrin, C. B., Eber, G. B., Rubenstein, L. S., Beyrer, C., & Saloner, B. (2023). "It was like you were being literally punished for getting sick": Formerly incarcerated people's perspectives on liberty restrictions during COVID-19. *AJOB Empirical Bioethics*, 1–12. https://pure.johnshopkins.edu/en/publications/it-was-like-you-were-being-literally-punished-for-getting-sick-fo
Swanwick, R., Oppong, A. M., Offei, Y. N., Fobi, D., Appau, O., Fobi, J., & Frempomaa Mantey, F. (2020). The impact of the COVID-19 pandemic on deaf adults, children and their families in Ghana. *Journal of the British Academy*, *8*, 141–165.
Taremwa, I. M., Ashaba, S., Naggayi, B. R. K., Kayongo, B., Nimwesiga, C., Ayebazibwe, C., … & Frank, J. (2023). Psychosocial challenges of the coronavirus disease-2019 pandemic among frontline health care providers and their coping mechanisms at Mbarara Regional Referral Hospital, Southwestern Uganda. *Psychology Research and Behavior Management*, *16*, 549–560. doi: 10.2147/PRBM.S399687
Tate, K. A., Fallon, K. M., Casquarelli, E. J., & Marks, L. R. (2014). Opportunities for action: Traditionally marginalized populations and the economic crisis. *Professional Counselor*, *4*(4), 285–302.
Vigo, D., Patten, S., Pajer, K., et al. (2020). Mental health of communities during the COVID-19 pandemic. *The Canadian Journal of Psychiatry*, *65*(10), 681–687.
Vindrola-Padros, C., Andrews, L., Dowrick, A., Djellouli, N., Fillmore, H., Gonzalez, E. B., … & Johnson, G. (2020). Perceptions and experiences of healthcare workers during the COVID-19 pandemic in the UK. *BMJ Open*, *10*(11), e040503.
Wang, Y., Pan, B., Liu, Y., Wilson, A., Ou, J., & Chen, R. (2020). Health care and mental health challenges for transgender individuals during the COVID-19 pandemic. *The Lancet Diabetes & Endocrinology*, *8*(7), 564–565.
Washington Group. (2019). Question Sets of the Washington Group.
World Health Organization. (2011). *World report on disability 2011*. Geneva: World Health Organization.
Yap, J., Chaudhry, V., Jha, C. K., Mani, S., & Mitra, S. (2020). Are responses to the pandemic inclusive? A rapid virtual audit of COVID-19 press briefings in LMICs. *World Development*, *136*, 105122.
Zokaei, K. (2011). How systems thinking provides a framework for change: A case study of disabled facilities grant service in Neath Port Talbot County Borough Council. *Systems Thinking: From Heresy to Practice: Public and Private Sector Studies*, 17–39.

## Glossary of Key Terms and Concepts

**Direct Disability Inclusive Measures** attempt to ensure the well-being of disabled people from the impact of the pandemic (Rotarou et al., 2021).

**Disability** defined as preventing or slowing action, in a manner which is atypical in function, and results in a lack of independence, perceived as a socially constructed obstacle (Friedman & Owen, 2017).

**Disablism** may be defined as discourses and practices that exclude, discriminate against, and/or otherwise oppress disabled people (Rotarou et al., 2021).

**Indirect Disability Inclusive Measures** the purpose of indirect measures is to protect the general population, and in this manner, disabled people as well from the impact of the pandemic (Rotarou et al., 2021).

**Knowledge Gap Hypothesis** The knowledge gap hypothesis posits that pre-existing health disparities will worsen when information flows to those in high socioeconomic status (the "haves") before reaching those in the lower socioeconomic status (the "have nots") (Gaziano, 2017).

**Marginalized Populations** are groups as well as communities of people that have been historically oppressed as a result of unequal power relationships (Tate et al., 2014).

**Systems Thinking** may be understood as a set of synergistic analytic skills working together as a system that are employed to improve the capability of identifying and understanding systems, as well as predicting their behaviors, and devising modifications to them in order to produce desired effects (Arnold & Wade, 2017).

## Discussion Questions

1 How do Samuels et al.'s (2020) project illuminate our understanding of how multimedia can be used to develop innovative treatment models for substance abusers with limited access to COVID-19 pandemic?
2 Based on past studies of the relationship between social support and recidivism what may we predict about the impact of COVID-19 restrictions on family visitations for individuals serving long-term incarceration on future violent behaviors and likelihood of committing future crimes? Explain.
3 How can we create more inclusive digital technologies? Please use illustrations.
4 Please watch the TED Talks 'Systems Thinking is Not Optional: Lessons from a Pandemic: Steve Woodsmall' at: https://www.youtube.com/watch?v=yuvHvi84TFw

   Has this presentation convinced you of the feasibility of a systems thinking approach regarding the COVID-19 pandemic? Why or why not?

## Role-Playing Exercises

1 Get into two groups of two. Pretend one pair are parents who are incarcerated. Pretend the remaining pair are children visiting your parents in jail. Write down what questions you would have and what you would like to say during your visit. Now role play the visit as a face-to-face interaction. Role play as a video-based meeting. What changed? How were the two meetings different without touch/physical presence? Was it easier to communicate in one method over the other? Explain.

# 9

# LESSONS LEARNED FROM PAST PANDEMICS

## Introduction

The COVID-19 pandemic is an ongoing global health crisis with, as of this writing, over 700 million confirmed cases and over 7 million deaths world-wide. Tragically, COVID-19 is not the world's first pandemic. In recent history, our universe has dealt with other pandemics, including the Spanish flu (1918–1919), SARS outbreak (2003), the H1N1 flu (2009–2010), and Ebola outbreak (2014–2016).

Choi and Powers (2021) describe the nature of the pandemic to be an exemplar of what they consider to be a wicked problem. From a communications perspective, decision-makers are faced by the challenge of implementing measures without the presence of definitive knowledge; given the possibility of ongoing outbreaks that cannot be realistically predicted with certainty. On the other side, the public lacks an ability to understand how to react and respond, given their rising level of confusion, which, in turn, perpetuates fear and the spreading of more misinformation about the virus. In essence, Choi and Powers (2021) argue that effective communication strategies are central to a successful pandemic response and that such strategies need to focus on proper education that increases public awareness of the virus but also with a focus on effectively preventing the spread of inaccurate information for this same purpose.

This chapter presents a compilation of lessons learned based on the results of studies we have reviewed in previous chapters combined with exploration of the response styles of countries which have successfully and not so successfully dealt with the COVID-19 pandemic. We begin this review with a discussion of a study that analyzed the successful strategies used by South Korea in

DOI: 10.4324/9781003394983-9

their management of the COVID-19 pandemic. The main findings of that study serve to highlight central aspects of communication that went well, and enabled the citizens of Korea to feel understood, empowered, and ultimately in a position to take action in preventative health measures. We next turn our attention to a study that analyzed certain communication breakdowns in how the COVID-19 pandemic was handled in Italy, a country that is known world-wide for being heavily impacted by the virus, especially during the early phases of the pandemic. The study identified five major communication weaknesses. It is through detailed analyses of these breakdowns that we hope to provide insights into how to improve communications during future pandemics or other world disasters. After this, we review a paper which analyzes the positive and negative aspects of the healthcare system in Quebec, Canada during the early stages of the COVID-19 pandemic to gain additional insights into how communication takes place and information is exchanged during such a global level crisis event. This study was selected as an illustration of a mixed success story as it comprised a number of interesting strengths and weaknesses. First, as the authors state, given Quebec is the second largest province in Canada, a country that is well endowed with high quality and quantity of resources, and was hard hit in terms of mortality and prevalence of the virus, it may be considered a 'textbook case' for analysis of how prepared a healthcare system is to deal with a crisis situation of this magnitude. Second, a robust methodology was employed given that data were obtained from multiple sources such as testimonials from clinical and managerial sources, in addition to information gathered by Google and Google Scholar about government and other organizations that managed the COVID-19 pandemic. Finally, strength of this analysis is that the authors of the reflections and testimonials comprise a background of considering breadth, including expertise in health technology assessment, researchers in public health, health crisis management, as well as practitioners such as physicians.

The chapter concludes with recommendations that focus on various societal level aspects of communication in the management of the COVID-19 pandemic, in large part, based on reviews of the literature from previous chapters of this book. It is our hope that the compilation of these recommendations will be informative to those working in the area of disaster management, as well as policy makers and health communication experts.

## Good Communication Styles: What to Do

In their exploration of positive pandemic communication employed by South Korea, Choi and Powers (2021) identified high degrees of transparency and coherence as two major success factors. Basing their review on social marketing concepts, defined as seeking to influence social behaviors in a manner that does not necessarily benefit the marketer, but to rather benefit the target audience and the general society at large. It is a technique that has been used extensively in international health programs (Weinreich, 2006). Choi and Powers (2021) discuss the system-level communication strategies using the theoretical framework of social marketing concepts. Before proceeding further, it is important to first understand what is meant by the concept of social marketing. Choi and Powers (2021) explain that in social marketing, the focus is to bring about change across different levels of the society which will ultimately lead to holistic change and changes in long-term health behavior. This concept is related to a systems thinking approach which was discussed earlier in Chapter 1 about the importance of a holistic approach in effective communication during a crisis event.

## What Not to Do: Uncoordinated Communication

During the first phases of the outbreak of the coronavirus disease in Italy, a lack of coordination between political and scientific levels and the media and other agencies making claims about the pandemic, suggests a mismanagement of the crisis during the first phases of the outbreak. The outbreak management suffered from the five communication weaknesses identified by Reynolds et al. (2002), related to (i) mixed messages from multiple messengers; (ii) delay in releasing information; (iii) biased attitudes (paternalistic) in information content, (iv) lack of immediate reaction to rumors or inability to distinguish between accurate and misinformation, and (v) political confusion. A common theme in these analyses of communication breakdowns is inaccuracy of information about the coronavirus, and uncertainty of information about the coronavirus irrespective of where this uncertainty stems from.

In their discussion of lessons learned in the management of the COVID-19 pandemic from the Italian experience, Romagnani et al. (2020) stressed the importance of testing strategies in virus containment, and how a lack of definitive procedures and protocols further increased the transmission of the virus and its subsequent consequences. This highlights the importance of good communication strategies in building clear and strong plans of action for the management of the virus. However, as Romagnani et al. (2020) also note the smooth development of these strategies is contingent on proper and quick access to information. Quick access to information is contingent upon a plethora of factors related to patients‘ conditions and environments, which requires access to hospital and other important records that are clear to understand and easily accessible. This highlights the need for synchronous access and sharing of important information among multiple stakeholders during a global crisis.

### *Analysis of a Canadian Healthcare System: Lessons Learned*

Issues related to surveillance and monitoring of the COVID-19 crisis by the Quebec healthcare system in Canada included missing and/or inconsistent international data, lack of reliable monitoring and information; the researchers speculated that these issues impacted the ability to take action and implement recommendations. Some successes of communication included having a trio-led communication strategy (comprising the Quebec Prime Minister, the Minister of Health and Social Services and the National Public Health Director who presented information to the public in an informal tone that was widely disseminated by social and other media and was given additional credence by support from scientific authority figures, especially during the first wave). Communication failures that were noted in this analysis included some distrust in the information given but especially a refusal to accept the media as the primary source of information. For this reason, greater transparency was called for in addition to a greater ability to coordinate across various stakeholders compiling the information about the virus, including but not limited to clinicians, managers working directly in the field, such as the Minister of Health and Social Services in Quebec (MSSS).

Alami et al.'s (2021) analysis of the successes and failures of Quebec's healthcare system during the COVID-19 pandemic is instructive as it illustrates that the benefits of good communication strategies in maintaining rapport with the public is ultimately limited if information is missing or not located in a timely manner during a crisis situation.

## Future Thoughts and Recommendations

Our review of the large corpus of theory and studies about the COVID-19 pandemic has provided some insights into the underlying nature of communication breakdowns. Considering the social origins of mental functioning (Brown et al., 2021), especially when our environment is unpredictable, scholars advocating the socio-cultural perspective highlight the collaborative nature of knowledge. Applied to epidemic management, we need to consider resources and responsibility hand-off (i.e., do we have sufficient resources and if so, how do we most efficiently distribute these resources to human agents?) (Margherita et al., 2021). To date, as declared by the authors in 2021, and to the best of our knowledge as of this writing in November, 2023, Margherita et al.'s (2021) study presents an important analysis on how to adopt a coordination science approach when analyzing and articulating the dynamics of flow dependencies, defined as an instruction being dependent on the result of a previous action, which characterize a pandemic. Following a purposive sampling approach, nine domain experts were consulted in the creation of their analysis; the selection criteria included at least 15 years of cumulative experience in the healthcare industry which comprised direct experience with COVID-19 issues in their current work. Their work depicts the shared flow, fit and shared dependencies involved in the management of disaster event that can help to maximize efficient communication and information sharing. Twelve coordinated mechanisms are discussed in detail in their work with each flow comprising a right place, a right thing, a right time and a corresponding management criterion. In the case of flow 2 for example, the management criterion of an emergency coordination unit comprises hospitals or other temporary health facilities (right place), bio-contained and authorized units (right thing), and is event-driven (right time).

The flow dependencies illustrate many concepts previously discussed that relate to effective communication including the importance of information availability and coordination. First, information has to be available, and other areas/organizations need to be aware of this. Arguably, a situational awareness needs to be present. Second, this information needs to be accessible. As columns two, three, and four show, the right time, place, and right thing need to work in harmony. And finally, management criteria need to be present: there has to be a practical manner of transferring information.

In this book we have attempted to present a scholarly discussion of the COVID-19 pandemic that helps to address the questions of what went right and what went wrong. Of particular note are key disparities in access to healthcare and information about the pandemic, discussed in Chapters 5 and 8. In Chapter 5, ample evidence was presented regarding a notable absence of female presence in COVID-19 decision-making committees (Bali et al., 2020; Cevik et al., 2020; Van Daalen et al., 2020), which was associated with a rhetorical style of government management that encouraged a team-spirit approach where the public was encouraged to participate in the fight to contain the virus. Chapter 8 highlighted the barriers to communication as well as access to information about the COVID-19 pandemic for a number of vulnerable populations including older people (Banovic et al., 2022), the hearing impaired (Jesus et al., 2020; Kuper et al., 2021) and migrants (Abba-Aji et al., 2022; Cox et al., 2021; Etti et al., 2021). These barriers included but were not limited to masks and other protective equipment reducing speech volume, and difficulty in seeing and reading nonverbal cues during communication, language barriers, and difficulty employing digital communication to access information, as well as underrepresentation in research. Chapter 5 also discussed leadership styles and how certain factors and rhetorical styles can impede or facilitate public trust in government during public crises such as the COVID-19 pandemic.

Based on some of the communication success stories and failures we have reviewed in this book, we conclude our final chapter with a list of recommendations that may be of service for future pandemics. For ease of presentation, the recommendations to follow will be presented in the following categories: Information about the Coronavirus (e.g., accuracy, equal access to data, clarity, knowledge synthesis), Communication (e.g., transparency, knowledge sharing) and Information Action Ratio (e.g., how information can lead to action).

## Recommendations Regarding More Efficient Information Sharing About The Coronavirus

### *Create a Consensus-Based Global Standard for an International Data Entry System*

The importance of data standardization has has been pointed out by several authors in the field of situation awareness (Ouverson et al., 2021; Usbeck et al., 2015).

#### *Recommendation 1: Creating More Equal Access to Data*

As aforementioned, there is a plethora of evidence to suggest lack of access, especially for certain marginalized and/or vulnerable groups in society to healthcare and information about the COVID-19 pandemic (Abba-Aji et al., 2022; Banovic et al., 2022; Cox et al., 2021; Etti et al., 2021; Jesus et al., 2020; Kuper et al., 2021).

#### *Recommendation 2: Global System of Information Databases*

We have discussed many examples of countries where mismanagement of the pandemic may have been largely attributed toward certain bodies of government being unaware of important information that was not shared, especially in a timely manner for more efficient and collaborative decision-making.

## Recommendations Regarding the Creation and Communication of Information

### *Recommendation 3: The Need for More Gender-Inclusive Decision-Making*

Despite evidence that suggests that women, especially minority women, are disproportionately affected in pandemics, it has been found that women from minority ethnic groups are consistently under-represented in health and humanitarian leadership (Bali et al., 2020). We found evidence supporting this in Chapter 5, where we explored gender differences in leadership styles when managing the COVID-19 pandemic. Indeed, Much has been written to substantiate the benefits of a more balanced gender-based influence on the creation of policies and strategies aimed at effective management of the pandemic (Huang, 2021). Alrich and Lilito (2020) found female leaders to communicate better and respond faster to COVID-19 policies than male leaders. Faster responsiveness of female leaders during the pandemic was a finding echoed by Coscieme et al. (2020), in addition to eliciting more compliance from the public with a stronger focus on equity, human needs, and generosity. Windsor et al. (2020) in their exploration of national data for 175 countries around the world found that countries led by women performed better during the pandemic.

### *Recommendation 4: Working with Religious Organizations as Part of the Solution*

It has been stated that governments need to rely on organizations and resources such as schools, health facilities, schools and clerics to quickly promote public education of COVID-19 (Djaante et al., 2021). If no government has the resources to mass campaign alone (Djante et al., 2021) and needs the assistance of other organizations to do so effectively, this may include the support of religions/religious leaders. Djante and colleagues (2021) further posit how religion can be seen as a solution rather than a problem during pandemics

(Djante et al., 2021). Indeed, given the pivotal role of religious leaders in certain cultures, communities, and countries, religious leaders formed part of the consultation and decision-making process. An inspiring example of using a religious organization (the MUI in Indonesia) to help shape narratives that promote adherence to safety procedures during the pandemic is the condemnation of self-serving behaviors of hoarding food, or masks and other essential items (Djanate et al., 2021).

## Recommendations Regarding New Approaches About Knowledge Creation

It has been noted by scholars that policy questions are often framed to be rooted where simply pulling the right levers will get the economy and society back on track after a crisis (Hynes et al., 2020). The limitation of this approach according to Hynes et al. (2020) is that issues that arise during a crisis situation are often treated separately within different fields of specializations what they refer to as scientific and institutional "silos" (Hynes et al., 2020, p. 174). Serious disease outbreaks such as Covid-19, it is argued, are the result of **emergence** which is defined as a process whereby a situation arises through the interaction of a number of actors and influences. What is needed to build long-term resiliency in infrastructures, is the integration of a range of policies such as educational, demographic, employment, well-being, and technology by means of a systems approach, where proper attention is given to the presence and influence of crucial linkages between issues that take place during crisis situations (Hynes et al., 2020).

### *Recommendation 5: Incorporating Systems Mapping and Systems Modeling for Communicating Health Information for Planetary Emergencies*

When considering the viral nature of COVID-19 misinformation and disinformation scholars need to take into account the need for more complex systems to more effectively communicate health information (Lee et al., 2023). According to Lee et al. (2023), because it is difficult for humans to see and fully understand complex systems, certain systems and methods such as systems mapping and systems modeling, can help facilitate communicating public health-related information. **Systems Mapping/Systems Modeling** may be defined as a set of elements that are interconnected and that is coherently organized in a way that achieves something within a representation of physical space (Meadows, 2008). This, in turn, can lead to the development of more tailored, precise, and proactive communications, while at the same time, leaving less opportunity for misinformation and disinformation to spread (Lee et al., 2023).

### *Recommendation 6: Multiple Stakeholders/Information Sharing*

It has also been suggested that collaborating with community-based organizations that serve individuals from varying geographic, racial/ ethnic, age, religious/faith backgrounds may ultimately help to increase vaccine acceptance rates from different communities (Salmon et al., 2021).

### *Recommendation 7: Regarding Transforming Information into Action*

Studies have found that while people report being relatively informed about the coronavirus, a large minority do not feel news media or the government have explained what they can do in response to the pandemic (Nielson et al., 2020; Turi & Varig, 2021). Indeed, in an intriguing study information gaps during the pandemic were identified by Pitch et al. (2023). In their qualitative analysis of Dear Pandemic (DP), an online ad hoc risk communication platform created to directly address common health questions including those about the pandemic, Pitch et al. (2023) identified the following four themes: the need to clarify other sources; a lack of trust in information; recognizing possible misinformation; and questions related to personal decision-making. The authors noted that as the DP question box gathered the informational needs of DP readers during the course of the COVID-19 pandemic, the results of the study could help organizations improve communication efforts for similar contexts in the future in digital spaces. This leads to the following recommendations:

### *Recommendation 8: Ensure Information Is Clear, Accurate, and Honest*

Include sources of information so the public can check the veracity of information and believe if it is true (Finset et al., 2021).

### *Recommendation 9: Make It Clear for What the Public Needs to Do and Explain What Is NOT Known*

For example, use jargon-free language and make appropriate socio-linguistic changes. In other words, make pandemic guidelines part of everyday lexicon (Finset et al., 2021).

### *Recommendation 10: Avoid Politicalization of Information about COVID-19*

Scholars have pointed out that when messages disseminated through diverse communication channels are politicized, this may result in individuals' sharing information with more restricted members of a homogeneous group (Kim & Kreps, 2020).

### *Recommendation 11: The Need for More Dynamic Risk Assessment Tools*

Not all risk assessment tools will be applicable for every country. This was pointed out by Mishra (2020) in the case of India where certain conventional disaster risk assessment tools used to assess incidence of the spread of the virus and estimate the risk of spread of diseases in different locations were deemed inadequate for decision-making. First the information was not granular enough in certain cases, meaning in the Indian context a district also might have been too large a unit of analysis in the sense that a district may be "red" and consequently close down all its economic activity according to the assessment, whereas in reality, the risk may have been confined to a small part of the district. A second factor noted by Mishra (2020) was that the information from an assessment tool may not have been dynamic enough; given that smaller time steps at which the updates could be provided were needed given the rapid spread of the virus. Third the analyses from these risk assessment tools were determined to not adequately be informed by the local drivers of risk. From these three factors, Mishra (2020) recommended that disaster risk management community should take stock of these lessons and refine these tools to meet future needs.

### *Recommendation 12: Reaching a Wider Audience*

In the context of public health crises, studies highlight the importance of reaching the least educated segments of the population with campaign messages. Studies suggests these messages can help to close gaps between the more and less educated group in their intentions to engage in preventive behaviors (McAbee et al., 2021; Peña-Lillo & Guzman, 2022).

### *Recommendation 13: The Need for Multiple-Issue Campaigns.*

Citing findings that diversity of reasons have been given for vaccine hesitancy, scholars have argued against the effectiveness of single-issue mass campaigns as likely to bring about large shifts in COVID-19 vaccine hesitancy; this was the case for Bates et al. (2022) in Equador and Venezuela where it was found that addressing structural changes and issues relating to interpersonal communication would have a greater impact on vaccine uptake.

### *Recommendation 14: Advocating a More Culture-Centered Approach (CCA)*

Such an approach is recommended as it draws upon placed-based articulations of meanings of health and culture-centered theorizing comprises ongoing dialogs to identify problems and co-develop localized solutions through the formation of community advisory boards and involve engaging in ongoing reflexivity, listening, and dialog with community members, the CCA foregrounds community-led solutions (Casillas et al., 2022; Dutta, 2008).

Ultimately our recommendations may be condensed into the following key recommendations:

**KEY RECOMMENDATIONS**

- Ensure information is clear, jargon-free and easily understood.
- Make action plans that are clear and accessible to a broad audience base that vary in levels of education including marginalized groups, where people understand exactly what needs to be done.
- Create a holistic understanding of the pandemic where the gestalt or 'big picture' can be seen without complication.
- Ensure your information is framed in a manner where gains and losses are easily understood.
- Ensure you are willing to adapt information about the pandemic as needed and keep information accurate and updated.

- Share information with stakeholders and involve key influencers in society as much as possible. Ensure information is empirically based and the public recognizes this and trusts the validity of information they are given.
- Be transparent in how information is shared and create trust with the public and government.

## Bibliography

Abba-Aji, M., Stuckler, D., Galea, S., & McKee, M. (2022). Ethnic/racial minorities' and migrants' access to COVID-19 vaccines: A systematic review of barriers and facilitators. *Journal of Migration and Health, 5*, 100086.

Alami, H., Lehoux, P., Fleet, R., Fortin, J. P., Liu, J., Attieh, R., Cadeddu, S. B. M., Abdoulaye Samri, M., Savoldelli, M., & Ag Ahmed, M. A. (2021). How can health systems better prepare for the next pandemic? Lessons learned from the management of the COVID-19 pandemic in Quebec (Canada). *Frontiers in Public Health, 9*, 671833. doi: 10.3389/fpubh.2021.671833

Aldrich, A. S., & Lotito, N. J. (2020). Pandemic performance: Women leaders in the Covid-19 crisis. *Politics & Gender, 16*(4), 960–967.

Bali, S., Dhatt, R., Lal, A., et al. (2020). Off the back burner: Diverse and gender inclusive decision- making for COVID-19 response and recovery. *BMJ Global Health*, 5, e002595. doi: 10.1136/ bmjgh-2020–002595

Banovic, S., Sinanovic, O., Jankovic, S., Patkovic, N., & Smajlovic, S. (2022). Communication of the elderly during the COVID-19 pandemic. *Acta Informatica Medica, 30*(4), 324.

Bates, B. R., Villegas-Botero, A., Costales, J. A., Moncayo, A. L., Tami, A., Carvajal, A., & Grijalva, M. J. (2022). COVID-19 vaccine hesitancy in three Latin American countries: Reasons given for not becoming vaccinated in Colombia, Ecuador, and Venezuela. *Health Communication, 37*(12), 1465–1475.

Brown, M. E., & Finn, G. M. (2020). Intra-COVID collaboration: Lessons for a post-COVID world. *Medical Education, 55*(1), 122–124.

Casillas, A., Flores-Uribe, E., Abhat, A., Moreno, G., Brown, A., Szilagyi, P. G., & Norris, K. (2022). The language of COVID-19: Health systems must now prioritize responsive in-language and culturally-tailored messaging. *International Journal of Disaster Risk Reduction, 77*, 103077. doi: 10.1016/j.ijdrr.2022.103077. Epub 2022 Jun 2. PMID: 35673629; PMCID: PMC9159962.

Cevik, M., Haque, S. A., Manne-Goehler, J., Kuppalli, K., Sax, P. E., Majumder, M. S., & Orkin, C. (2020). Gender disparities in international COVID-19 clinical trial leadership. *Clinical Microbiology and Infection: The Official Publication of the European Society of Clinical Microbiology and Infectious Diseases, 27*(7), 1007–1010. doi: 10.1016/j.cmi.2020.12.025.

Choi, S., & Powers, T. L. (2021). COVID-19: Lessons from South Korean pandemic communications strategy. *International Journal of Healthcare Management, 14*(1), 271–279.

Coscieme, L., Fioramonti, L., Mortensen, L. F., Pickett, K. E., Kubiszewski, I., Lovins, H., … & Wilkinson, R. (2020). Women in power: Female leadership and public health outcomes during the COVID-19 pandemic. *MedRxiv*, 2020–07. https://doi.org/10.1101/2020.07.13.20152397

Cox, A., Iedema, R., Li, S., Sabbe, M., Salaets, H., & Dauby, N. (2021). Adding barriers to barriers during the COVID-19 pandemic: A call for interdisciplinary research on communication with migrant patients in the emergency department. *European Journal of Emergency Medicine*, *28*(1), 5–6.

Van Daalen, K. R., Bajnoczki, C., Chowdhury, M., Dada, S., Khorsand, P., Socha, A., … & Rajan, D. (2020). Symptoms of a broken system: The gender gaps in COVID-19 decision-making. *BMJ global health*, *5*(10), e003549.

Desson, Z., Lambertz, L., Peters, J. W., Faulkenbach, M., & Kauer, L. (2020). Europe's Covid-19 outliers, German, Austrian and Swiss policy responses during the early stages of the 2020 pandemic. *Health Policy and Technology*, *9*, 405–418.

Djalante, R., Lassa, J., Setiamarga, D., Sudjatma, A., Indrawan, M., Haryanto, B., Mahfud, C., Sinapoy, M. S., Djalante, S., Rafliana, I., Gunawan, L. A., Surtiara, G. A. & Warsilah, H. (2020). Review and analysis of current responses to COVID-19 in Indonesia: Period of January to March 2020. *Progress in Disaster Science*, 100091

Dresler-Hawke, E., & Veer, E. (2006). Making healthy eating messages more effective: Combining integrated marketing communication with the behaviour ecological model. *International Journal of Consumer Studies, 30*(4), 318–326.

Dutta, M. J. (2008). *Communicating health: A culture-centered approach*. Polity Press.

Etti, M., Fofie, H., Razai, M., Crawshaw, A. F., Hargreaves, S., & Goldsmith, L. P. (2021). Ethnic minority and migrant underrepresentation in Covid-19 research: Causes and solutions. *London: EClinicalMedicine*, *36*. doi: 10.1016/j.eclinm.2021.100903

Finset, A., Bosworth, H., Butow, P., Gulbrandsen, P., Hulsman, R. L., Pieterse, A. H., … & van Weert, J. (2020). Effective health communication–a key factor in fighting the COVID-19 pandemic. *Patient Education and Counseling*, *103*(5), 873.

Huang, P. H. (2021). Put more women in charge and other leadership lessons from COVID- 19. *FIU Law Review*, *15*, 353.

Hynes, W., Trump, B., Love, P., & Linkov, I. (2020). Bouncing forward: A resilience approach to dealing with COVID-19 and future systemic shocks. *Environment Systems and Decisions*, *40*, 174–184.

iSMA. (n.d.). What is Social Marketing 2020 [cited 2020 June 25]. Available from: https://isocialmarketing.org/

Jacobsen, K. H. (2020). Will COVID-19 generate global preparedness? *Lancet, 395*, 1013–1014. doi: 10.1016/S0140–6736(20)30559-6

Jesus, T. S., Kamalakannan, S., Bhattacharjya, S., Bogdanova, Y., Arango-Lasprilla, J. C., Bentley, J., … & of the American, I. N. G. (2020). People with disabilities and other forms of vulnerability to the COVID-19 pandemic: Study protocol for a scoping review and thematic analysis. *Archives of Rehabilitation Research and Clinical Translation*, *2*(4), 100079.

Kim, D. K. D., & Kreps, G. L. (2020). An analysis of government communication in the United States during the COVID-19 pandemic: Recommendations for effective government health risk communication. *World Medical & Health Policy*, *12*(4), 398–412.

Kuper, N., Modersitzki, N., Phan, L. V., & Rauthmann, J. (2021). The situation during the COVID-19 pandemic: A snapshot in Germany. *PLoS ONE*, *16*(2), Article e0245719. doi:10.1371/journal.pone.0245719

Lee, B. Y., Greene, D., Scannell, S. A., McLaughlin, C., Martinez, M. F., Heneghan, J. L., … & Bartsch, S. M. (2023). The Need for Systems Approaches for Precision Communications in Public Health. *Journal of Health Communication, 28*(sup1), 13–24.
Lee, K.-M., & Jung, K. (2019). Factors influencing the response to infectious diseases: Focusing on the case of SARS and MERS in South Korea. *International Journal of Environmental Research and Public Health, 16*(8), 1432. https://doi.org/10.3390/ijerph16081432
Margherita, A., Elia, G., & Klein, M. (2021). Managing the COVID-19 emergency: A coordination framework to enhance response practices and actions. *Technological Forecasting and Social Change, 166*, 120656.
McAbee, L., Tapera, O., & Kanyangarara, M. (2021). Factors associated with COVID-19 vaccine intentions in eastern Zimbabwe: A cross-sectional study. *Vaccines, 9*(10), 1109.
Meadows, D. (2008). *Thinking in systems: A primer*. Chelsea Green Publishing.
Mishra, P. K. (2020). COVID-19, Black Swan events and the future of disaster risk management in India. *Progress in Disaster Science, 8*, 100137.
Nielson et al. (2020). The Reuters Institute for??? https://reutersinstitute.politics.ox.ac.uk/sites/default/files/2020-06/DNR_2020_FINAL.pdf
Palmedo, C. (2023). What did we learn about pandemic communication? *Journal of Health Communication, 28*(sup1), 1. soi: 10.1080/10810730.2023.2221067
Peña-Y-Lillo, M., & Guzmán, P. (2022). Can high exposure help to close gaps? The influence of COVID-19 preventive messages on behavioral intentions by educational attainment in Chile. *Health Communication, 37*(12), 1544–1551.
Piltch-Loeb, R., James, R., Albrecht, S. S., Buttenheim, A. M., Dowd, J. B., Kumar, A., … & Aronowitz, S. (2023). What were the information voids? A qualitative analysis of questions asked by dear pandemic readers between August 2020-August 2021. *Journal of Health Communication, 28*(sup1), 25–33.
Ouverson, K. M., Ostrander, A. G., Walton, J., Kohl, A., Gilbert, S. B., Dorneich, M. C., ... & Sinatra, A. M. (2021). Analysis of communication, team situational awareness, and feedback in a three-person intelligent team tutoring system. *Frontiers in Psychology, 12*, 553015.
Reynolds, B., Galdo, J. H., Sokler, L., & Freimuth, V. S. (2002). *Crisis and emergency risk communication*. Centers for Disease Control and Prevention (U.S.). https://stacks.cdc.gov/view/cdc/6574
Romagnani, P., Gnone, G., Guzzi, F., Negrini, S., Guastalla, A., Annunziato, F., Romagnani, S. & De Pal, R. (2020). The COVID-19 infection: lessons learned from the Italian experience. *Journal of Public Health Policy, 41*, 238–244.
Salmon, D., Opel, D. J., Dudley, M. Z., Brewer, J., & Breiman, R. (2021). Reflections on governance, communication, and equity: challenges and opportunities in COVID-19 vaccination: Article examines the engagement and communication steps necessary to strengthen the COVID-19 vaccine roll out by federal, state, and local governments. *Health Affairs, 40*(3), 419–425.
Turi, G., & Virag, A. (2021). Experiences and lessons learned from COVID-19 pandemic management in South Korea and the V4 countries. *Tropical Medicine and Infectious Disease, 6*(4), 201. doi: 10.3390/tropicalmed6040201
Usbeck, K., Gillen, M., Loyall, J., Gronosky, A., Sterling, J., Kohler, R., ... & Canestrare, D. (2015, May). improving situation awareness with the Android Team Awareness Kit (ATAK). In *Sensors, and Command, Control, Communications, and Intelligence (C3I) Technologies for Homeland Security, Defense, and Law Enforcement XIV* (Vol. 9456, pp. 172–193). SPIE.

Udemy. (2023). Emergence key concept in systems thinking. Retrieved on November 19, 2023 from https://www.udemy.com/course/emergence/

Weinreich, N. K. (2006). What is social marketing. *Weinreich Communications, 10.* https://www.social-marketing.com/whatis.html

Windsor, L. C., Yannitell Reinhardt, G., Windsor, A. J., Ostergard, R., Allen, S., Burns, C., … & Wood, R. (2020). Gender in the time of COVID-19: Evaluating national leadership and COVID-19 fatalities. *PLoS One, 15*(12), e0244531.

## Glossary of Key Terms and Concepts

**Emergence** a process whereby a situation arises through the interaction of a number of elementary parts are put together to create a new patterns of organization (Udemy, 2023).

**Social Marketing** seeks to influence social behaviors in a manner that does not necessarily benefit the marketer, but rather benefits the target audience and the general society at large. It is a technique that has been used extensively in international health programs (Weinreich, 2006).

**Systems Mapping/Systems Modeling** a set of elements that is interconnected and that is coherently organized in a way that achieves something within a representation of physical space (Meadows, 2008).

## Discussion Questions

1 Now that you have finished reading this textbook about communication breakdowns during the COVID-19 pandemic, what do you feel are the main lessons on how to improve communication for future pandemics?
2 With a partner, please refer to Appendix B which provides summaries of strengths and weaknesses of how various countries in the world managed the pandemic. Select three countries that did well, and
3 Three countries that did not do as well. What do the successful management styles have in common? What do the unsuccessful countries have in common? Discuss.

# CONCLUDING THOUGHTS

The COVID-19 pandemic has been described as a crisis on every level where its impact has been felt socially, culturally, environmentally, politically, and economically. It comprised a complex entanglement of people, other living things, places, spaces, objects, time, discourse, and culture (Lupton & Willis, 2021). We began this book with the thought-provoking prediction of the COVID-19 pandemic that Bill Gates articulated in his TED Talk in the April of 2015. Even with the ideas expressed in his presentation, the world could hardly have prepared itself for the millions of people who were impacted by this devastating pandemic.

The subject area of risk communication is highly complex and multi-faceted (Peterson & Thompson, 2010). First, credible information is needed to make informed decisions. Yet, during disaster events, one is often bombarded by a plethora of information, much of which comprises misinformation. Second, good decision analysis skills are founded on the ability to determine what is the most relevant information (Morgan et al. 2001). Due to the nature of a disaster event, such as in the case of a pandemic, information often comes quickly, may be subject to change and may not be completely reliable. In such an environment where there is typically much chaos and panic, individuals need to turn information they receive into decisions and ultimately actions taken to best survive an ever evolving situation (Lindgaard et al., 2010).

In his analysis of the structure and function of communication, Lasswell (1948) states that an act of communication answers these questions: who, says what, in which channel, to whom, with what effect? He further describes how different scholars specialize in these various aspects and thus content analysis

DOI: 10.4324/9781003394983-10

may require greater focus upon what is said, whereas media scholars may place greater focus on the media and the audience, and so forth.

Given the complexity of the COVID-19 pandemic, or any disaster at the global level, understanding how communication breakdowns take place is a massive undertaking. Effective coordination of a public health system is difficult and challenging. In their analysis of the institutional landscape of COVID-19, Fierbeck and Hardcastle (2020) point to the importance of incorporating agility and flexibility into the decision-making process. It seems the problem in learning from past pandemics is that all pandemics are different.

> Some lessons—such as the need to share data as quickly and as comprehensively as possible—seem to have been poorly learned; other lessons (most painfully, that all pandemics are different) highlight the need to build agility and flexibility into decision-making. That long-term care homes rather than hospitals would be the epicenter of many of the biggest outbreaks, for example, was not appreciated soon enough by many jurisdictions: SARS had been limited to hospitals and, as those most vulnerable to H1N1 were younger rather than older cohorts, H1N1 did not force our attention to long-term care homes. But lessons are not just for governments; they are for all those involved in pandemic responses. And, as political decision makers have learned that they must listen and respond to front line workers, so too must those at the front line understand that pandemics are not simply a moment in time, but rather exist within a specific political context, one that constrains the political choices available to those at the helm.
>
> *(Fierbeck & Hardcastle, 2020, p. 35)*

A key lesson from this analysis is that better preparation for future pandemics may require a re-structuring of government infrastructures. At present, in some countries, certain bodies have needed information, while other bodies and agencies have the power of decision-making. Clearly having agencies that have both (decision-making authority in addition to current information) would facilitate communication as this would eliminate to transfer information across agencies such that a central authority could manage both.

In order to elucidate the various factors which contribute toward the complexity with which communication typically takes place during such events, this book asks several questions adopting Communication and Psychology lenses. We explored various themes pertinent to efficient communication, including

- The kinds of information we have
- How we understand this information
- How we make decisions about adopting proactive safety measures from this information

Through examining how the COVID-19 pandemic was managed, we analyzed successful and not-so-successful management styles to promote a better understanding of effective communication. We also explore the experiences of various groups during the pandemic to better understand how they may have been further marginalized and issues of access to healthcare. In a post-pandemic world, we are interested in how communication patterns may have changed for the general populace as well as for these marginalized groups to promote a better understanding of how to promote inclusivity.

## Our Post-Pandemic World

### *The Impact on Future Professions and Marginalized Groups*

Socially and economically disadvantaged people rely on certain professions more than the populace at large. For those involved in birthing, the case of Doulas is a good example. Doulas provide support to their clients through a variety of manners, such as nonverbal communication (conveying acceptance of a birthing person's decisions for their medical care, touch and facial expressions, etc.) and also play a role in improving the communication between their clients and medical professionals; some of their work is physical involving tools such as birth balls and Rebozos (a traditional Mexican garment or large woven scarf) to help shift bodies into more comfortable positions. For low SES mothers to be, they are a recognized source of prenatal education (Nguyen et al., 2022).

A study conducted by Nguyen et al. (2022) found that not only did virtual communication (the primary manner of communication during the pandemic) limit many of the traditional manners of communication that Doulas practiced during the birthing process, the lack of physical communication made establishing a trusting relationship between Doulas and their clients more problematic. These raise questions about the future of professions such as the Doulas – more research is needed to explore new opportunities and challenges that have arisen as modes of communication change in such professions.

### *COVID-19's Impact on Pre-Existing Health Inequalities: Next Steps for the Future*

There is much evidence to suggest that COVID-19 has worsened pre-existing health inequalities (Bilal et al., 2021; Cortenez et al. 2022; Dutta et al., 2022; Kim et al., 2020). What is problematic, as Dutta et al. (2022) have pointed out is that considering that the dominant approach to health communication has typically centered on a message-centric individualistic behavior change framework (Nan & Thompson, 2020) this does little to improve structural inequalities in access to healthcare. Let us consider, for example, how the added cost of healthcare during the pandemic and the more limited time of interaction can be worsened in the case of single parents. During in-person consultations who are already facing language barriers, and given support staff may not be allowed, the consultation becomes even more psychologically isolating with even more difficulty in communication experienced by all parties present (Dutta et al., 2022).

This case scenario illustrates how some threads of care in marginalized communities are based on face to face interaction, which begs the question: how can they or should they be considered in a post-pandemic world? Dutta and colleagues emphasize on the need for culture centered approach (CCA) where community members have a greater voice in negotiating structures and ongoing dialogs to help identify problems in the system and co-develop localized solutions (Dutta et al., 2022).

### *Post-Pandemic Shifts in Power Dynamics*

When discussing post-pandemic shifts in communication it is important not to disregard the importance of how power-dynamics may have been altered when considering union/employee voice. Marchington (1981, 1992, 2017) for example, in advocating against a 'one size fits all' approach considers how external environments shape conceptualizations of a work context that is free from discrimination. This helps to illuminate why uniform trajectories often cannot be accurately predicted during times of crisis. As Marchington (cited in Budd, 2022) elaborates:

> 'waves' theory allows us to explain uneven firm responses to COVID, some of which might be more EIP-favouring than others. That is, firms are not predicted to necessarily respond to the early crisis points of the pandemic by curtailing voice nor would they consistently respond to shifts in worker voice preferences as the pandemic wore on by improving participation arrangements. And, crucially, employers would be expected to behave in non-uniform ways, determined by how external factors are filtered through the internal dynamics of the organisation and the specific unique decision-making processes of leaders and line managers. Moreover, Marchington's research on informal voice reminds us that we should expect to see these dynamics resulting in varying trajectories of both formal and informal mechanisms.
>
> *(Budd, 2022, p. 545)*

We may recall that it was previously stated how this book has employed macro as well as micro analyses of the impacts of COVID-19 pandemic in altering communication in a global context. The unpredictability of global level disaster events makes it near impossible to explain consistency in behavior across countries. For example, while it may have been speculated that social partnership and dialog would decrease post-pandemic, the opposite occurred and there is much evidence to suggest that cooperation styles varied between countries (Budd et al., 2023).

Shifting back to a micro-analysis, Lai and Cai's (2023) analysis of personal interaction between service staff and managers within the hospital sector, during and after the COVID-19 pandemic, highlighted various psychological issues that emerged from a prolonged uncertain period. Namely, their investigation found that a holistic strategy, transparent decision-making strategy, and sympathetic behaviors from managers and leaders helped service staff to develop more effective coping mechanisms during a crisis management situation.

### *An Altered World*

A large component of communication is the concept of trust and in this book we have discussed how the COVID-19 crisis has altered how trust may be taking place in society. Historically, trust has taken place with the development of time, through repeated exposure of reliable behavior between two or more interacting parties. The unexpected, ever-changing nature of a global public health disaster such as the COVID-19 pandemic has altered this conceptualization of what we understand to be trusted on several levels: the public's trust in the government as well as in each other, given that information is ever changing and is not always credible. With school closures around the world, the pandemic has resulted in higher rates of obesity for many children as a result of online learning. Much scholarship has investigated the new world of COVID-19 children (de Miranda et al., 2020) and, indeed, the pandemic has been found to impact how children communicate (Charney et al. 2021), word choice, and even types of play (The Economist, 2023). There is much scope for future research to explore this in further depth.

## *A Grand Challenge*

Scholars have highlighted the importance of an international perspective to approach things holistically and not just rely on lessons learned from one or two countries given the extreme manner in which the world is interconnected. As an example, Budhwur and Cumming (2020) note that while studies from specific regions may contribute important insights, when it is possible to adopt a broader view that informs a more global audience, then this route should be taken instead.

Indeed, the COVID-19 pandemic has been described as a "grand challenge" by academics (Bacq et al., 2020; Fu et al., 2023; Howard-Grenville, 2021) and considering that they do not neatly fit into either stable specifications nor straightforward solutions we need to recognize grand challenges as 'seemingly intractable' puzzles (Ferraro et al., 2015, p. 367). Ferraro et al. (2015) have described grand challenges as inherently complex and uncertain in that interactions and constraints are not only multiple but only partially visible to any given actor at any time. This makes grand challenges difficult when we consider the complexity for the existence of any single set of criteria, upon which individuals may reach a consensus about a given problem, let alone agree upon a solution (Howard-Grenville, 2021).

The pandemic has also demonstrated how grand challenges can infiltrate rapidly into other domains. For example we may consider that the pandemic originated as a global health crisis, but later changed the world's conceptions and understanding of workplaces, which have arguably raised further questions around broader social issues such as inequality, gender, health (Howard-Grenville, 2021) as well as the ethics of how marginalized groups are treated and valued in our society. There are many more ways the COVID-19 pandemic has changed our understanding of the world including our conceptions of others and how we communicate that remain to be explored by future scholars.

This book is an important step toward elucidating how communication has taken place during the COVID-19 pandemic. As stated by the Director General of the WHO, Dr. Tedros Adhanom Ghebreyesus, "[O]ur greatest enemy right now is not the virus itself. It's fear, rumors and stigma. And our greatest assets are facts, reason and solidarity." Such words may serve as a warning that favors a pragmatic approach in understanding the massive changes that have taken place in our social structures on a global level. We need to better comprehend how we are persuaded toward action in a disaster event, favoring adherence to fact-based information rather than false information. We need to develop the critical evaluation skills that will help us to do this should we face another pandemic such as the COVID-19 pandemic in the future.

## Bibliography


Ahluwalia, S. C., Edelen, M. O., Qureshi, N., & Etchegaray, J. M. (2021). Trust in experts, not trust in national leadership, leads to greater uptake of recommended actions during the COVID-19 pandemic. *Risk, Hazards & Crisis in Public Policy, 12*(3), 283–302.

Ahmad, W. N. W., & Ali, N. M. (2018). A study on persuasive technologies: The relationship between user emotions, trust and persuasion. *International Journal of Interactive Multimedia and Artificial Intelligence, 5*(1), 57–61. http://www.ijimai.org/journal/sites/default/files/files/2018/02/ijimai_5_1_7_pdf_14509.pdf

Bacq, S., Will, G., Matthew, J., Regan, S., & Trenton, A. W. (2020). The COVID-19 virtual idea blitz: Marshaling social entrepreneurship to rapidly respond to urgent grand challenges. *Business Horizons, 63*(6), 705–723.

Bilal, U., Alfaro, T., & Vives, A. (2021). COVID-19 and the worsening of health inequities in Santiago, Chile. *International Journal of Epidemiology, 50*(3), 1038–1040.

Boyle, C. A., Fox, M. H., Havercamp, S. M., & Zubler, J. (2020). The public health response to the COVID-19 pandemic for people with disabilities. *Disability and Health Journal, 13*(3), 100943.

Budd, J. W., Johnstone, S., & Lamare, J. R. (2023). Never 'one-size-fits-all': Mick Marchington's unique voice on voice, from micro-level informality to macro-level turbulence. *Human Resource Management Journal, 33*(3), 539–550.

Budhwar, P., & Cumming, D. (2020). New directions in management research and communication: Lessons from the COVID-19 pandemic. *British Journal of Management, 31*(3), 441.

Charney, S. A., Camarata, S. M., & Chern, A. (2021). Potential impact of the COVID-19 pandemic on communication and language skills in children. *Otolaryngology–Head and Neck Surgery, 165*(1), 1–2.

Cortinez-O'Ryan, A., Moran, M. R., Rios, A. P., Anza-Ramirez, C., & Slovic, A. D. (2020). Could severe mobility and park use restrictions during the COVID-19 pandemic aggravate health inequalities? Insights and challenges from Latin America. *Cadernos de saude publica, 36*, e00185820.

de Miranda, D. M., da Silva Athanasio, B., Oliveira, A. C. S., & Simoes-e-Silva, A. C. (2020). How is COVID-19 pandemic impacting mental health of children and adolescents?. *International Journal of Disaster Risk Reduction, 51*, 101845.

Devine, D., Gaskell, J., Jennings, W., & Stoker, G. (2021). Trust and the coronavirus pandemic: What are the consequences of and for trust? An early review of the literature. *Political Studies Review, 19*(2), 274–285.

Dutta, M. J., Jayan, P., Elers, P., Elers, C., Rahman, M. M., & Pokaia, V. (2022). Receiving healthcare amidst poverty during the COVID-19 lockdowns: A culture-centered interrogation. *Health Communication, 37*(12), 1503–1509.

Ferraro, F., Etzion, D., & Gehman, J. (2015). Tackling grand challenges pragmatically: Robust action revisited. *Organization Studies*, 36, 363–390.

Fierbeck, K., & Hardcastle, L. (2020). Have the post-sars reforms prepared us for COVID-19? Mapping the institutional landscape. In C. M. Flood, V. MacDonnell, & J. Philpott (Eds.), *Vulnerable: The law, policy and ethics of COVID-19* (p. 628). University of Ottawa Press/Les Presses de l'Universitéd'Ottawa.

Flood, C. M., MacDonnell, V., & Philpott, J. (2020). *Vulnerable: The law, policy and ethics of COVID-19* (p. 628). University of Ottawa Press/Les Presses de l' Université d'Ottawa.

Fu, X., Fu, X., Ghauri, P. N., & Khan, H. (2023). Tackling exigent grand challenges through corporate social innovation: Evidence from the COVID-19 pandemic. *Journal of Product Innovation Management.*

Gagnon, J. C. (2020). The solitary confinement of incarcerated American youth during COVID-19. *Psychiatry Research, 291*, 113219.

Henry, B. F., Mandavia, A. D., Paschen-Wolff, M. M., Hunt, T., Humensky, J. L., Wu, E., … & El-Bassel, N. (2020). *COVID-19, mental health, and opioid use disorder: Old and new public health crises intertwine* (Vol. 12, No. S1, p. S111). Educational Publishing Foundation.

Howard-Grenville, J. (2021). Grand challenges, Covid-19 and the future of organizational scholarship. *Journal of Management Studies, 58*(1), 254.

Hwang, T. J., Rabheru, K., Peisah, C., Reichman, W., & Ikeda, M. (2020). Loneliness and social isolation during the COVID-19 pandemic. *International psychogeriatrics, 32*(10), 1217–1220.

Iturri, F., Gale-Bentz, E., Reinhard, E. E., Hunter, T. B., McCann, C. N., Zaman, A., … & Tellez, A. (2020). Incarceration and pandemic-related restrictions during COVID-19:

An empathic understanding of two worlds. *Psychological Trauma: Theory, Research, Practice, and Policy, 12*(S1), S233.

Kearns, R. (2021). Narrative and metaphors in New Zealand's efforts to eliminate COVID-19. *Geographical Research, 59*(3), 324–330.

Kendall, E., Ehrlich, C., Chapman, K., Shirota, C., Allen, G., Gall, A., ... & Palipana, D. (2020). Immediate and long-term implications of the COVID-19 pandemic for people with disabilities. *American Journal of Public Health, 110*(12), 1774–1779.

Kim, E. J., Marrast, L., & Conigliaro, J. (2020). COVID-19: Magnifying the effect of health disparities. *Journal of General Internal Medicine, 35*, 2441–2442.

Lai, Y. L., & Cai, W. (2023). Enhancing post-COVID-19 work resilience in hospitality: A micro-level crisis management framework. *Tourism and Hospitality Research, 23*(1), 88–100.

Lasswell, H. D. (1948). The structure and function of communication in society. *The Communication of Ideas, 37*(1), 136–139.

Lindgaard, G., Sen, D., Stojmenovic, M., Lundahl, S., Noonan, P., Dudek, C., ... & Seguin, P. (2010, May). Deriving user requirements for a CBRNE support system. In *ISCRAM*. https://idl.iscram.org/files/lindgaard/2010/708_Lindgaard_etal2010.pdf

Lupton, D., & Willis, K. (Eds.). (2021). *The COVID-19 crisis: Social perspectives*. London: Routledge.

Marchington, M., & Armstrong, R. (1981). Employee participation: Problems for the shop steward. *Industrial Relations Journal, 12*(1), 46–61. doi: 10.1111/j.1468-2338.1981.tb00249.x

Marchington, M., & Dundon, T. (2017). The challenges for fair voice in liberal market economies. In D. Grimshaw, C. Fagan, G. Hebson, & I. Tavora (Eds.), *Making work more equal. A new segmentation approach* (pp. 90–107). Manchester University Press.

Marchington, M., Goodman, J., Wilkinson, A., & Ackers, P. (1992). New developments in employee involvement. Employment Department Research Paper Series No 2. HMSO.

Milliman, R. E., & Fugate, D. L. (1988). Using trust-transference as a persuasion technique: An empirical field investigation. *Journal of Personal Selling & Sales Management, 8*(2), 1–7.

Morgan, M. G., Fischhoff, B., Bostrom, A., & Atman, C. J. (2001). *Risk communication: A mental models approach*. Cambridge: Cambridge University Press.

Pancani, L., Marinucci, M., Aureli, N., & Riva, P. (2021). Forced social isolation and mental health: A study on 1,006 Italians under COVID-19 lockdown. *Frontiers in Psychology, 12*, 663799.

Peterson, T. R., & Thompson, J. L. (2010). Environmental risk communication: Responding to challenges of complexity and uncertainty. In H. D. O'Hair and R. L. Heath (Eds.). *Handbook of Risk and Crisis Communication*, Mahway, NJ: Lawrence Erlbaum.

Pietrabissa, G., & Simpson, S. G. (2020). Psychological consequences of social isolation during COVID-19 outbreak. *Frontiers in Psychology, 11*, 2201.

Ramchurn, S. (2004). Multi-agent negotiation using trust and persuasion. Doctoral dissertation, University of Southampton.

Rahman, M., Ahmed, R., Moitra, M., Damschroder, L., Brownson, R., Chorpita, B., ... & Kumar, M. (2021). Mental distress and human rights violations during COVID-19: A rapid review of the evidence informing rights, mental health needs, and public policy around vulnerable populations. *Frontiers in Psychiatry, 11*, 603875.

Schoeneborn, D., Vásquez, C., & Cornelissen, J. P. (2022). Theorizing the role of metaphors in co-orienting collective action toward grand challenges: The example of the Covid-19 pandemic. In *Organizing for Societal Grand Challenges* (pp. 69–91). Emerald Publishing Limited.

Siegrist, M., & Zingg, A. (2014). The role of public trust during pandemics. *European Psychologist*.

The Economist. (2023). COVID-19 has given children new words and ideas to play with. Retrieved on October 30, 2023 from https://www.economist.com/culture/2022/02/04/covid-19-has-given-children-new-words-and-ideas-to-play with?utm_medium=cpc.adword.pd&utm_source=google&ppccampaignID=18798097116&ppcadID=&utm_campaign=a.22brand_pmax&utm_content=conversion.directresponse.anonymous&gclid=Cj0KCQjwqP2pBhDMARIsA JQ0Czr-pK2BHLZqiyhvDuYG4cGZsrzNAjpqsDoRnIQlwpBBVH8tK1biS7 RoaAhlpEALw_wcB&gclsrc=aw.ds

# INDEX

www.ingramcontent.com/pod-product-compliance
Ingram Content Group UK Ltd.
Pitfield, Milton Keynes, MK11 3LW, UK
UKHW022353190926
475702UK00015B/2276
* 9 7 8 1 0 3 2 4 9 6 8 2 5 *